TWAYNE'S WORLD AUTHORS SERIES

A Survey of the World's Literature

Sylvia E. Bowman, Indiana University

GENERAL EDITOR

FRANCE

Maxwell A. Smith, Guerry Professor of French, Emeritus
The University of Chattanooga
Former Visiting Professor in Modern Languages
The Florida State University

EDITOR

Arthur Rimbaud

TWAS 369

Photo Harlinque-Viollet

Arthur Rimbaud

ARTHUR RIMBAUD

By F. C. ST. AUBYN

University of Pittsburgh

TWAYNE PUBLISHERS

A DIVISION OF G. K. HALL & CO., BOSTON

Library of Congress Cataloging in Publication Data

St. Aubyn, Frederic Chase, 1921–
    Arthur Rimbaud.

    (Twayne's world authors series ; TWAS 369 ; France)
    Bibliography: pp. 185–92
    Includes index.
    1. Rimbaud, Jean Nicolas Arthur, 1854–1891.
PQ2387.R5Z87 1976   841'.8   75–14427
ISBN 0–8057–6192–6

To Phyllis and Barbara

Contents

About the Author

F. C. St. Aubyn received his B.A. from Southwest Missouri State University and the M.A. and Ph.D. from Yale University. After teaching at Harpur College, the University of Delaware, and Elmira College, he went to the University of Pittsburgh where he is presently Chairman of the Department of French and Italian. Dr. St. Aubyn is the author of Twayne's World Authors Series volume on *Stéphane Mallarmé* and is preparing the volume on *Charles Péguy* for the same Series. Co-editor of two textbooks, Jean-Paul Sartre's *Les Mouches* and *Trois Pièces Surréalistes,* his numerous articles on modern French literature have appeared in England, France, and Italy, as well as the United States. He has published more than fifty book reviews and in 1967–68 was the recipient of a Fellowship from the American Council of Learned Societies. The results of his research that year will appear in the near future in France under the title *Essai de Bibliographie de Michel Butor: 1954–1972.* The bibliography includes more than 1,000 items in twenty-two languages.

Preface

The present book is intended as a critical and analytical introduction to the poetry of Rimbaud for students and teachers in high schools, colleges, and universities as well as for the general public. The attempt has been to present, with the simple aid of a dictionary, a straightforward and logical interpretation that in no way precludes other possible interpretations.

A chronology and brief biography have been provided, but, because of the severe limitations of space imposed by the format of this series, I have commented on only twelve of the most representative and complex of the early poems as well as the Seer Letters and "Le Bateau ivre." Among the poems supposedly written after "Le Bateau ivre," I have analyzed only the seven included in *Une Saison en enfer,* reserving most of the space for the two major works.

Also because of space limitations, the poem could not be provided in its entirety. It is hoped the student will read the poem, then read my comments, and finally, reread the poem in the light of those comments. He can then bring the same critical approach to his reading of the other poems. The conclusion includes an attempt to assay Rimbaud's accomplishments and influence while a selective bibliography is offered as a guide to further study and enjoyment of Rimbaud's poetry.

I take this opportunity to express my profound gratitude to Professor Henri Peyre, who suggested the subject of my doctoral dissertation on Rimbaud, and to Professor Kenneth Cornell, who so patiently and kindly saw it through to its successful completion.

F. C. St. Aubyn

University of Pittsburgh

Chronology

September: accepts Verlaine's invitation to Paris and brings with him "Le Bateau ivre."

1872 July: Rimbaud and Verlaine in Brussels and later, London. September 14: "Les Corbeaux" published in *La Renaissance littéraire et artistique.*

1873 After two trips to London, Rimbaud and Verlaine meet in Brussels where Verlaine shoots Rimbaud in the hand on July 10. Verlaine condemned to two years in prison. Rimbaud returns to Charleville.

October: *Une Saison en enfer* printed in Brussels but never distributed and not discovered until 1901.

1874 Rimbaud travels to London with Germain Nouveau.

1875 From this date until his death, Rimbaud travels widely, returning home only periodically.

1878 January: "Petits Pauvres" (later called "Les Effarés") published in *The Gentleman's Magazine,* probably by Verlaine.

November 17: death of father in Dijon.

1880 December 13: arrives at Harar in Ethiopia, where he spends most of the rest of his life.

1882 Félicien Champsaur publishes stanzas 3 and 4 of "Les Chercheuses de poux" in his novel *Dinah Samuel.*

1883 October–November: Verlaine publishes "Les Poètes maudits: Arthur Rimbaud" in *Lutèce;* this marks the beginning of Rimbaud's renown.

1884 Verlaine publishes *Les Poètes maudits: Tristan Corbière, Arthur Rimbaud, Stéphane Mallarmé.*

December 10: Rimbaud's "Rapport sur l'Ogadine" published in *Comptes rendus des séances de la Société de Géographie.*

1886 April–June: "Les Premières Communions" and *Illuminations* published in *La Vogue.*

Illuminations published separately, edited and prefaced by Verlaine.

September: *Une Saison en enfer* published in *La Vogue.*

1887 August 25 and 27: "M. Rimbaud au Harar et au Choa" published in *Le Bosphore égyptien* in Cairo.

November 4: "Itinéraire d'Antotto à Harar" published in *Comptes rendus des séances de la Société de Géographie.*

Chronology

1888 "Le Dormeur du val" and "Le Buffet" published by Lemerre in his *Anthologie des poètes français du XIXe siècle*.

1889 January–February: "Le Mal," "A la musique," "Sensation," and "Ma Bohème" published in *La Revue indépendante*.

1890 March 15: "Au Cabaret vert" published in *La Revue d'aujourd'hui*.

September 15: "Paris se repeuple" in *La Plume*.

1891 April: Rimbaud, suffering from a swollen right knee, is transported by litter from Harar to Aden.

May 20: Arrives at the hospital in Marseilles.

May 27: His leg is amputated.

July 23: He returns to Charleville.

August 24: Rimbaud goes back to the hospital at Marseilles.

November 1: "Venus anadyomène" and "Bal des pendus" in the *Mercure de France*.

November 1: "Lettre de Charles d'Orléans à Louis XI" published in *Revue de l'Evolution sociale, scientifique et littéraire*.

November 10: Rimbaud dies at Marseilles.

November 14: buried at Charleville.

November 20: a collection of his poetry under the title *Reliquaire* appears in Paris, causing a scandal because of the unauthorized preface.

1895 Verlaine published the *Poésies complètes d'Arthur Rimbaud*.

CHAPTER 1

Introduction: *A Poet's Life*

JEAN-NICOLAS-ARTHUR RIMBAUD was born October 20, 1854,[1] in the small town of Charleville in northeastern France a few miles from the Belgian border. By the time of Rimbaud's birth his father, Frédéric, had worked his way up through the ranks of the infantry to the grade of captain. Also by that time the family of Rimbaud's mother, Vitalie Cuif, had worked its way up from the peasantry to the provincial bourgeoisie of the small landowner.

After siring two sons, Frédéric in 1853 and Arthur in 1854, Captain Rimbaud took part in the Crimean campaign of 1855–1856. He returned to Charleville long enough to beget three daughters: Vitalie who was born and died in 1857; a second Vitalie born in 1858, who died at the age of seventeen in 1875; and Isabelle born in 1860, who lived until 1917. Two months after the birth of Isabelle, the captain rejoined his garrison and retired from the infantry four years later. He died in Dijon in 1878 without ever having seen his family again, as far as we know.

Life for Madame Rimbaud after 1860 could not have been easy. In the eyes of the citizens of Charleville she was a dour figure abandoned with four children. In her own eyes she already considered herself a widow, although she was to live for eighteen years with the knowledge that her husband was very much alive. She did have the last laugh on her errant mate, however, because she lived to collect her pension as an army officer's widow for twenty-nine years.

Nevertheless, the care of the children was her responsibility alone. Given the limits of her education and personality, she did as well as she could. Although she maintained appearances by dint of careful management, money was not her greatest problem. Timid and proud, she found herself with her little brood perched perilously on the edge of bourgeois society. Harsh and domineering, she could not express her real feelings for fear of revealing the kindness and weakness hidden behind this wall of hostility. Her Catholicism was a rigid Jansenism allowing no deviation. Her penny-pinching within the confines of strict morality made life possible if not always pleasant for her children and herself.

Strangely enough, Rimbaud's personality when he matured was a curious amalgam of that of both his parents. Traveling widely like his father, he never, like his father, really created a home for himself. Like his mother, he pinched pennies all his life in the hopes of creating a fortune and became more and more practical, withdrawn, and laconic. Nevertheless, no matter how widely he wandered he always, right up to the year of his death, kept returning to Charleville as if there were something there he had missed. Born near a foreign border, he spent his life crossing frontiers in his poetry and in his travels, apparently without ever finding what it was he was searching for on the other side.

When he was finally permitted to attend school in 1862, Rimbaud quickly proved a model student, a teacher's and mother's delight. He completed nine years in eight, earned an impressive number of prizes, and saw three poems in Latin published in the *Official Bulletin of the Academy of Douai* of January 15, June 1, and November 15, 1869. Five months later a translation of twenty-six lines from Lucretius' *De natura rerum*, two poems in Latin as well as a Latin composition appeared in the *Bulletin* of April 15, 1870. Unfortunately Rimbaud had plagiarized the translation from the well-known poet Sully-Prudhomme. Scholars find the fifteen year old's translation something of an improvement over that of his elder.[2] Another composition by Rimbaud entitled "Letter from Charles d'Orléans [to Louis IX] beseeching clemency for Villon, threatened with the gallows," probably written in February or April, 1870, has also been preserved. But by that time Rimbaud had published his first poem in French, "Les Etrennes des orphelins," in *La Revue pour tous* of January 2, 1870.

For eight years the model student Rimbaud had gone off to school each day and marched off to church each Sunday in the little family regiment closely supervised by his mother. He learned his lessons and read his Bible and then fate intervened, first in the form of a twenty-two-year-old teacher named Georges Izambard, who began his career at Charleville in January, 1870. Before Rimbaud could collect his school prizes in August, fate intervened again. France declared war on Prussia July 18 and the disastrous Franco-Prussian War was underway. Education in Charleville was suspended, because the town lay in the path of the invading army. That was the end of Rimbaud's formal schooling.

We know from Rimbaud's schoolboy compositions and the curricula of the two schools he attended that he received the typical classical education of the France of the 1860s. We also know from his performance that he profited from his studies scholastically and that they account for many of the ideas and allusions in his works. If we had not learned from accounts of his childhood by his sister Isabelle and others, we could see from his poetry that Rimbaud passed no small amount of time thumbing the Bible under his mother's eye. Although Victor Hugo was born fifty-two years before Rimbaud, he did not die until fifteen years after Rimbaud had ceased to write, thus keeping alive the influence of the Romantic revolution of the 1830s brought about by Lamartine, Musset, Vigny, and others. Izambard introduced Rimbaud to the poets of the Parnassian movement shortly before Rimbaud began to read insatiably in the Charleville library. Thus Rimbaud's early poems are, almost inevitably, a pastiche of all of these influences.

His first poem, "Les Etrennes des orphelins," appeared in January, 1870, the month Izambard arrived in Charleville. On May 24 Rimbaud sent three poems, "Sensation," "Credo in unam" (Soleil et chair), and "Ophélie," to Théodore de Banville in Paris in hopes of being published in the second *Parnasse contemporain*. In his letter Rimbaud described himself as seventeen when he was fifteen and a half, and if he flattered the Parnassians outrageously, Banville had only to read the poems to learn that imitation is indeed the sincerest form of flattery. Unfortunately we do not have Banville's reactions to these poems by a young provincial. The second *Parnasse* was delayed by the war but when it did appear, Rimbaud's poems were not included.

I *The Flight to Anywhere*

During 1870 and before his departure for Paris, Rimbaud wrote some forty poems, most of which are almost impossible to date accurately. He enjoyed Izambard's company and influence little more than six months, for soon after war was declared in July, 1870, Izambard returned to his home in Douai, expecting to be called into service. Rimbaud collected his school prizes in early August and later in the month, with Izambard gone and nothing to hold him in Charleville, he took the train to Paris by a circuitous route because of the war. He was arrested when he got off the train for not having paid the complete fare and taken to Mazas Prison, where he remained for several days. During his incarceration the empire fell. In answer to Rimbaud's plea, Izambard sent the money necessary for his release and the trip to the home of Izambard's aunts, the Gindre sisters, in Douai northwest of Charleville, where he spent two happy weeks. But late in September Izambard, at the behest of Madame Rimbaud, was obliged to conduct Rimbaud home.

Rimbaud remained there hardly more than a week before he took off again, this time for Belgium. He looked for work as a journalist in Charleroi. Disappointed, he went to Brussels and finally made his way back to the warm hospitality of the Gindre sisters. While staying there about ten days he copied out twenty-two of his poems for his friend Paul Demeny, a young poet he had met through Izambard. The collection remains one of the principal sources of our knowledge of Rimbaud's early works. Early in November Madame Rimbaud ordered the police to return her son to Charleville.

When school could not open because of the war, Rimbaud spent a great deal of time reading in the library. Late in December Mézières, the twin city of Charleville, was bombarded by the Prussians, and early in January both cities were occupied. The armistice was signed January 28, 1871, and one month later Rimbaud fled to Paris. He may have seen the victorious Germans marching in the Champs-Elysées, but we know he was penniless, wandering through the streets and reading the news bulletins, and undoubtedly going hungry. By March 10 Rimbaud had returned to Charleville on foot.

Thus in something like six months Rimbaud had run away from home three times, each escape a sort of flight to anywhere—anywhere away from his mother and Charleville. All sorts of conjectures can be made as to why he ran away: the desire to be free of his mother's tyranny, the hopes of finding a job, adventure, excitement—the same reasons, in other words, why most boys run away from home. Upon his return he again read in the library—historians like Thiers and Michelet, socialists like Proudhon and Louis Blanc, and many others. On March 18 the Commune was declared in Paris. Rimbaud had thus missed by one week the greatest revolutionary event of his life.

The socialist Commune persevered in its struggle against the reactionary forces of Thiers from March 18 to May 28. Where Rimbaud was during that time is uncertain. We know that he was still in Charleville on April 17 and by his Seer Letters that he was there again on May 13. Many scholars are convinced by little or no evidence that Rimbaud visited the capital between those dates and participated in the Commune. Until further evidence is discovered, I am convinced he remained in Charleville. Several of his poems attest to his socialist fervor and there can be no doubt that by this time, Rimbaud had been totally transformed. The model schoolboy had become a long-haired tramp, wearing dirty, disreputable clothes, smoking his pipe upside down, writing blasphemous slogans on park benches, cadging beers from his acquaintances, and making a foulmouthed nuisance of himself. What actually caused the transformation is also a matter of conjecture. Perhaps part of the answer lies hidden in the poem "Le Coeur volé."

In any event Rimbaud wrote his astonishing Seer Letters on May 13 and 15, addressing the first to Izambard and the second to Demeny. In spite of the bombast and rhetoric, they remain an incredible creation by a boy of sixteen. On June 19 Rimbaud wrote Demeny asking him to burn all of the poems he had given him. He also sent along three new poems. On August 15 Rimbaud sent his poem "Ce qu'on dit au poète à propos de fleurs" to Banville. Late in August or early in September he wrote Verlaine. sending him five poems. Without waiting for a reply he sent off three more a few days later. Properly impressed, Verlaine invited Rimbaud to come to Paris. On September 10 Rimbaud

left Charleville with the blessings of his mother. Obviously little
was known in the provinces about Verlaine's private life or
Madame Rimbaud might have had second thoughts. At least this
was Rimbaud's first flight to somewhere, to Paris, to the literary
center of the world, to fame, and perhaps fortune.

II *The Flight to Somewhere*

Yet Rimbaud's comportment in Paris belies such aspirations.
He began by alienating Verlaine's in-laws, the straitlaced Mautés
who had been kind enough to take him in. Verlaine introduced
Rimbaud to his artist and writer friends, several of whom paid
for Rimbaud's lodging after the Mautés showed him the door. On
October 30 Verlaine's son was born, but, in spite of the happy
event, Verlaine's life deteriorated into a series of brutal drunken
scenes with his young wife. On November 15 Edmond Lepel-
letier, theater critic and gossip columnist, published a newspaper
account of an evening at the theater that left no doubt in the
public mind about the nature of the Verlaine-Rimbaud relations.

Rimbaud had been invited to attend the monthly dinners of
the Parnassians who called themselves the "Vilains Bonshommes."
Rimbaud read his "Bateau ivre," which impressed the group.
He collaborated with them on the satirical *Album zutique,* but
late in December or early in January, 1872, the drunken Rimbaud caused such a scene by interrupting the poet who was
reading his works and by threatening the life of the photog-
rapher Etienne Carjat that he was invited never to return. In
late February or early March Rimbaud left Paris for Charleville
as the price for an attempted reconciliation between the Verlaines.

Rimbaud was back in Paris by May, however. Under the influence of Verlaine he continued to write the first poems of his
late period that had begun the previous months in Charleville.
As irony would have it, by then he was known to literary Paris
only as the perpetrator of that infamous hoax "Voyelles" and
considered nothing more than a dangerous fraud. Although Rimbaud and Verlaine could not have known it, their abrupt departure for Brussels in early July was the beginning of a series
of peregrinations that would bring them back to Brussels and the
fatal denouement of their friendship. Verlaine's mother and

wife joined the poets in Brussels in the hopes of taking Verlaine
back to Paris. He eluded the nice ladies at the last minute,
however, and in September he and Rimbaud left for London.
They mingled briefly with the refugees of the Commune, but
Rimbaud was unhappy and returned to Charleville in November
or December. In January, 1873, Verlaine fell ill. His mother
sent Rimbaud the money to rejoin him. In March Rimbaud took
out a reader's card at the British Museum. The following month
they were back in France. They remained there barely a month
before they were again crossing the Channel. In June they placed
advertisements in the newspaper as tutors in French but in
July a quarrel broke out and Verlaine went off to Brussels.

Rimbaud followed him there and in a drunken bout Verlaine
fired at Rimbaud, wounding him slightly in the hand. Rimbaud
was taken to the hospital where the wound was treated. Everything might have been all right but on the way to the railroad
station Verlaine made a movement which Rimbaud interpreted
as an attempt to reach for his gun. In a panic Rimbaud sought
the protection of the nearest policeman. Verlaine was arrested
and held in prison for trial. Rimbaud returned to the hospital
to have the bullet removed. While there he signed the withdrawal of his complaint against Verlaine. But it was too late.
Rimbaud returned to Charleville July 20, and on August 8 Verlaine was fined and sentenced to two years in prison.

Rimbaud refused to participate in the work of the family on
his mother's farm at Roche. Instead, he scribbled furiously at
Une Saison en enfer, which he had begun in April. The book
must have been completed well before October because by then
it had been printed by J. Poot in Brussels. Rimbaud received a
few author's copies which he sent to friends, but he was unable
to pay the printing costs and the whole edition remained in
the publisher's attic until it was discovered by accident in 1901.
Une Saison was Rimbaud's last attempt at literary publication.
The flight to somewhere thus really ended in the attic of a
Brussels printer.

III *The Flight to Nowhere*

The flight to nowhere gave promise of being a continuation
of the flight to somewhere. In the sense that it gave us some of

the *Illuminations,* the flight was a success. But that was more or less in spite of Rimbaud.

He probably met the young poet Germain Nouveau late in 1873. We know they were in London in March, 1874, because on April 4 they took out reader's cards at the British Museum. In July Madame Rimbaud and sister Vitalie visited them in London. Rimbaud left, perhaps for Scarborough, and by November 7 he was in Reading, where he offered his services in the newspaper as a traveling companion. By the end of 1874 Nouveau had left Rimbaud, and the latter was back in Charleville where he took his first piano lessons.

In February, 1875, Rimbaud went to Stuttgart to learn German. Verlaine, released from prison and converted to ardent Catholicism, visited Rimbaud in Stuttgart, the last time the two friends met. In late April Rimbaud left Germany, crossed Switzerland and the Alps, and made his way to Milan. He wanted to visit central Italy, but in June he had to ask the French consul at Leghorn for assistance. He got to Paris, looked up friends, found a job, and saw his mother and two sisters. He attempted to call upon Verlaine's mother, but she was not at home. By October Rimbaud was back in Charleville. In December his sister Vitalie died.

By April, 1876, Rimbaud was in Vienna. Robbed by a cab driver, he was conducted to the Austro-German border by the police. He walked across Germany to Charleville. On May 19 he signed up with the Dutch colonial army at Harderwijk in Holland and sailed on June 10 for Java by way of Southampton, Gibraltar, Naples, Suez, and Aden. This last city thus makes its first appearance in Rimbaud's itinerary, a port of call to which he will return many times. His ship arrived at Batavia (modern Djakarta) July 19, but by August 15 Rimbaud had been declared a deserter. He had signed up on a British ship and returned to Charleville in December by way of the Cape of Good Hope, Ireland, and Paris.

On May 10, 1877, Rimbaud was in Bremen, where he attempted to join the American marines. In June he was in Stockholm describing himself first as an agent and later as a seaman. He showed up in Copenhagen, perhaps traveled to Norway, and in September went to Marseilles where he sailed for Civita-Vecchia, visited Rome, and returned to Charleville.

Early in 1878 Rimbaud was in Hamburg doing what we do not know. Witnesses claim to have seen him in Paris at Easter. He spent the summer on his mother's farm and actually helped with the work. In October he crossed the Vosges Mountains, Switzerland, and the St. Gothard Pass on foot, getting as far as Lugano. He took the train to Milan and from Genoa he sailed for Alexandria on November 19. Shortly after arriving in Egypt he left for Cyprus, where he found a job on December 16 as foreman in a marble quarry. His father had died in Dijon on November 17. Unknown to Rimbaud someone, probably Verlaine, published "Les Effarés" in an English review, *The Gentleman's Magazine,* in January, 1878; it was the first hint that Rimbaud's literary career would continue in spite of him.

In May, 1879, Rimbaud took sick and returned to Charleville, where the doctor diagnosed typhoid fever. He again passed the summer at Roche, again helped with the work, and saw his old friend Delahaye. With the approach of winter Rimbaud hoped to return to a warm climate. He got as far as Marseilles but fell ill again. As a result he again spent the winter at Roche.

Rimbaud left Charleville for Cyprus in March, 1880. He found another job, this time as foreman of a construction crew building a summer residence for the British governor, but resigned on July 20 for health and financial reasons. He looked for work in Alexandria and then pushed on to several African ports on the Red Sea. In one of them he met an agent of the Mazeran, Viannay, Bardey Co., whose headquarters were in Aden. He arrived there on August 7 and was hired immediately. On November 2 he was assigned to the branch office at Harar in Abyssinia, now Ethiopia. He sailed for Zeilah in British Somaliland, where he joined a caravan and made the 150-mile trip overland to Harar, arriving December 13. He was home at last for he spent most of the remaining ten years of his life in this outpost in the wilds of eastern Ethiopia.

Although he began as early as September, 1881, to request reassignment, he spent a year in Harar, where the humidity and work were not to his liking. The only excitement was an ivory expedition in May and June. He left Harar in December for Aden, where life was so dull he was happy to accept the position of director of the agency at Harar in September, 1882. Rimbaud was unaware that the novelist Félicien Champsaur had chronicled one of his visits to Paris in a *roman à clef* about Sarah Bernhardt called *Dinah Samuel* in 1882. Champsaur called him Arthur Cimber and quoted two stanzas of "Les Chercheuses de poux."

Rimbaud left Aden for Harar in March, 1883. If he found living and working conditions more bearable, the conduct of business was complicated by the political situation. While Rimbaud was organizing commercial expeditions to various parts of Ethiopia, Verlaine was preparing his book on *Les Poètes maudits*. The section on Rimbaud appeared in the October and November issues of *Lutèce* and marked the beginning of Rimbaud's fame.

To add to Rimbaud's woes, his company was declared bankrupt in 1884. Rimbaud left Harar for Aden in March and learned in April that his contract had been canceled. Alfred and Pierre Bardey formed the new company of Bardey Brothers and hired Rimbaud for six months. In Paris Verlaine published *Les Poètes maudits* in book form. Rimbaud published a "Rapport sur l'Ogadine," the account of a trip made the previous year, in the *Comptes rendus des séances de la Société de Géographie* on December 10.

Rimbaud worked for the Bardeys until October, 1885, when he decided to make his fortune selling arms. The Emperor Jean and King Ménélik of the Choa were preparing for war. Jean was getting his arms from the English, Ménélik from the French and Italians. In October Rimbaud signed a contract with a Pierre Labatut to arrange for the first caravan. He went to Tadjoura in French Somaliland to make his preparations.

Rimbaud planned to leave Tadjoura on January 11, 1886, but was forced to cool his heels until April, waiting for authorization. He obtained the necessary license, but Labatut was stricken with cancer, returned to France, and died. That same month *La Vogue* in Paris began the publication of Rimbaud's "Les Premières Communions" and *Illuminations*. Rimbaud went into association with a Paul Soleillet, who in turn died of a stroke in September. The same month *La Vogue* published *Une Saison en enfer,* while Verlaine published the *Illuminations* in book form that year. Rimbaud finally left Tadjoura in October.

After four months of incredible hardships the caravan arrived in Ankober to discover that Ménélik had been defeated by the Emir of Harar and had retreated to Entotto. Rimbaud left for Harar with the French explorer Jules Borelli. There the Ras Makonnen paid for the goods in the form of drafts. By July, 1887, Rimbaud was back in Aden. He decided to go to Cairo with his servant Djami. On August 5 he stopped in the Ethiopian port of Massaoua to cash Makonnen's drafts, but was not able to get to Cairo until August 20 because of red tape. He remained there about five weeks. He put his money in a French bank, and his article "M. Rimbaud au Harar et au Choa" was published by a Cairo newspaper, *Le Bosphore égyptien,* in its issues of August 25 and 27. In Cairo Rimbaud complained of rheumatism in his left thigh and pains in his right knee. He was back in Aden by October 8, and on November 4 his "Itinéraire d'Antotto à Harar" appeared in the *Comptes rendus* of the geographical society.

Early in 1888 Rimbaud was preparing another shipment of arms. In March he returned to Harar, covering 375 miles on horseback in eleven days. He was in Aden on April 4, and on April 16 he landed in Zeilah. On May 3, twelve days after he arrived in Harar, he learned that his permission to transport arms had been denied. He decided to set up his own company in Harar in conjunction with a businessman in Aden, César Tian, and the Bardey Brothers. Back in Paris Rimbaud's poetry was anthologized for the first time. Alphonse Lemerre published "Le Dormeur du val" and "Le Buffet" in his *Anthologie des Poètes français du XIXe siècle.*

In January and February, 1889, Rimbaud's poems, "Le Mal," "A la musique," "Sensation," and "Ma Bohème," were published in *La Revue indépendante.* Early that same year the Emperor Jean was defeated by Ménélik, who thus became the Emperor Ménélik II and founder of modern Ethiopia. Rimbaud was able to continue in business with some success during 1889 and 1890, unaware that "Au Cabaret-vert" had been published in *La Revue d'aujourd'hui* on March 15, 1890, and "Paris se repeuple" in *La Plume* on September 15.

Rimbaud began to suffer terrible pains in his right knee in February, 1891. By March he was directing his affairs from a bed. He decided to go to the coast to consult the doctors. To make the trip, he had a litter constructed and hired bearers to carry him the 150 miles to Zeilah. The trip took twelve agonizing days. From there he went to Aden where the doctors at the English hospital advised him to return to France. He arrived in Marseilles on May 20. The doctor ordered amputation of Rimbaud's right leg. Madame Rimbaud arrived on May 23, and the operation took place four days later. She left for Roche early in June, followed by Rimbaud in late July. Late in August he returned to Marseilles with his sister Isabelle. By this time the cancer had spread throughout his body. In a third attempt a priest finally saw Rimbaud on October 14. He confessed but was not given communion. On November 1 "Vénus anadyomène" and "Bal des pendus" were published by the *Mercure de France*, and the "Lettre de Charles d'Orléans à Louis XI" appeared in the *Revue de l'Evolution sociale, scientifique et littéraire*. Rimbaud became delirious and on November 9 dictated an incoherent letter indicating his desire to leave Marseilles by boat. The following day he died.

Just ten days after his death a collection of his poetry appeared under the title *Reliquaire*. The unscrupulous editor Léon Genonceaux had published the poetry, collected by a young poet and Rimbaud enthusiast, Rodolphe Darzens, along with the notes of a projected preface by Darzens while the latter was in Marseilles attempting to interview Rimbaud. Darzens had the edition confiscated, Genonceaux escaped to Belgium, and the book was republished without the preface. Thus the first scandal in Rimbaud's posthumous career took place only six days after he had been buried in Charleville. Verlaine published the first *Poésies complètes d'Arthur Rimbaud* in 1895 just three months before he himself died, thus closing the circle on a turbulent friendship.

Who could believe the story of Rimbaud's life if we did not have the facts so patiently dug up by indefatigable scholars? No wonder Breton called Rimbaud "a Surrealist in the practice of life and elsewhere."[3] In ten years Rimbaud had amassed thirty thousand francs, worth about 150,000 francs in 1971,[4] or roughly thirty thousand dollars. He had created a small fortune but had killed himself in the process. He had, in the words of the late W. H. Auden, "dreamed / Of a new self, a son, an engineer, / His truth acceptable to lying men."[5] Rimbaud's life after death is even more fantastic, based as it is on a collection of poems easily printed on 150 pages. The flight that Rimbaud had determined to be a flight to nowhere became in spite of him a flight to almost everywhere, which would last much longer than the thirty-seven years he lived. To discover how and why Rimbaud should have had such enormous influence after his death, we must turn to his poetry.

CHAPTER 2

Early Songs

ALTHOUGH several of his schoolboy compositions appeared in an academic bulletin in 1869, Rimbaud published only three poems during his lifetime. The first was "Les Etrennes des orphelins" (The Orphans' New Year's Gifts) that appeared on January 2, 1870, when Rimbaud was fifteen. The second, "Trois Baisers" (Three Kisses), later called "Première Soirée" (First Party), came out in August of the same year. The last was "Les Corbeaux" (The Ravens), published in July, 1872. Someone, probably Verlaine, printed his "Petits Pauvres" (Poor Little Ones), now known as "Les Effarés" (The Bewildered Ones), in *The Gentleman's Magazine* in England in January, 1878. But by 1875 Rimbaud had already begun the peregrinations that ended only with his death in 1891.

Any grouping of Rimbaud's early poems would be arbitrary. While an analysis in chronological order can reveal something about his evolution, precise dates are almost impossible to determine, and in any case the time span was so short that chronology is rendered less meaningful.[1] Something can be gained, perhaps, by discussing selected poems in the accepted chronological order within groups that treat similar subjects.

I Songs of Satire

Rimbaud satirizes many aspects of French life. One of his earliest targets was Charleville's "Society" which gets its due in "A la musique" (To Music). The title carries the notation "Place de la gare, à Charleville" (Station Square, Charleville). The poem, nine quatrains of alexandrines rhyming *a b a b*, probably dates from shortly after the public concert of July 7, 1870, and has sources in Pétrus Borel, Baudelaire, and Glatigny,[2] but Rimbaud's treatment is his own. The tone is set by the first line: "On

28

the square cut up in niggardly little patches of lawn" (*Sur la place taillée en mesquines pelouses*). Everything is narrow and correct in appearance, even "the trees and the flowers" (*les arbres et les fleurs*), but behind this facade "the wheezy bourgeois" (*les bourgeois poussifs*) are wearing "their jealous stupidities" (*leurs bêtises jalouses*), the local "dandy is parading around up front" (*aux premiers rangs, parade le gandin*), the natty "notary is hanging from his monogrammed watch fob" (*Le notaire pend à ses breloques à chiffres*), the rich are keeping time to the musical squawks with their lorgnettes (*Des rentiers à lorgnons soulignent tous les couacs*), "the big beefy bureaucrats are dragging along their fat wives" (*Les gros bureaux bouffis traînent leurs grosses dames*) who in turn are followed by their "officious elephant-keepers" (*officieux cornacs*) dressed in "marked-down flounces" (*dont les volants ont des airs de réclames*).

Whole "clubs of retired grocers" (*des clubs d'épiciers retraités*) with their limited intelligence "are very seriously discussing treaties" (*Fort sérieusement discutent les traités*) but soon go back to dipping in their silver snuff boxes (*Puis prisent en argent*). The ellipsis of this last expression will become the rule rather than the exception in Rimbaud's later poems. Another "honest" bourgeois, the roundness of whose backside is flabbergasting (*Epatant sur son banc les rondeurs de ses reins*), "is enjoying his clay pipe" (*Savoure son onnaing*). The *onnaing* is a more expensive type of clay pipe from the village of that name near the Belgian border. Of course the bourgeois' tobacco is "contraband" (*c'est de la contrebande*). With all the explosive "b's" in the stanza, *banc, bourgeois, bouton, bedaine, tabac, brins, déborde, contrebande*, the reader can hear the bourgeois' buttons popping. Local hoodlums always attend such free concerts, spoiling the pleasure of others with their snickering (*ricanent les voyous*), while the soldiers (*les pioupious*), carried away by the trombones (*rendus amoureux par le chant des trombones*), chuck the babies under the chin in order to get into the good graces of the nursemaids (*Caressent les bébés pour enjôler les bonnes*). In his close observation Rimbaud has caricatured in the first six stanzas no less than ten types to be found in Charleville society.

The contrast is heightened when the poet turns to his preoccupation with the young girls in the last three stanzas. He is completely "disarrayed" (*débraillé*) by "their eyes full of indiscreet things" (*leurs yeux tout pleins de choses indiscrètes*). He can only watch without saying a word (*Je ne dis pas un mot*), their "white necks" (*cous blancs*), "stray locks" (*mèches folles*), blouses (*corsage*), "fragile finery'" (*frêles atours*), their "divine backs" (*dos divin*), and "the curve of their shoulders" (*la courbe des épaules*). He works his way down to their feet (*J'ai bientôt déniché la bottine*), and when he does he begins to "reconstruct their bodies, burning as he is with a fine fever" (*Je reconstruis les corps, brûlé de belles fièvres*). The girls find him "comical" (*drôle*) while he "feels kisses forming on his lips" (*Et je sens les baisers qui me viennent aux lévres*). Rimbaud seems to be asking, will this teenager, caught up in his first desires, become just another "wheezy bourgeois" or is he asking, did these repulsive characters really once share this young man's torments? The contrast is between youth and age with the pitiless eye of youth revealing hypocrisy where it finds it.

The reader has done more than turn a page in going from "A la musique" to "Les Assis" (The Seated Ones). The language of the later poem, probably written after October, 1870,[3] exhibits an unexpected vigor and originality. Rimbaud uses the term of the title, *assis*, so awkward to translate into English, in a pejorative sense to indicate the bureaucrats who do nothing but dictate from their chairs without venturing anywhere. The eleven quatrains of alexandrines rhyming *a b a b* offer a complete description of these bureaucrats including their eyes (stanzas 1,3,7,8), fingers (1), feet (2,7), skin (3), knees (5), teeth (5), noodle (*caboche*, slang for head, 5), heads (7), hand (8), fist (9), chin (9), arm (10), and finally leg (11). The technical terminology includes femur (thighbone, 1), sinciput (forehead, 1), ossature (skeleton, 2), skeleton (2), kidneys (4,6), omoplate (shoulderblade, 6), and tonsils (9). If their foreheads are leprous, their loves are epileptic and the rungs of their chairs rachitic. Epilepsy for the human and rickets for the chair bring the sitter and his seat together making of them one diseased entity. The neologisms include fingers that are "knobby" (*boulus*), foreheads covered with "ugly spots" (*hargnosités*, from *hargneux*, "ill-tempered"), and a skin that would become as thin as "percale" (*percaliser*) if exposed to the sun. These dour denizens may tremble like a toad but will rumble like a cat that has had its ears boxed if they are forced to move. The "chairs" (*chaises*) of stanza two become "seats" (*sièges*) in stanza three and when capitalized (*les Sièges*) in stanza four, they almost become a Holy See, but return again to "seat" in the fifth and to the "seats" and "chairs" they really are in the tenth. If these "green pianists" tap out (Rimbaud uses *clapoter*, "the sound of lapping water") boat songs (*barcarolles*) with their fingers on the bottoms of their chairs in stanza five, they create in the sixth the effect of a veritable "shipwreck" (*naufrage*) if they are disturbed.

Rimbaud develops his references to their eyes, which are in the first stanza "circled with green / Rings" (*cerclés de bagues / Vertes*), to powerful effct in stanzas seven (*de prunelles fauves / Qui vous accrochent l'oeil du fond des corridors*) and eight (*leur regard filtre ce venin noir*), but he is not completely unsympathetic. In stanza two he notes that they are cramped in their chairs "from morning to night" (*pour les matins et pour les soirs*), and in the ninth "from dawn to dusk" (*de l'aurore au soir*). In the last two stanzas their dreams of chairs become "true little loves of chairs on a leash" (*De vrais petits amours de chaises en lisière*) like children and one day "proud offices" will be lined with them. In his conclusion Rimbaud switches to an unexpected flower image according to which the spattered ink of these seated scribblers becomes "Flowers of ink spitting forth pollen in the shape of commas" (*Des fleurs d'encre crachant des pollens en virgules*) "along the squatting calyxes [that is, the seated ones] / Like a flight of dragonflies along a row of gladioli" (*le long des calices accroupis / Tels qu'au fil des glaïeuls le vol des libellules*). The liquid "l's" of *fleurs, pollens, virgules, Les, le long, calices, Tels, fil, glaïeuls, le vol,* and *libellules* hardly prepare the reader for the sharp prick in the leg the seated one gets from a sliver of straw in the chair seat. The unrelenting eye of Rimbaud has created an unforgettable satire of tight little minds holding tight to their tight little chairs.

In the final stanza of "Les Assis" Rimbaud describes his subjects as "squatting calyxes" (*des calices accroupis*). Thus *assis* and *accroupissements* are both pejorative, an idea reinforced by

the poem titled "Accroupissements" written before May, 1871.[4]
This satire on religious life contains many unusual words and
even more unusual images. Its seven five-line stanzas rhyme
a b a b a while the stately alexandrines heighten the irony. Poor
Brother Milotus! His stomach is upset (*l'estomac écoeuré*)
and the sun "gives him a migraine and makes him dizzy" (*lui
darde une migraine et fait son regard darne*). The colloquial
term *darne* of the Ardennes will be used again by Rimbaud.
When Brother Milotus performs his natural functions on his
chamber pot "his knees are next to his stomach" (*ses genoux
à son ventre*), the fetal position also mentioned in "Ma Bohème"
(*un pied près de mon coeur*) and "Les Assis" (*genoux aux dents*).
He is surrounded by filth (*crasse*) and as in a nightmare his foot-
stools become "strange toads" (*crapauds étranges*) while his
sideboards seem to have "the gaping maws of singers" (*des
gueules de chantres*) that are opened by "a sleep full of horrible
appetites" (*un sommeil plein d'horribles appétits*). A Surrealist
image fifty years before the fact: "He listens to the hairs grow
on his clammy skin" (*Il écoute les poils pousser dans sa peau
moite*). But again Rimbaud is not totally unsympathetic, for
in the final stanza he uses a flower image (*un fond / De neige
rose ainsi qu'une rose trémière*) as he had in "Les Assis" and
notes that while Brother Milotus sits there "in the evening in
the light of the moon" (*le soir, aux rayons de la lune*), "his
nose follows the star of Venus" (*un nez poursuit Vénus*), the star
of the goddess of love, an emotion Milotus will never know.

Another religious satire, "Les Premières Communions" (First
Communions), is usually dated July, 1871.[5] These "First Communions" are both the sacred and the profane. Rimbaud shows
how the pious sentimentalities of the former have corrupted the
latter. The poem is divided into nine parts, Parts I and II containing seven and one stanzas respectively of six alexandrines
rhyming *a b a b a b*. Parts III through IX contain from one to five
quatrains rhyming *a b a b* for a total of thirty stanzas of 136
lines. The first three stanzas of Part I describe the simple country
church and its close relationship to the place and people it
serves. If the children are "fifteen ugly brats" (*quinze laids
marmots*), the priest "A grotesque in black" (*Un noir grotesque*),
and the mass nothing more than "divine babbling" (*divins*

babillages), the church represents for Rimbaud true religion solidly based in community life. After his first communion the communicant has his "first black suit" (*Le premier habit noir*), the wonderful communion dinner (*le plus beau jour de tartes*), and a "pious picture" (*Quelque enluminure*) placed under the tarts (*Sous le Napoléon ou le Petit Tambour*), a picture that will later "join two maps on a school day" (*Et que rejoindront, au jour de science, deux cartes*) to be put away among his treasures, as the "only sweet souvenirs that remain for him of the great Day" (*Ces seuls doux souvenirs lui restent du grand Jour*). Ironically, that evening when the curate hears the music celebrating the day he can hardly keep his feet from tapping "in spite of the celestial prohibitions" (*en dépit des célestes défenses*).

In Part II the priest picks out one girl and that marks the beginning of her problems. Overcome by anxiety at the thought of all that is required, she awakens at midnight in Part V and suffers so intensely she goes outside to pass the rest of this "holy night" (*sainte nuit*) in the latrine. Rimbaud asks in Part VII what she has suffered at the hands of these "dirty fools / Whose divine work still deforms the world" (*sales fous / Dont le travail divin déforme encor les mondes*). She awakens in Part VIII after the first night of conjugal love to realize that she will never be able to experience profane but true love because of the sacred and mystical love that has claimed her soul. Part IX includes one of Rimbaud's most quoted lines: "Christ! Oh Christ, eternal thief of energy" (*Christ! ô Christ, éternel voleur des énergies*). He has "for two thousands years" (*pour deux mille ans*) kept the foreheads of women (*les fronts des femmes*) "nailed to the ground with shame and headaches" (*Cloués au sol, de honte et de céphalalgies*) or "overcome . . . with grief" (*renversés . . . de douleur*). Whatever Rimbaud's final attitude toward women he said that in their defense a hundred years before women's liberation.

Details of language raise questions of interpretation. Rimbaud speaks of *rosiers fuireux* with *fuireux* a colloquial expression for *foireux* which can mean either "jittery" or "diarrhetic." I can see the rose bushes as jittery if they are disturbed by the wind. I can also see them as diarrhetic if the wind is causing them to lose their petals in a diarrhetic stream. The familiar expression *font du genre* emphasizes the actions of the boys who are no sooner out of church than they are "doing their thing," the things boys usually do when they get together. The expression *catéchistes* in Part II rhymes with itself, an oversight difficult to explain. In addition, a *catéchiste* is the teacher of the catechism while a *catéchumène* is the student. Rimbaud obviously meant student in both cases. In Part III he speaks of *Vierges nitides* using a Latin ending in imitation of church Latin, a device that underlines the irony of the "resplendent Virgins." In the following stanza he speaks of "Latin endings" (*terminaisons latines*) almost as if to draw attention to his cleverness. Rimbaud uses the Latinism *illunés* in Part V incorrectly to mean "illuminated by the light of the moon." Whatever the language, Rimbaud makes a strong indictment of the church in its treatment of women.

II *Songs of Love and Hate*

Generally no poem is more romantic than a sonnet dedicated to Venus. According to Roman mythology she emerged from the sea on a shell as typified by Botticelli's beautiful painting "The Birth of Venus." Rimbaud took the occasion, however, to satirize the subject by drawing a brutally realistic portrait of a contemporary "goddess." His poem, "Vénus anadyomène" (Venus Emerging from the Waves), which is dated July 27, 1870, and which owes something to Glatigny and Coppée,[6] depicts Venus emerging from her bath. In the first line her cast-iron bathtub painted green is compared to a coffin (*Comme d'un cercueil vert en fer blanc*), thus setting the tone. She emerges not gracefully but "slowly and stupidly" (*lente et bête*) to reveal a body of incomparable repulsiveness "giving off a strangely horrible / Taste" (*le tout sent un goût / Horrible étrangement*). As Rimbaud zeroes in with his magnifying glass (*la loupe*) he reveals the reason for the awful odor. His Venus has "Clara Venus" (Illustrious Venus) tattooed on her "broad behind" which is also "Hideously beautiful with an ulcer of the anus" (*sa large croupe / Belle hideusement d'un ulcère à l'anus*). The "hideously beautiful" becomes a hallmark of Rimbaud's later poetry.

With "Le Coeur volé" (The Stolen Heart) we arrive at a turning point in Rimbaud's literary production. He included the
poem under the title "Le Coeur supplicié" (The Tortured Heart)
in his Seer Letter of May 13, 1871, to his former teacher
Izambard. He sent it to Paul Demeny on June 10 under the title
"Le Coeur du pitre" (The Clown's Heart).[7] Rimbaud put his
poetic theory into words in the Seer Letters and the theory into
practice in the poems he sent with them. After these letters and
poems Rimbaud's poetry was never again quite the same.

The expression *coeur volé* is found twice in the text. The
idea of the clown is in keeping with the form, the triolet, a fixed
form in which the first line of the eight-line stanza is repeated
in the fourth, and the second and third lines are repeated in the
seventh and eighth. With its frequently repeated rhymes,
a b a a a b a b, the triolet belongs to the oral tradition often recited
or set to music. Rimbaud's use of the octosyllable rather than
the alexandrine reinforces this songlike effect. The subject of the
poem, no matter how it is interpreted, does not coincide with its
lighthearted form. The progression is from a heart that is "sad"
(*Mon triste coeur*) and "full of tobacco" (*plein de caporal*)
in the first stanza to a heart that has been "depraved" (*Leurs
insultes l'ont dépravé*) in the second to a heart that has been
"stolen" (*ô coeur volé*) in the third. Rimbaud uses one of his
favorite verbs *baver* ("to slobber"), but what is a heart that
"slobbers at the stern" (*bave à la poupe*)? What is a heart that
is "full of tobacco?" Who are "They" (*Ils*) and what are their
"spurts of soup" (*jets de soupe*)? Tobacco juice? Sperm? Both?
"They" could be soldiers (*la troupe*), but the word can also mean
simply "band" or "gang." While the first half of the first stanza
seems to describe an action that is almost undeniably physical
and sexual, the last half describes an anguish that is mental and
moral as the narrator suffers under the "jibes" (*Sous les quolibets*)
and the "universal laughter" (*un rire général*).

Caporal means both tobacco and a corporal in the military
sense while in the second stanza the idea of soldiers is heightened
by another of Rimbaud's favorite words *pioupiou* ("soldier"),
this time in the form of *pioupiesques* ("soldier-like"). But when
the expression is added to *Ithyphalliques*, which refers to an
amulet in the form of an erect phallus used in the feast of

Bacchus, and both are applied to "insults," then the latter become crudely sexual, erect like both a phallus and a ramrod-stiff soldier. Again in the second stanza the reader has to ask, who are "they?" Most interpreters conclude that the pronoun refers to the soldiers casting lewd shadows against the wall in the evening light. Grammatically it refers to the insults which could be so vivid in the narrator's mind that "In the evening light" they seem to form "Phallic and ramrod-like / Frescoes" (*A la vesprée ils font des fresques / Ithyphalliques et piou-piesques*) on the walls of his soul. Using the expression "abra-cadabra" much as it is used in English as an incantation, he asks the "magic waters" (*flots abracadabrantesques*) to "take his heart" and cleanse it so "that it may be saved" (*Prenez mon coeur, qu'il soit sauvé*).

In the final stanza the antecedent of "they" in the first line is again ambiguous. Logically it seems to refer to the soldiers, but grammatically it again refers to the insults of the last line of the preceding stanza. "When they have exhausted their tobacco quids" (*Quand ils auront tari leurs chiques*), when the insults have at last dried up, his heart will have been so sullied he will not know what to do (*Comment agir, ô coeur volé*). The laughter of the first stanza has become "drunken songs" (*refrains bachiques*), and the narrator will suffer his disgust physically, wanting to vomit (*des sursauts stomachiques*) because his heart has been humiliated and debased (*ravalé*). But *ravaler* also means "to swallow again" or "to choke down" which continues the image of *sursauts stomachiques*. The expression of the first stanza, *Mon triste coeur*, becomes *mon coeur triste* in the last, a nuance almost impossible to translate into English. The former might be "sad" or "unhappy," whereas the latter could be "sor-rowful" with the feeling for what has been forever lost. The harsh sound of the dominant rhyme in -*iques* heightens the feeling of disgust become dismay. The poem speaks of more than a simple loss of childhood or even a painful loss of innocence and is, as a contemporary poet put it, one of "the darkest and most dangerous"[8] of all of Rimbaud's poems. It lies at the heart of darkness of Rimbaud's poetry and what comes after can only stem from it at least in part.

III   *Letters to the World*

The first of Rimbaud's two Seer Letters,[9] that of May 13, 1871, to Izambard, is in some ways a prelude to the second. The letter remains important, however, for several reasons. Rimbaud states baldly: "I am cynically making of myself a *kept* man" (italics Rimbaud's) and in order to do so "all that I can invent that is stupid, obscene, evil, in action and in words, I deliver up. . . ." But he is careful to note that he is doing it out of the same principle as Izambard who had become a teacher out of a sense of the individual's debt to society. Another distinction Rimbaud draws in this letter that is not treated in the second is the difference between subjective and objective poetry. The subjective poet is one who, like Izambard, can only sing of himself. The objective poet is quite another breed. As Rimbaud puts it, "I am corrupting myself as much as possible" because "I want to be a poet and I am working at making of myself a *Seer*." According to his method "It is a question of arriving at the unknown by deranging *all of the senses.* The suffering is enormous but one must be strong, be born a poet, and I have realized that I am a poet." Rimbaud makes the prophetic statement, "I shall be a worker," but for the moment he is "on strike." What Rimbaud goes on to say about the objective poet may not be terribly original. The German and French Romantics had expressed a similar idea at least two generations earlier in their personifications of the muse of poetic inspiration. But Rimbaud's way of stating it was absolutely new, with a psychological insight that antedated by a quarter of a century the first works of Freud, Rimbaud's contemporary. The poet wrote: "It is false to say: I think: one ought to say I am thought," and adds his now famous dictum: "The I is another" (JE *est un autre*). In this letter he uses the illustration of wood that could just as well have been a chair but which finds itself a violin. So the poet is a man made of the same stuff as other men but fashioned differently so as to be able to put into words the visions of mankind. The poet no longer recounts his subjective self but creates an objective reality that is true for all men.

The second letter, which one critic has called "the birth certificate of modern poetry,"[10] is addressed to Paul Demeny and dated May 15, 1871. It opens with the bold declaration: "I have resolved to give you an hour of new literature" and that Rimbaud proceeds to do. In a sweeping panorama Rimbaud makes many rash judgments that only youth has the courage to make. He asserts that all ancient poetry culminated in Greek poetry whose rhythms gave cadence to action. Between the Greeks and the Romantics the so-called poets produced only "rhymed prose," including that "Divine Fool" Racine. The Romantics are important because they "prove so well that the song is very infrequently the work, that is to say the thought sung *and understood* by the singer." Here Rimbaud repeats his dictum, "The I is another," and this time uses the example of brass that awakens to find itself a bugle. The poet's task is to reveal as much of the "universal intelligence" as he is able. To date all writers have been nothing more than bureaucrats, functionaires: "author, creator, poet, this man has never existed." The Greeks would have readily recognized Rimbaud's first principle: "The first study by the man who wants to be a poet is his own knowledge, all of it: he searches his soul, inspects it, puts it to the test, learns it. Once he knows it, he must cultivate it." He must make his "soul monstrous." Rimbaud then expands on the idea of the seer expressed in his first letter:

I say he must be a *seer*, must make himself a *seer*.

The Poet makes himself a *seer* by a long, immense, and reasoned *deranging* of *all the senses*. All forms of love, suffering, madness; . . . An ineffable torture for which he needs all the faith, all the superhuman force possible, as a result of which he becomes among all men the great sick one, the great criminal, the great damned one,—and the supreme Learned One——For he arrives at the *unknown!*

The echo of Baudelaire's "Le Voyage" whose last line reads, to plunge "To the bottom of the Unknown in order to find the *new*" is unmistakable. One almost has the impression he is reading Nietzsche's *Zarathustra* almost fifteen years before its publication.

As I indicated, the German Romantics propounded the idea of the poet as seer while the French Romantics credited their inspiration to a divine muse. Rimbaud's emphasis is, however, quite different. True, the poet is a new Prometheus, "the thief of fire," who brings with him warmth and light and thus enlightenment. But if the poet is thus somehow privileged, he is also responsible "for humanity, even for *animals.*" The poet creates form, even giving a formless form to the formless. He must find a universal language that all will understand, a language that will be "of the soul for the soul, summarizing everything, perfumes, sounds, colors." Both the idea of the infinite expansion of the senses by any and all means and this synthesis of senation Rimbaud had obviously found in Baudelaire. But again Rimbaud goes beyond his predecessor. The true poet is responsible not only for the moral but also the physical well-being of mankind for "he would be *a multiplier of progress*" in a future which "will be materialistic" and when "Poetry will no longer give cadence to action: it will be *in advance*" of action, creating the cadence to which the reality of action will adapt itself in spite of itself and in spite of the poet.

Rimbaud also devotes a paragraph to women. He may well have been inspired by the Illuminists who were among the early feminists. When woman's "endless bondage" will have at last been broken and she can live "for herself and through herself," then "she too will be a poet. Women will find the unknown, ... strange, unfathomable, repulsive, delicious things" that everyone can use. Although the paragraph is hardly more than an aside in this long letter, the mention of woman as something other than an object of poetic inspiration is, like the sentiments expressed in "Les Premières Communions," a revolutionary idea on Rimbaud's part a hundred years before women's liberation.

Thereafter Rimbaud evaluates the poets beginning with the Romantics. The early Romantics were seers without knowing it. Hugo's novel *Les Misérables* is "a true *poem*" but his poetry is loaded with the extraneous, whereas Musset is the worst villain of all, corrupting and perverting generations of would-be poets. The later Romantics, whom we should call Parnassians, like Gautier, Leconte de Lisle, and Banville, are great visionaries but Baudelaire alone is "king of poets, *a true God,*" though he was too much the dandy to have the courage to free himself from the constraints of French poetics. Rimbaud concludes that the Parnassian School, what we have since termed the Symbolist School, "has two seers: Albert Mérat and Paul Verlaine." After Rimbaud's estimate of Baudelaire which is still valid a hundred years later, the reader is stumped by this pairing of a name no one recognizes today with that of Verlaine. Rimbaud had admired Mérat to the extent of borrowing from him in his early poetry so perhaps we can forgive him one error in judgment, and, considering his age, perhaps several.

In the Seer Letters Rimbaud offers us, as a critic put it, "no philosophy (clairvoyance is only a discipline), no explanation of the world, but the liberating realism of poetry."[11] French poets and their critics frequently make extravagant claims for the power of poetry. The fact is that the poetry Rimbaud created more or less according to his theory has exerted as much influence over Western poetry as that of any other writer since his time. If poetry has any power at all then "the liberating realism" of Rimbaud's poetry is still a force in the world in which we live.

CHAPTER 3

More Early Songs

BETWEEN January, 1870, and the summer months of 1871, that is, between Rimbaud's first published poem in French and his first long masterpiece, "Le Bateau ivre," he wrote several poems that are "poetic exercises." The earlier texts resemble the set pieces almost all poets compose on popular subjects. The later poems tend to treat more and more the subject of poetry itself, or better, poetry as a creative act, poetry as creation. The subject is central to his two long poetic works in prose, links them to the works of Mallarmé, and provides us today with some justification for calling both Mallarmé and Rimbaud Symbolist poets.

I Songs of a Poet

One of the most original of the early set pieces is the sonnet "Oraison du soir" (Evening prayer) which dates from after October, 1870,[1] and which is among the first to exhibit Rimbaud's malicious delight in the profane and scabrous. The disdain Rimbaud displayed toward those who lead a sedentary life in "Les Assis" is evident here from the first words: "I live seated, like an angel in a barber's chair" (*Je vis assis, tel qu'un ange aux mains d'un barbier*). This ironic reference to an angel in the first line, particularly after the "prayer" of the title, alerts the reader to the satire to come. The narrator is sitting there with "beer in hand" (*Empoignant une chope*), his "hypogastrium" (*L'hypogastre* being the lower region of the abdomen, another of Rimbaud's technical terms) and neck thrown out (*cambrés*), a pipe in his mouth (*un Gambier / Aux dents*, a *Gambier* being a cheaper pipe than the *onnaing* of "A la musique"), "beneath thick clouds," one might say "sails" or "veils," of smoke in the café (*sous l'air gonflé d'impalpables voilures*).

The reader is not prepared for the strong image in the second quatrain of "A Thousand Dreams" (*Mille Rêves*) compared to "the hot droppings" (*les excréments chauds*) of pigeons that "softly singe" (*font de douces brûlures*) his soul. In the second half of the quatrain his "sorrowful heart" (*mon coeur triste*) is compared to "sapwood" (*un aubier*, again a technical term), which is the younger, softer, outer portion of wood that is more permeable, less durable, and usually lighter in color than the heartwood of the harder central core. Thus his heart is like the white sapwood that is turned yellow by some plant disease (*Qu'ensanglante l'or jeune et sombre des coulures*, with *coulures* still another technical term for an accident that prevents the fertilization of flowers).

The conclusion of the tercets comes when he has "carefully choked down his dreams" (*quand j'ai ravalé mes rêves avec soin*, *ravalé* having been used in "Le Coeur volé") or as one might say, according to the exaggeration of youth, drowned them "with thirty or forty beers" (*ayant bu trente ou quarante chopes*). He must then, like most beer drinkers, "see to his natural functions" (*lâcher l'âcre besoin*). He feels as "Sweet as the Lord of cedar and hysops" (*Doux comme le Seigneur du cèdre et des hysopes*), two aromatic plants mentioned in the Bible, the former continuing the image of the *aubier* and the latter adding the idea of the purificatory sprinkling rites of the ancient Jews. Thus his "evening prayer" is the act of urinating "very high and very far" (*très haut et très loin*) "With the consent of the tall heliotropes" (*Avec l'assentiment des grands héliotropes*), a figure that underscores the irony of the purificatory sprinkling rites and prolongs the figure of *coulures*, blights caused by heavy rains that damage the pollen and thus prevent fertilization. Rimbaud's bitter humor is thus stated in a vocabulary that is as accurate as it is biting and in images that are as unexpected as they are original.

If poets are not born but made, then Rimbaud's poem, "Les Poètes de sept ans" (The Seven-Year-Old Poets), probably written between May 15 and June 10, 1871,[2] remains one of the best analyses of the phenomenon. Its sixty-four alexandrines in rhymed couplets are arranged in groups of four, twelve, fourteen, and thirty-four. The opening quatrain, which sets the scene, begins with the word "And" (*Et*) like a Classical tragedy, creating the impression with the reader that he is participating in an action that has already begun. Such is the case for "the Mother" (*la Mère*) closes the Bible (*le livre du devoir*) which she has been reading to her children and goes off, very "satisfied and very proud" of herself (*satisfaite et très fière*) for a duty well done. She does not notice that the soul of her son, the reason for her reading, is "filled with loathing" (*livrée aux répugnances*) behind "his blue eyes" (*les yeux bleus*) and "forehead covered with bumps" (*le front plein d'éminences*). The reference to the forehead has aroused many interpretations. One critic thinks Rimbaud meant that it was full of the unusual gifts that foretell the poet.[3] If Rimbaud's poet were a little older than seven I should think he meant simply a pimply forehead. Even more simply, could he mean a bony forehead? Why not. The point is that this satisfied and proud mother has not the vaguest idea of what is going on in her son's mind.

In the next group of twelve lines Rimbaud enumerates the character traits of this repressed child. He wears the cloak of obedience all day long (*Tout le jour il suait d'obéissance*) but just as with most repressed children, sooner or later psychological "tics" (*des tics noirs*) begin to manifest themselves and reveal his "acrid hypocrisy" (*prouver en lui d'âcres hypocrisies*). In the musty corridors he sticks out his tongue (*En passant il tirait la langue*) at his classmates, "his two fists lowered" (*les deux poings / A l'aine*) but ready for action. He would close his eyes so tight he saw stars (*dans ses yeux fermés voyait des points*). In the evening he could be seen pouting on the stairway above as the last light of day poured through a dormer window (*On le voyait, là-haut, qui râlait sur la rampe, / Sous un golfe de jour pendant du toit*). In the hated heat of summer he would lock himself up in the latrine where it was a little cooler (*A se refermer dans la fraîcheur des latrines*) in order to think and regale his nostrils (*Il pensait là, tranquille et livrant ses narines*). Rimbaud also described this attraction of the excremental when speaking of the young girl in "Les Premières Communions."

In the third group of fourteen lines Rimbaud reveals that his poet likes winter no better than summer. The little garden is "bathed in moonlight" (Rimbaud again uses the Latinism *s'illunait* incorrectly as he did in "Les Premières Communions"). The poet is "lying in the dirt at the foot of the wall, / Squeezing his eyes until he is dizzy in order to provoke visions" (*Gisant au pied d'un mur, enterré dans la marne, / Et pour des visions écrasant son oeil darne*). Rimbaud uses the colloquial expression *darne* as he did in "Accroupissements" and just as the priest "listened to the hair grow on his clammy skin," so the poet "listened to the teeming of the mangy fruit trees" (*Il écoutait grouiller les galeux espaliers*). His only friends are the poor children who "spoke with the sweetness of idiots" (*Conversaient avec la douceur des idiots*). Rimbaud has used ten lines to set the scene for the appearance of the mother who disapproves of his friendship with these ragamuffins (*l'ayant surpris à des pitiés immondes, / Sa mère s'effrayait*). His compassion is "foul" (*immondes*) only in her eyes. The poet will throw his profound tenderness in the astonished face of his mother (*les tendresses, profondes, / De l'enfant se jetaient sur cet étonnement*), because he knows that, in spite of her Bible and self-satisfaction, she is a hypocrite (*Elle avait le bleu regard,—qui ment*).

The last group of thirty-four lines recounts the visions, dreams, and experiences of the poet. Most poets and most seven year olds make up stories (*il faisait des romans*) about exotic and faraway places, for they represent freedom (*où luit la Liberté ravie*) from this constraining life. The young poet finds inspiration in the illustrated magazines (*Il s'aidait / De journaux illustrés*) where he saw laughing Spanish and Italian women (*il regardait / Des Espagnoles rire et des Italiennes*). He also has his first sexual experience when the eight-year-old neighbor, "the daughter of workers next door" (*la fille des ouvriers d'à côté*), dressed "in Indian robes" (*en robes d'indiennes*) right out of his picture books, "jumped on his back" (*elle avait sauté, / Dans un coin, sur son dos*) and attacked him (*par elle meurtri des poings et des talons*). In self-defense "he bit her on the buttocks / For she never wore panties" (*il lui mordait les fesses, / Car elle ne portrait jamais de pantalons*). He "took back with him to his room the taste of her skin" (*Remportait les saveurs de sa peau dans sa chambre*). If he detested summer, he also feared winter when he had to spend the pallid Sundays reading the Bible with its cabbage-green pages in front of the fireplace (*Il craignait les blafards dimanches de décembre, / Où, pommadé, sur un guéridon d'acajou, / Il lisait une Bible à la tranche vert-chou*). This juxtaposition of the sexual experience with the reading of the Bible highlights the realism of the former and the hypocrisy of the latter.

He was oppressed by the contradiction of his dreams (*Des rêves l'oppressaient*), for if "he did not love God" (*Il n'aimait pas Dieu*), he did love the workers whom he saw coming home in the evening, "dirty, in their working clothes" (*Noirs, en blouse*). Can one not love God and still love his fellow man? If one loves his fellow man does he automatically love God? Liberty is indeed ravished if these men have no choice but to work all day only to return home dirty and dog-tired. In the face of the reality before him "he dreamed of amorous prairies where luminous / Swells, wholesome perfumes, golden pubescences, / Make a calm movement and take flight" (*Il rêvait la prairie amoureuse, où des houles / Lumineuses, parfums sains, pubescences d'or, / Font leur remuement calme et prennent leur essor*). Rimbaud again uses a technical term, *pubescences*, which describes the state of plant stems and leaves when they begin to be covered with a down of fine, short hairs, a development necessary for the full blooming of the plant. Perhaps no one line better describes Rimbaud's poetic method than this one in which all of the lovely visions make one small, calm movement and suddenly take flight before the reader's eyes. The young poet returns to his room to relive has fantasies. The contrast in the final three lines is between the reality of "the sounds of the city / Down below" (*la rumeur du quartier, / En bas*) and the poet up in his room "sitting on a piece of ecru-colored / Cloth, and violently foreseeing sails" (*couché sur des pièces de toile / Ecrue, et pressentant violemment la voile*). All the poet needs is a scrap of cloth in order to dream of ships and exotic lands. Another key word is *violemment* for if Rimbaud's images suddenly take flight, they do so with a violent wrench of the imagination. If any one poem foretells the Rimbaud to come, "Les Poètes de sept ans" is it.

In "Les Soeurs de charité" (Sisters of Charity), probably written before June, 1871,[4] it is a question of both charity, one of the keys to *Une Saison en enfer*, and a genie, who plays an important role in the *Illuminations*. The opening quatrain describes the physical attributes of a young man so handsome that "an unknown Genie in Persia might have worshipped him beneath the moon" (*qu'eût.... sous la lune / Adoré, dans la Perse, un Génie inconnu*). The second quatrain reveals some of his psychological attributes for he is "Impetuous with charms" that are both "virginal / And black" (*Impétueux avec des douceurs virginales / Et noires*). The enjambment of the adjective "black" serves to underline the sense of guilt he suffers for impulses that in their newness are essentially "pure." Like most young men he is "proud of his first pigheaded enthusiasms" (*fier de ses premiers entêtements*). The second half of the quatrain in which his enthusiasms are compared "to young seas, tears of summer nights / That turn on beds of diamonds" (*Pareil aux jeunes mers, pleurs de nuits estivales / Qui se retournent sur des lits de diamants*) is a dazzling vision. In the third quatrain "the young man" finds himself "face to face with the ugliness of this world" (*Le jeune homme, devant les laideurs de ce monde*), "full of the eternal and profound wound" (*plein de la blessure éternelle et profonde*) that is birth into, and knowledge of, this world, and at that moment he "begins to desire his sister of charity" (*Se prend à désirer sa soeur de charité*).

Rimbaud spends three quatrains demonstrating how and why woman cannot be that sister of charity. She is nothing more than a "heap of entrails" and "sweet pity" (*monceau d'entrailles, pitié douce*). In spite of her physical attractions (*regard, ventre, doigts, seins, prunelles*), she "is never the sister of charity" (*Tu n'es jamais la soeur de charité*), whereas all physical love is "only a question" (*Tout notre embrassement n'est qu'une question*) because it satisfies the need but momentarily. He who would depend upon her finds that woman is dependent upon him (*C'est toi qui pends à nous*) and must be cradled (*Nous te berçons*), "charming and grave Passion" (*charmante et grave Passion*) that she is. In spite of the misogyny Rimbaud goes on to explain woman's dependence, the first reason being the brutal moral and physical subjugation she has suffered at the hands of man (*les brutalités souffertes autrefois*). The second reason is physiological. She "gives her all" (*Tu nous rends tout*) including the excess of blood of menstruation (*Comme un excès de sang épanché tous les mois*). This spilling of blood is quite the opposite of malicious, so that woman is like the dark night that covers us "but without malevolence" (*ô Nuit pourtant sans malveillances*).

In the last four quatrains the narrator turns to other possible sisters of charity. Frightened by the dependence of woman (*Quand la femme, portée un instant, l'épouvante*), he considers for a moment "Love, the call of life, and the song of action" (*Amour, appel de vie et chanson d'action*). Then "come the green Muse and burning Justice" like an "august obsession" (*Viennent la Muse verte et la Justice ardente / Le déchirer de leur auguste obsession*). One critic sees the green Muse as the Muse of Nature and burning Justice as the anarchy of Prudhon.[5] Another sees them as absinthe and revolution.[6] Why cannot the green Muse be simply that inspiration which creates something new that is tender and green like a shoot in the soil and which grows into an idea that changes the world? Certainly burning Justice represents Rimbaud's desire for justice for all as demonstrated in "Les Poétes de sept ans," "Les Pauvres à l'église," and many other poems. And certainly poetic creation and revolution were obsessions with him. "Endlessly perturbed by the splendors and the calms" (*sans cesse altéré des splendeurs et des calmes*) of these obsessions, "Abandoned by these two inplacable Sisters" (*Délaissé des deux Soeurs implacables*), he turns "whimpering / Tenderly to knowledge with its nourishing arms" (*geignant / Avec tendresse après la science aux bras almes, almes* being a somewhat awkward Latinism based on *alma*, "nourishing"). But knowledge with its "black alchemy and holy studies" (*la noire alchimie et les saintes études*) is repugnant to this man wounded by life because it does not fill his "atrocious solitude" (*d'atroces solitudes*).

Rimbaud's conclusion is something of a Romantic letdown. There is only one sister of charity who can aid this man and "Although he believes in vast ends, immense Dreams or / Promenades through the nights of Truth" (*Qu'il croie aux vastes fins, Rêves ou Promenades / Immenses, à travers les nuits de Vérité*), he calls upon her "with all his body and soul" (*t'appelle en son âme et ses membres malades*). She is none other than "mysterious Death" (*O Mort mystérieuse*), the ultimate sister of charity who delivers us from the servitude of life. The poem reveals the extremes to which Rimbaud will go in his search for inspiration while the mention of charity, the Genie, and alchemy hint at concepts used in his later poetry.

II   Song of the Vowels

The fourteen lines of Rimbaud's sonnet of the "Voyelles" (Vowels), written before September, 1871, have caused more comment than any other single short work.[7] Unfortunately most of the "discoveries" about the poem are inconclusive and the results of their detailed application unconvincing. Taking the poem for what it seems to say, almost no reader could doubt that the assigning of colors to vowels is an exercise in synesthesia. Many artists before Rimbaud discussed the possibility, but his immediate source was obviously Baudelaire. In the "Salon" of 1846 Baudelaire quoted E. T. A. Hoffmann, who was convinced of "an analogy and an intimate connection between colors, sounds, and perfumes." Baudelaire chose the order "Perfumes, colors, and sounds" in his sonnet "Correspondances." But Baudelaire spoke of "sounds" while Rimbaud writes of "vowels." The use of vowels may have been suggested to him by a colored alphabet book rediscovered or remembered from childhood. If so, the correlation between the vowels, their colors, and their examples is striking but not precise. Even if Rimbaud borrowed the image of the black fly buzzing around cruel stenches from the fourth and fifth quatrains of Baudelaire's "Une Charogne" (Carrion) where it is a question of stench (puanteur), buzzing flies (Les mouches bourdonnaient), "this putrid stomach" (ce ventre putride) that suggests Rimbaud's "gulfs of shadow" (golfes d'ombre), and "black battalions" (de noirs batallions), as one critic has suggested,[8] the idea of synesthesia breaks down because Rimbaud does not illustrate the color of the vowel with examples that include the sound of the vowel. The point of departure was thus synesthesia, but the demonstration was not synesthetic.

The next thing the reader notices is that Rimbaud did not list the vowels in the usual order but rather, A, E, I, U, O, so that he could use the Greek Alpha and Omega for the beginning and end. Later, however, when he refers to the poem in "Alchimie du verbe" in *Une Saison*, he lists them in the usual order. The reader also notices that Rimbaud named five colors, black, white, red, green, and blue, the first two of which are not colors of the spectrum since black is the absence of all color and white the presence of all color, although the two do provide Rimbaud with the sharp distinction of opposites. Red, green, and blue, nevertheless, follow the usual order of the spectrum while violet, the last of the order, appears in the last line of the sonnet. If the black of the vowel remains the black fly of the example, white becomes "candors" (*candeurs*, from the Latin *candor*, "whiteness"), red becomes purple, green becomes *virides* (a neologism from the Latin *viridis*, "green"), while blue becomes the violet of the last line.

What, then, is the correlation between the form of the vowel and the example? Critics are content with the Roman *A* as symbolic of the fly and its wings (*noir corset velu des mouches*). The *I* in its vertical narrowness does suggest a stream of blood (*sang craché*) or in its horizontal narrowness the lips (*rire des belles lèvres*). The *U* does suggest cycles and the undulations of sea and pasture (*cycles, vibrements divins des mers virides, / Paix des pâtis*) as well as, perhaps, the wrinkles in a studious forehead (*paix des rides / . . . aux grands fronts studieux*), particularly those between the eyebrows caused by squinting. And certainly *O* does symbolize the opening of the bell of the bugle (*Clairon*) as well as eyes (*Ses Yeux*). But what about *E?* Critics who are content with the Roman *A* insist that Rimbaud really meant the Greek epsilon ε. If you lay it on its front side ⌒ you get the mounds of rising morning vapors and the forms of tents and glaciers as well as the rounded flower cluster of the umbel (*ombelles*, from the same stem as umbrella). If you lay it on its back ⌣ you get the lances (*Lances*). The kings (*rois blancs*) are more difficult to see but perhaps they are standing up straight or sitting up on horseback like lances. What else has been discovered in the innocent epsilon in this position beggars description.[9] Much of this speculation on form is fun but it turns out to be mostly fun.

What about the phonetic and moral attributes connected with the vowels? Certainly there is an *A* in *noir* and *éclatant* plus

the nasal *A* repeated in *puanteurs,* but the sounds are hardly pure
and insistent as one might expect. The sound suggested is that
of "buzzing" (*bombinent,* a form already used by Rimbaud in
"Les Mains de Jeanne-Marie"). The adjective "cruel" (*cruelles*)
would seem in Rimbaud's lexicon to refer to the color black
rather than the vowel, if we remember Rimbaud's "black blood
of belladonnas" in "Les Mains de Jeanne-Marie." Buzzing hardly
suggests the vowel *A* to me. The acute *E* is present only in *et,
des* (twice), and *glaciers,* the grave *E* in *fiers* and *ombelles,*
the mute *E* in *tentes, lances,* and *ombelles,* while the soft sound
of œ is insisted upon in the repetition *candeurs-vapeurs,* hardly
a dramatic demonstration of the vowel *E* in any of its pronuncia-
tions. The moral and physical attributes are guilelessness (*candeurs*), pride (*fiers*), and the shivering (*frissons*) of flowers in
the wind. *I* suggests the sharp sound of laughter (*rire,* which
does include the vowel) and, while the lips are beautiful
(*belles*), the laughter is that of anger (*colère*) or, what is worse,
"penitent drunkenness" (*ivresses pénitentes,* both of which include the vowel). The first tercet describes *U* by using the sound
only twice in the thirty-six syllables, in the first which names
it and in the last, *studieux.* Otherwise the vowel is absent. The
sibilant cycles (*cycles*), "the divine vibrations of the green seas"
(*vibrements divins des mers virides,* with *vibrements* a neologism
based on the verb *vibrer*), the "Peace of pastures sown with
animals, the peace of wrinkles" (*Paix des pâtis semés d'animaux,
paix des rides*), are formed in the quiet pursuit of knowledge.
The mention of alchemy (*l'alchimie*) sent scholars into a flurry
of activity in an attempt to uncover all Rimbaud knew about the
subject. Certainly he knew something about it, possibly from
primary sources but more probably from secondary sources. The
discovery that Eliphas Lévi had used the expression "angels
and worlds" while Rimbaud had written "Worlds and Angels"
(*des Mondes et des Anges*) was sufficient to encourage critics
to attempt total interpretations according to the occult sciences,
none of which is very convincing.

In the final tercet the *O* is the sound of the "supreme Trumpet full of strange stridencies" (*suprème Clairon plein des
strideurs étranges; strideurs* is a rare word Rimbaud had used in
"Paris se repeuple"), that is, the trumpet of the Last Judgment.

The stridencies are intermingled with the "Silences traversed by the Worlds and the Angels" (*Silences traversés des Mondes et des Anges*). The line is ambiguous and can be read as the "traversed silences" of the Worlds and the Angels, that is, their silences that are full of movement like the heavens which the planets and angels inhabit or it can mean that the silences are traversed by the worlds and angels themselves. "Worlds" is also ambiguous, since it could mean planets, but in opposition to angels it could also mean the worlds of mortal men who will be the victims of the Last Judgment as opposed to the angels who will be spared. The last line of the sonnet is a final irony because it offers the ultimate ambiguity, "O the Omega, violet rays of His [or Her] Eyes" (*O l'Oméga, rayon violet de Ses Yeux*). Some critics are convinced it must be "Her Eyes" since Rimbaud obviously had in mind the violet eyes of a girlfriend who had recently ditched him. What girl? Well, there may have been one if not several. Other critics read it as "His Eyes," the eyes of the Lord on the Day of Judgment which I find, because of the capitals and because of the association of God with omega, more consistent with the cataclysmic tone of the final tercet. Or the line may be nothing more, as a critic has suggested,[10] than a plagiarized line from Leconte de Lisle's poem "Péristèris" which reads, "The golden ray which swims in her violet eyes" (*Le rayon d'or qui nage en ses yeux violets*).

Almost all of these conjectures contain some germ of truth, and almost all of them are incorrect if they are insisted upon in detail. I can agree with René Etiemble's evaluation of the sonnet as an "incoherent poem, loosely constructed, stuffed with literary allusions, Latinisms, [and] bookish images" (p. 233). Yet I am also convinced that readers will always be attracted to this poem, which moves from a cruel view of physical death to the apocalyptic vision of the Last Judgment in passing by the peaceful vapors that rise from and around tents in the early morning, the glimmer of proud glaciers and white kings, and the gentle movement of flowers in the wind, to the excesses of blood and anger and passion, to the divine undulations of the sea and the pastures with their lowing herds, and the mysterious quiet of the alchemist's study. Something about the sounds and the sights, this kaleidoscope of visions, will continue to draw readers in spite of its apparent lack of logical meaning. Whatever meaning the poem has, the reader brings it to the poem and as long as there are new readers, there will be new meanings.

III *A Poet's Song to a Poet*

On August 15, 1871, Rimbaud sent a second letter to Banville inclosing the poem "Ce qu'on dit au poète à propos des fleurs" (What One Says to the Poet about Flowers), dated July 14, 1871, and signed Alcide Bava (again from *baver*, to slobber). Although the poem is long and contains several obvious borrowings from Banville as well as parodies of Armand Silvestre, Albert Mérat, Leconte de Lisle, and others,[11] it is far from just more poetic "slobbering." The title presents the first problem. Some critics believe that the "one" (*on*) of the title is a typical bourgeois telling the poet what he thinks of poeticizing about flowers. I find that the poet of the title is Rimbaud himself and the *on* the "they" of his contemporaries and predecessors who wrote extravagantly about flowers. Rimbaud is repeating all the ridiculous things "they" have written on the subject. In the poem Rimbaud gives his analysis of the situation of the poet in contemporary society at the moment he himself was beginning to write according to the concepts of the Seer Letters, just before the composition of "Le Bateau ivre" and his departure from Charleville to realize his poetic ambitions.

The poem's forty quatrains of octosyllables rhyming *a b a b* are grouped in five sections containing six, nine, seven, eleven, and seven quatrains. Part I begins with the adverb "Thus" (*Ainsi*), which is usually reserved for the conclusion of a poem. Rimbaud's parody will "thus" be the conclusion to the long history of the poet's use and abuse of flowers beginning with the lily. After two lines filled with Parnassian "black azure / Where trembles the sea of topazes" (*l'azur noir / Où tremble la mer des topazes*), Rimbaud quickly sets the satirical tone by using the very "functional" verb "will function" (*Fonctionneront*) to refer to delicate "Lilies" (*Les Lys*) and tops it off with the parenthetical expression "these enemas of ecstasies" (*ces clystères d'extases, clystères* being the technical term), thus creating an unexpected shower of flowers. In our more practical epoch (*notre époque*) when plants are expected to work for us (*Quand les Plantes sont travailleuses*) like the palm trees (*sagous*) that produce starch, the lily can only suffer (*boira les bleus dégoûts*) as the subject of the poet's religious extravagances (*Dans tes Proses religieuses*) with *Proses* as an indication of what Rimbaud thinks about such poetry. The lily as the "fleur de lys" long served the political purposes of defenders of the monarchy like Monsieur de Kerdrel while the lily along "with the carnation and the amaranth" (*avec l'oeillet et l'amarante*) was the reward of the minstrel (*Ménestrel*), a term from the Middle Ages, a period much in vogue with the Romantics of the generation of 1830 (*Le Sonnet de mil huit cent trente*). Although few lilies are actually to be seen (*On n'en voit pas*), they "are always shivering" (*Toujours frissonnent*) in the poet's verses like the quivering "sleeves / Of soft-stepping Sinners" (*les manches / Des Pécheresses aux doux pas*). Rimbaud addresses these poets with the ironic "My Dear" (*Cher*) and points out that while the poet blathers on about lilies, the same "morning breezes" that sweep "over the lowly forget-me-nots" (*brises du matin / Sur les myosotis immondes*), lowly and therefore unclean (*immondes*) and beneath the poet's contempt, sweep over him when he, who considers himself to be of the lily family, must take his bath just like any other mortal. And his bathrobe, just like anyone else's, billows out with the morning drafts (*Ta chemise ... / Se gonfle*). The only thing the poet's "love will allow to pass through his tollbooths are / Lilacs" (*L'amour ne passe à tes octrois / Que les Lilas*) which all poets call "swings" (*balançoires*) as they balance in the breeze, and "Wood Violets" (*les Violettes du Bois*) which all poets call the "Sugary spittle of black Nymphs" (*Crachats sucrés des Nymphes noires*). So much for lilies.

Rimbaud speaks of roses in Part II. Poets are content only when they have enormously "puffed-up Roses" (*Roses soufflées*), "inflated" with the music "of a thousand octaves" (*Et de mille octaves enflées*). Only a Banville can cause roses to snow down (*Quand BANVILLE en ferait neiger*), "streaked with blood" because they are red (*Sanguinolentes*) and "swirling" (*tournoyantes*). Woe to "the stranger / With his ill-disposed interpretations" (*l'étranger / Aux lectures mal bienveillantes*), for Ban-

ville will "poach his mad eye" (*Pochant l'oeil fou*) like an egg.
Most poets are like "peaceful photographers" (*paisibles pho-
tographes*), because the flora they depict are "about as diverse /
As carafe stoppers" (*diverse à peu près / Comme des bouchons
de carafes*). All that ordinary poets can talk about are "French
vegetables, / Ill-tempered, consumptive, ridiculous" (*les végétaux Français, / Hargneux, phtisiques, ridicules*), so lowly that
"the stomach of basset hounds / Navigates peacefully" through
them "at sundown" (*le ventre des chiens bassets / Navigue en
paix, aux crépuscules*). Or such poets take inspiration "from
frightful drawings" full of exotic flowers like "blue Lotus or
Sunflowers" (*d'affreux dessins / De Lotos bleus ou d'Hélianthes*)
and from "rosy prints with holy subjects" (*Estampes roses, sujets
saints*) like Rimbaud must have received for his first communion.
An ode on the mythological Indian plant, the Açoka, "fits in
nicely with the / Stanza on a prostitute's window" (*L'Ode Açoka
cadre avec la / Strophe en fenêtre de lorette*) and is about as
poetic, while "heavy butterflies" (*lourds papillons*) "Discharge
on a Daisy" (*Fientent sur la Pâquerette*). All of this "Old
greenery" (*Vieilles verdures*) is for sale as cheaply as the "Old
clothes" of the old-clothes dealer's cry which included "old
lace" (*vieux galons*). The poetry is nothing more than "vegetable
pastries" (*croquignoles végétales*) because it is made of flowers,
perhaps the fantastic flowers (*Fleurs fantasques*) made of
feathers or shells found "in old Salons" (*des vieux Salons*).
This poetry is as harmless as the buzzing of june bugs, not
at all like the rattle of the dangerous rattlesnake (*Aux han-
netons, pas aux crotales*). The poems are "chubby vegetable
babes in tears" (*Ces poupards végétaux en pleurs*) that a
dreadful artist like Jean Gérard, called Grandville, would have
put on a leash (*Que Grandville eût mis aux lisières*) and that
"evil stars with visors" (*De méchants astres à visières*)
"suckled with colors" (*qu'allaitèrent de couleurs*) about as
colorful as milk. These "smudges from musical pipes / Make
precious glucoses" (*vos bavures de pipeaux / Font de précieuses
glucoses*). The poems are mere ink smudges intended to be
musical. *Précieuses* can be taken in the seventeenth-century
meaning or in the sense that glucose is a necessity of life. Glucose is many things, for example, the organic substance synthe-

sized by green plants during the assimilation of chlorophyll and
thus consistent with the flower theme. But it can also be described as a thick, starchy syrup or as nothing more than
sugared water. All of these definitions fit the poem. Rimbaud
terminates Part II with a magnificent figure. All of these flowers,
these "Lilies, Açokas, Lilacs and Roses" (*Lys, Açokas, Lilas et
Roses*) are nothing more than a "Pile of fried eggs in old hats"
(*Tas d'oeufs frits dans de vieux chapeaux*).

In Part III Rimbaud calls the poet a "white Hunter" (*blanc
Chasseur*) "who runs stockingless / Through the panic pasture"
(*qui cours sans bas / A travers le Pâtis panique*) in search of
rhymes. The word *panique* comes from the name Pan, Greek
god of the forests, pastures, and flocks. Surely the poet should
know his botany a bit better (*Ne peux-tu, ne dois-tu pas / Con-
naître un peu ta botanique*). Rimbaud fears that the poet will
substitute the exotic for the ordinary, "Catharis [Spanish fly, an
aphrodisiac of dried beetles] for crickets" (*Aux grillons roux les
Cantharides*), "The gold" of South American rivers "for the blue
of the Rhine" (*L'or des Rios au bleu des Rhins*), warm and
flowery Floridas for cold and barren Norways (*aux Norvèges les
Florides*). Rimbaud mentions Norway several times in his poetry
and uses *Florides* in "Le Bateau ivre." The time has passed when
the poet's art can reduce "the astonishing Eucalyptus / Of the
boa constrictors to a line of six feet" (*l'Eucalyptus étonnant /
Des constrictors d'un hexamètre*). Rimbaud plays on the idea
of constriction in the word *constrictors* as well as on the idea of
a snake six poetic feet long. The poet speaks "As if Mahogany /
Only served, even in Guiana" (*Comme si les Acajous / Ne
servaient, même en nos Guyanes*), as a home for monkeys in the
"heavy delirium of tropical vines" (*Au lourd délire des lianes*).
The liquid *l*'s of *lourd, délire,* and *lianes* suggest the flowing
movements of the monkeys and the vines. "In short" (*En somme*),
the time has come when all this poetic prattle about "a Flower,
Rosemary / Or Lily, dead or alive" (*une Fleur, Romarin / Ou
Lys, vive ou morte*), is not worth a "seabird's excrement" (*Un
excrément d'oiseau marin*) or the "single tear of a candle" (*un
seul pleur de chandelle*). When Rimbaud speaks of "seabird's
excrement" is he thinking of South American guano so useful as
fertilizer? He is also probably saying that it is not worth wasting

a single drop of candlewax on the writing of this flowery poetry. In the last two quatrains Rimbaud maintains that even if such poets were to visit these faraway places in order to find inspiration, they would spend their time "seated down there, in a / Bamboo hut with the shutters / Closed" (*assis là-bas, dans une / Cabane de bambous—volets / Clos*). Rimbaud again uses *assis* pejoratively and insists that even in this exotic setting such poets would "polish off flowery offerings / Worthy of the extravagant Oise" (*Tu torcherais des floraisons / Dignes d'Oises extravagantes*), the Oise being a peaceful river that flows from Belgium through northern France to the Seine, hardly an exotic sight. Rimbaud concludes that the reasons for writing such poetry are "No less laughable than they are arrogant" (*Non moins risibles qu'arrogantes*).

In Part IV, the longest of the poem, Rimbaud enumerates the subjects the poet should treat according to the practical and mercenary spirit of the age. Rimbaud first uses "Speak" (*Dis*, three times), then "Let us know" (*Sachons*, once), and finally "Discover" (*Trouve*, five times), as exhortations to the poet so that he will be able to "serve us" (*sers-nous*, once) his pitiful findings. He should speak to us not of "terrifying revolts" (*d'épouvantables révoltes*) but of "exotic harvests" (*exotiques récoltes*) like "tobacco and cotton" (*les tobacs, les cotonniers*) that will make money. Rimbaud called the poet a "White Hunter." Now that he has gone off on his expedition his "white forehead" has been "tanned by Phoebus," the Greek god both of the sun and poetry (*front blanc que Phébus tanna*). He should tell us how many dollars it will cost to exploit Cubans like Pedro Velasquez and Havana itself (*combien de dollars se rente / Pedro Velasquez, Habana*). The poet should "Smother with excrement the sea surrounding Sorrento" (*Incague la mer de Sorrente*), where "thousands of Swans" take refuge (*Où vont les Cygnes par milliers*). *Incaque* is an obsolete verb from the Latin *incacare*, the source of the modern French child's expression for excrement, *caca*. The swan was, of course, one of the favorite symbols of the Parnassians.

The poet's stanzas (*strophes*) should be "publicity" (*des réclames*) "For the felling of mangroves / Ransacked by hydras and blades" (*Pour l'abatis des mangliers / Fouillés des hydres et des lames*). The poet's quatrain should "plunge into the blood-stained forests" (*plonge aux bois sanglants*), bloody because slashed by the blades just mentioned, in order to bring back useful products like "sugar, / Medicines and gums" (*de sucres blancs, / De pectoraires et de gommes*, with *pectoraires* a neologism referring to plants that provide drugs useful in treating respiratory diseases). The poet should be a scientist in order to determine "if the fairness / Of snowy Peaks, near the Tropics" (*si les blondeurs / Des Pics neigeux, vers les Tropiques*) is due to "egg-laying insects" (*des insectes pondeurs*) or "microscopic lichens" (*lichens microscopiques*). The poet as hunter (*Chasseur*) should find some sort of "perfumed plant" (*garances parfumées, garances* being the madder plant formerly used in dyeing) that nature herself would cause to bloom into pants for the army (*Que la Nature en pantalons / Fasse éclore!—pour nos Armées*). Or he should find near the edges of the "sleeping Forest" (*Bois qui dort*, which is a take-off on Sleeping Beauty, *La Belle au bois dormant*), flowers that will provide profitable oils for the hair (*des pommades d'or / Sur les cheveux*). Or he should find "in the mad meadows" (*aux près fous*) "pubescences" (*pubescences*, the technical expression Rimbaud used in "Les Poètes de sept ans" to designate the short hairs on plant stems) that could be turned into silver money (*argent*), or flower "calixes full of Eggs of fire / That cook in their own juices" (*Des calices pleins d'Oeufs de feu / Qui cuisent parmi les essences*), thus providing ready-prepared food. Or he should find other "cottony Thistles" (*des Chardons cotonneux*) from which material can be woven (*filer les noeuds*), or "Flowers that can serve as chairs" (*des Fleurs qui soient des chaises*). Or he should find "in the heart of the black veins / Some almost petrified flowers" (*au coeur des noirs filons / Des fleurs presque pierres*), in other words, precious stones the color of flowers and of course "valuable" (*fameuses*), that might also have "gemlike tonsils" (*des amygdales gemmeuses, gemmeuses* being a neologism based on *gemme*, "gem"). But what can the poet, this "Wag" (*Farceur*), serve up except "Stews of syrupy Lilies" (*Des ragoûts de Lys sirupeux*), which would at least be good to eat. Of course he would serve them "On a platter of splendid vermeil" (*Sur un plat de vermeil splendide*) to be eaten with "spoons of metal alloy" (*cuillers Alfénide*, the latter being an alloy used for tableware). Such are all the practical purposes to which the poet should dedicate himself.

The seven quatrains of Part V speak of heaven and hell, religion and the reality of contemporary life. Critics are divided over the meaning of the first quatrain. Some see it as a satire on religiosity according to which "the great Love" (*le grand Amour*) would be the love of God that steals for us from heaven "somber Indulgences" (*des sombres Indulgences*), remissions of sin and forgiveness. Others see this "great love" as the love Rimbaud will create (*dira*) in his poetry and that will, just as Prometheus stole fire from the heavens, be so great that it will steal indulgences and freedom for us from heaven. The first interpretation is more in keeping with the idea that even a writer like Renan—the symbol of adjustment to religious existence with his *Life of Jesus*—or the cat Murr of E. T. A. Hoffmann's two-volume *Kater Murr*—a philosophical dialogue between a tomcat and a mad musician in which the cat symbolizes the banal, complacent, and trivial—could never see "the immense Blue Thyrsi" (*les Bleus Thyrses immenses*), thyrsi being staffs surmounted by pine cones or bunches of leaves with grapes that were an attribute of Bacchus, the god of wine. Rimbaud found the cat's name as well as the rhyme *amour-Murr* in Banville's *Odes funambulesques*. Thus neither Renan nor Murr will ever know this great love or experience the visions induced by wine. Rimbaud asks the poet to arouse us to hysteria (*les hystéries*) "in our torpors, / By means of perfumes" (*dans nos torpeurs, / Par les parfums*), to exalt us (*Exalte-nous*) "to guilelessness / More guileless than Mary Herself" (*vers des candeurs / Plus candides que les Maries*). Rimbaud is playing on the double meaning of *candeurs* as whiteness, thus purity, and as guilelessness just as he did in "Voyelles." For a writer to be a poet in this modern world he must be a "Merchant, colonist, medium" (*Commerçant! Colon! Médium*) so that his "Rhyme will well up" (*Ta Rhyme sourdra*) "Like a ray of sodium, / Like rubber that pours out" (*Comme un rayon de sodium, / Comme un caoutchouc qui s'épanche*). He must be a juggler (*Jongleur*) so that "strange and electric flowers / And butterflies" (*d'étranges fleurs / Et des papillons électriques*) will escape (*s'évadent*) from his "black Poems" (*noirs Poèmes*) with their refractions of white, green, and red lights (*Blancs, verts, et rouges dioptriques*). The electric butterfly is another Surrealist image fifty years before the fact.

In the fifth quatrain Rimbaud foreshadows *Une Saison en enfer* by declaring "this is the Century of hell" (*c'est le Siècle d'enfer*) in which "telegraph poles / Will decorate,—a lyre with songs of iron, / [The poet's] magnificent shoulderblades" (*les poteaux télégraphiques / Vont orner,—lyre aux chants de fer, / Tes omoplates magnifiques*). To be truly popular the poet will have "to compose a poem / On the disease of potatoes" (*rime une version / Sur le mal des pommes de terre*) and in order to create "Poems full of mystery / That will be read from Tréguier / To Paramaribo" (*Poèmes pleins de mystère / Qu'on doive lire de Tréguier / A Paramaribo*)—Tréquier is the town where Renan was born and Paramaribo a city in faraway Surinam—he ought to "buy again the illustrated volumes of Figuier," whose large collection of *Tableaux de la nature* was published by Hachette in Paris (*rachète / Des Tomes de Monsieur Figuier, / —Illustrés!—chez Monsieur Hachette*). In other words, if you want to be a poet, look at picture books, says Rimbaud sarcastically, for that's about as much as the typical poet knows about nature.

Strangely enough, that is exactly what Rimbaud did in the composition of many of his poems and that is about how much he knew of the exotic places named in his poetry. But just as Rimbaud was unwilling to compromise with the tastes of his time in order to be a popular poet, so he incorporated many of the recent discoveries into his poetry, and thus was one of the first to create poetry inspired by unpoetic subjects. His poetry thus takes it place among the first truly urban works. Poetry was his religion during his short career just as it was Mallarmé's, so that both of them would agree with E. T. A. Hoffmann's conclusion to his short story "The Golden Pot": "Can anything but Poesy reveal itself as the sacred Harmony of all Beings, as the deepest secret of Nature?"[12] Rimbaud knew what earlier poets had said about flowers and was convinced that new subjects would have to be treated in a new way if poetry was to progress.

The explication of this poem has taken a good deal of space

because it is one of the longest and one of the first in which Rimbaud gave free rein to his fancy. This list of twenty-eight different types of flowers and plants plus almost endless variations on generic terms, combined with the images of the poached eye, the fried eggs in a hat, and the basset hound in the vegetables, seem to spring from Rimbaud's imagination with an ease and spontaneity that Mallarmé never managed. The reader can understand how Yves Bonnefoy found the poem to be one of Rimbaud's "most admirable" and "without doubt the one with his purest energy."[13] Mallarmé's poetry sometimes surpasses that of Rimbaud in beauty and finesse, but it almost never speaks with the vigor and urgency of Rimbaud's voice as it warns us that "this is the Century of hell."

IV A Song of Childhood

I cannot leave Rimbaud's early poems without speaking of at least one that treats of childhood since so many of them do. One of the most impressive is "Les Chercheuses de poux" (The Lice Seekers), whose date is still a conjecture.[14] Its five quatrains of alexandrines rhyming *a b a b* are full of visual, olfactory, tactile, and auditory sensations that heighten the contrast between the realism of what is being said and the poetic beauty of how it is being said. The first word of each quatrain has a special significance. The "When" (*Quand*) of the first quatrain finds its resolution in the "Then" (*Voilà que*) of the last. "The child" (*l'enfant*) is mentioned in the first line of both the first and second quatrains as well as in the next to the last line of the poem. Elsewhere the play of pronouns is between *Elles* ("They") as the first word of the second quatrain and the *Il* ("He") of the third and fourth. The contrast is also between the delightful sensations he is experiencing and the actions of the lice seekers, the former occasioned by the latter. The visual sensations include the colors of the "red turmoils" (*rouges tourmentes*) on his forehead caused by his scratching, "the white swarm of blurred dreams" (*l'essaim blanc des rêves indistincts*) taking place in his head, the seekers' "silvery fingernails" (*ongles argentins*), "the blue air" (*l'air bleu*) of the beautiful day, the rosy honey of their breath (*de longs miels végétaux et rosés*), the black of their eyelashes (*leurs cils noirs*), as well as the play on the word "gray" in the idiomatic expression "his be-fuddled indolence" (*ses grises indolences*).

The vision of the flashing fingers is intensified by descriptive terms like "frail" (*frêles*), "slender, terrible, and bewitching" (*fins, terribles et charmeurs*), "electric and gentle" (*électriques et doux*), while the fingernails are dubbed "royal" (*royaux*). The olfactory sensations are created by "a jumble of flowers" (*un fouillis de fleurs*), the odor of the seekers' breath "which smells like a long string of rosy, vegetable honey" (*Qui fleurent de longs miels végétaux et rosés*), and their "perfumed / Silences" (*les silences / Parfumés*). The auditory sensations include the song of their breath (*Il écoute chanter leurs haleines*), the whis-tling as they draw in their saliva (*un sifflement, salives / Reprises sur la lèvre ou désirs de baisers*), the sound of the beating of their eyelashes (*Il entend leurs cils nors battant*), another Sur-realist image, the crackling (*crépiter*) of the squashed lice, and the sigh of the harmonica (*Soupir d'harmonica*). The sibilants *s* and *z* of *sifflement, salives, Reprises, désirs,* and *baisers* heighten the sound of the whistling as does the sharp *i* of *sif-flement, salives, Reprises,* and *désirs*. The rhymes in the follow-ing quatrains, *silences-indolences* and *Paresse-caresses,* prolong this auditory sensation.

The tactile sensations include the blue air that bathes (*baigne*) the flowers, the touch of the seekers' fingers in his heavy hair (*dans ses lourds cheveux où tombe la rosée / Promènent leurs doigts*), and the slowness of their caresses (*la lenteur des caresses*). The troubled dreams of the child in the first quatrain become more and more erotic by the third where he sees "de-sires for kisses" (*désirs de baisers*) on their lips. His "befuddled indolence" of the fourth quatrain is increased by "the wine of Idleness" he feels rising in him (*Voilà que monte en lui le vin de la Paresse*) in the last quatrain, the wine combined with the sound of music that could cause him to go into ecstasy (*Soupir d'harmonica qui pourrait délirer*). The sensation of the caresses is so deliciously painful he feels "a desire to weep rise up and die down endlessly within him" (*Sourdre et mourir sans cesse un désir de pleurer*). The reader has difficulty re-membering that these " two tall charming sisters" (*deux grandes soeurs charmantes*) are hunting for lice in the child's hair. The magic of the verbal music with its subtle "wine of Idleness" lulls the reader with its sweet, sad song; it is a powerful performance by a poet of sixteen, or even eighteen years.

CHAPTER 4

Song of the Boat

DURING the summer of 1871 Rimbaud worked on his long poem "Le Bateau ivre" (The Drunken Boat) which continues to be one of his most popular. Scholars have found possible sources in Chateaubriand, Hugo, Edgar Allan Poe, Gautier, Leconte de Lisle, Baudelaire, Jules Verne, and Léon Dierx, to name only a few, plus several illustrated magazines.[1] In spite of the borrowings this vision by a boy who was not yet seventeen remains one of the most unusual poetic creations of the last thirty years of the nineteenth century. Some critics see it as Rimbaud's first avowal of failure to create poetry according to the concepts of the Seer Letters, an admission he seems to make again in his later works. Still others see it as a poetic prophecy of Rimbaud's own life, with its far-flung travels culminating in the final return to Charleville. Still others read it as simply a Symbolist poem with the voyage of the boat as the rather banal central symbol of the human experience. One of the best of the symbolic interpretations is that of the late Bernard Weinberg.[2] Most readers agree that the deluge of fantastic images expressed within the framework of the highly disciplined classical alexandrine constitutes a poetic feat realized by few writers of any age. Around September 10, 1871, Rimbaud accepted Verlaine's invitation to come to Paris. He took with him "Le Bateau ivre" to present to Verlaine as further proof of his talent. Verlaine and his poet-friends were impressed, as impressed as readers continue to be today.

The poem's twenty-five quatrains of alexandrines rhyming *a b a b* can be divided into three groups of five, nine, and seven plus four quatrains of conclusion. The tenses of the verbs reinforce this basic structure. The dominant tense of the first five quatrains is the imperfect indicating events that took place before the poem began. The second group of nine quatrains opens with the expression "since then" (*dès lors*) followed by the perfect tense. All but the first of these quatrains end with an exclamation point. The third group reverts to the imperfect with an unexpected switch back to the present tense in the last line of the group. This present tense prepares the reader for the perfect tense of the twenty-second quatrain which is a summary of the experiences of the voyage and which poses the question to which the conclusion replies. The last three quatrains move from the perfect tense to the present, to the results of this fabulous journey.

I *The Song of the River*

The first two quatrains describe the beginning of the trip as the boat was going down the rivers (*Comme je descendais des Fleuves*) to the sea. The rivers themselves remained "unmoved" (*impassibles*) by the great adventure that was about to begin, a reiteration of the Romantic indifference of nature to man's mortal plight. The haulers of Rimbaud's boat had dropped their towlines (*Je ne me sentis plus guidé par les haleurs*), thus allowing the boat to move freely with the current. The rivers must have been American because "Shouting Redskins had taken the haulers for targets, / Having nailed them naked to colored posts" (*Des Peaux-Rouges criards les avaient pris pour cibles / Les ayant cloués nus aux poteaux de couleurs*). In its newfound freedom the boat was unworried that it had no crew (*J'étais insoucieux de tous les équipages*) and happy that it was no longer anything so prosaic as a "Carrier of Flemish grains or English cottons" (*Porteur de blés flamands ou de cotons anglais*). Flemish and English contrast vividly with the Redskins just mentioned. The haulers must by now be dead for the shouting of the Indians has ended (*Quand avec mes haleurs ont fini les tapages*), leaving the boat to follow its course as it wished (*Les Fleuves m'ont laissé descendre où je voulais*). This part of the introduction thus ends as it began with the verb *descendre* and the imperfect tense (*voulais*). The rhyme of the first quatrain that includes the sharp sound of the French *i*, *impassibles-cibles*, is the first of ten such rhymes, one-fifth of the poem's total, which accentuate the drama.

The second stage in the development of the introduction begins with the mention of "tides" (*marées*) and continues for three quatrains. The boat was no longer being carried along by the river's current but had encountered the turbulent tug (*les clapotements furieux*) of the ocean's tides. Rimbaud says this took place "the other winter" (*l'autre hiver*), a remark that has caused considerable comment among scholars, comparable to that raised by the ambiguous expression *morts d'avant-hier* in "Les Corbeaux." Did Rimbaud mean "last winter" literally, the winter of 1870–1871 when he underwent a radical metamorphosis in his own life? Or did he simply mean that all of this took place at some time in the past? The naming of the season appears more significant than any possible autobiographical allusion. The boat survived the wintry rigors of its encounter with the open sea that lasted "Ten nights" (*Dix nuits*), as Rimbaud states later. The boat "ran through" (*Je courus*) these choppy waters with all the unheeding obstinacy of a determined child (*plus sourds que les cerveaux d'enfants*) and experienced "more tri-umphant hubbubs" (*tohu-bohus plus triomphants*) than those suffered by "floating Islands" (*les Péninsules démarées*). This encounter with the sea, the boat's "maritime awakening" (*mes éveils maritimes*), was blessed by the tempest (*La tempête a béni*). "Lighter than cork" (*Plus léger qu'un bouchon*) the boat "danced on the waters" (*j'ai dansé sur les flots*) and did it for "Ten nights" without once regretting the absence of the stupid shore lights that formerly guided it along the narrow river (*sans regretter l'oeil niais des falots*). As a result, the "fir shell" of the boat became thoroughly conditioned to "the green water" (*L'eau verte pénétra ma coque de sapin*) and, what is more important, thoroughly cleansed of its human filth (*Et des taches de vins bleus et des vomissures / Me lava*) and completely freed of the constraints of its "rudder and anchor" (*dispersant gouvernail et grappin*).

II *The Song of the Sea*

Now that the boat has undergone its purificatory rites and is totally free, the beginning of the action of the poem is announced by the expression "since then" followed by the perfect tense.

"Since then" the boat has "bathed in the Poem / Of the Sea" (*je me suis baigné dans le Poème / De la Mer*). For the first time Rimbaud indicates overtly that the voyage of the boat is symbolic. This symbolic sea is an unexpected amalgam of beauty and horror. It is "steeped with stars" (*infusé d'astres*) and thus "milky" (*lactescent*) with their light. The blue of the sky is assimilated by the green of the water (*Dévorant les azurs verts*). But also in this poetic sea something appears, "floating pale / And ravished" (*flottaison blême / Et ravie*), that proves to be "a pensive drowned person" (*un noyé pensif*) slowly "drifting down" (*descend*). In this same poetic sea "the bitter rednesses of love ferment" (*Fermentent les rousseurs amères de l'amour*), "suddenly staining the bluenesses" (*teignant tout à coup les bleuités, bleuités* being a neologism Rimbaud had used in "Les Premières Communions") of sea and sky. These eruptions of love are "frenzies / And slow rhythms under the brilliant glow of day, / Stronger than alcohol, more vast than the lyres" (*délires / Et rhythmes lents sous les rutilements du jour, / Plus fortes que l'alcool, plus vastes que nos lyres*) of poets. One critic feels that Rimbaud in this tortured stanza is comparing "the frenzies and rhythms of the waves to those of love, the sea thus becoming the source of life and fecundity."[3] Another critic thinks that "the rhythms of the sea, which is life, are troubled, agitated by love, poetry, and alcohol."[4] The feminine adjective *fortes* must refer either to *bleuités*, in which case the sea as poetry is stronger than alcohol and the lyres of poets, or to *rousseurs*, in which case the sun as the male love element is stronger than alcohol and poetry. The former reading is more logical for the sea of love poetry with its "frenzies and rhythms" has the boat-poet as its interpreter. By the use of the possessive *nos* (one manuscript reads *vos*) Rimbaud for the first time indicates overtly that the boat is the symbol of the poet.

The following seven quatrains enumerate the visions of the boat during its voyage. The first verb, "I know" (*Je sais*), is in the present tense but is used in the sense of "I have learned" or "I have gotten to know." The expression is repeated in the second line while the verb of the last line, "I have seen" (*j'ai vu*), is also repeated at the beginning of the next quatrain, forming parallel uses of the two verbs. Thus five quatrains all begin with a verb in the perfect tense: "I have seen" (*J'ai vu*), "I have dreamed" (*J'ai rêvé*), "I have followed" (*J'ai suivi*), "I have collided with" (*J'ai heurtè*), and return to "I have seen." Just as the second quatrain in this group is a continuation of the first, so the ninth quatrain is a continuation and completion of the series of things seen in the eighth. The first quatrain is filled with sky and sea beginning with "skies bursting with flashes of lightning" (*Je sais les cieux crevant en éclairs*). The soft sibilants of *sais-cieux* contrast with the hard *k* and liquid *r* of *crevant-éclairs*, which are separated by the repetition of the nasal *crevant-en*. The series continues with a list of maritime phenomena, "waterspouts" (*trombes*), "undertows" (*ressacs*), and "currents" (*courants*), but returns to the sky with the magnificent image of dawn rising up like a flight of doves (*L'Aube exaltée ainsi qu'un peuple de colombes*). Part of the exaltation of the image is the result of the contrast between night and day, that is, between the immediately preceding expression, "I know the evening" (*Je sais le soir*), and "The exalted Dawn," which are both "breakings" between night and day. The image had to be an unusual one to support the declaration of the final line of the first quatrain, the statement that forms the basis for all the extravagant visions to come: "I have sometimes actually seen what other men only thought they saw" (*j'ai vu quelquefois ce que l'homme a cru voir*), which is one of Rimbaud's most quoted lines.

The experiences are a fantastic miasma of color and movement. The first vision is caused by the reflections of the setting sun (*le soleil bas*) that create the effect of "long violet stains" (*de longs figements violets*) on the water. These stains so cohere that as they roll on the water in the distance (*Les flots roulant au loin*) they are like shutters opening and closing or going up and down (*leurs frissons de volets*). All of these movements are as erratic as those of a chorus of "actors in ancient dramas" (*Pareils à des acteurs de drames très-antiques*).

In this nightmare the reflections of the setting sun on "the dazzling snow" (*aux neiges éblouies*) bathe the night in a green light (*la nuit verte*). The sea as the source of life contains "unheard-of saps" (*des sèves inouïes*) that in their movement rise up sluggishly like a kiss to touch the stains now described as "the eye of the sea" (*Baiser montant aux yeux des mers avec lenteurs*). As these currents move beneath the surface of the sea they arouse the minuscule marine animals, the noctiluca, to yellow and blue phosphorescence, colors that seem to sing in the somber waters (*l'éveil jaune et bleu des phosphores chanteurs*).

If the initiation rites took ten nights, this part of the voyage took "many a month" (*des mois pleins*), during which the assault of the swelling seas on the reefs (*la houle à l'assaut des récifs*) was like a stampede of hysterical cattle (*pareille aux vacheries / Hystériques*). In all this confusion the boat did not give a thought to the legend that "the luminous feet of Mary" (*Sans songer que les pieds lumineux des Maries*) could calm the sea, a legend popular with French poets from Lamartine's "Le Lac" of 1820 to Mallarmé's "Hérodiade" of 1864–1867. Rimbaud's originality lies in returning to the cow image according to which the feet of Mary (and he uses the plural here as he had done in "Les Premières Communions") "could force open the muzzle of the wheezing Oceans" (*Pussent forcer le mufle aux Océans poussifs*), that is, show the way through the tempestuous sea by the light of her feet.

In the following quatrain Rimbaud returns to America when he notes that the boat collided with "incredible Floridas" (*d'incroyables Florides, Florides* being used also in the sense of flowered lands), where flowers mingled with men's watching eyes that were like panther eyes (*Mêlant aux fleurs des yeux de panthères à peaux / D'hommes*). The ominous atmosphere is relieved in the second half of the quatrain by the beauty of "rainbows stretched out like bridles / Beneath the horizon of the seas, to glaucous herds" (*Des arcs-en-ciel tendus comme des brides / Sous l'horizon des mers, à de glauques troupeaux*). With *troupeaux* Rimbaud has again returned to the cow image but this time with the meaning of schools of fish.

III   The Song of the Leviathans

The last two quatrains of this group enumerate the great convulsions that seem to take place in the sea, "the fermentation of enormous marshes" (*fermenter les marais énormes*) that are "traps / Where a whole Leviathan [a great Biblical sea monster] rots away in the rushes" (*nasses /Où pourrit dans les joncs tout un Léviathan*), great "downfalls of water in the midst of calm" (*Des écoulements d'eaux au milieu des bonaces*), and "faraway places cataracting into abysses" (*les lointains vers les gouffres cataractant*). Under these "Glaciers, silver suns, nacrous seas, glowing skies" (*Glaciers, soleils d'argent, flots nacreux, cieux de braises*) are found "hideous strands in the depths of brown gulfs" (*Echouages hideux au fond des golfes bruns*). The Leviathan has become giant serpents "devoured by bugs" (*dévorés des punaises*) that sink into the depths like twisted tree trunks (*choient, des arbres tordus*) with an odor of putrefaction like "black perfumes" (*avec de noirs parfums*).

The contrast to this cataclysmic adventure is established by the conditional perfect tense, "I should have liked" (*J'aurais voulu*), at the beginning of the next group of seven quatrains. The boat would have liked "to show to children spiny-finned sea breams" (*montrer aux enfants ces dorades*), "gold fish," and "singing fish" (*ces poissons d'or, ces poissons chantants*), for upon occasion "foams of flowers cradled it as it weighed anchor" (*Des écumes de fleurs ont bercé mes dérades, dérades* being a neologism based on *dérader*, "to lift anchor because of a storm") and "ineffable winds give it wings from time to time" (*d'ineffables vents m'ont ailé par instants*, and again *ailé* is a neologism).

The idea of *par instants* is repeated by *Parfois* so that in the midst of all the violent action upon occasion, when the boat felt itself a "martyr weary of poles and zones" (*martyr lassé des pôles et des zones*), the sob of the sea would soften its rolling (*le sanglot faisant mon roulis doux*) while the sea itself brought up toward the boat from its depths "flowers of shadow with yellow suckers" (*Montait vers moi ses fleurs d'ombre aux ventouses jaunes*) and the boat "remained like a woman on her knees" (*Et je restais, ainsi qu'une femme à genoux*).

At other times the boat was "almost an island, tossing about on its boards the quarrels / And droppings of mockingbirds with yellow eyes" (*Presque île, ballottant sur mes bords les querelles / Et les fientes d'oiseaux clabaudeurs aux yeux blonds*). As the boat was sailing along (*je voguais*) it was again haunted by "the drowned who sank down to sleep upside down" (*Des noyés descendaient dormir, à reculons*).

Sometimes the boat was lost amid the hair, that is, the reedy growths of the coves (*perdu sous les cheveux des anses*), sometimes "Tossed by the hurricane into the birdless ether" (*Jeté par l'ouragan dans l'éther sans oiseau*), that is, so high there were no birds. The boat was such "a water-logged carcass" (*la carcasse ivre d'eau*) that boats like the Monitor of American Civil War fame and the sailing ships of the Hanseatic League (*les Monitors et le voiliers des Hanses*) would not have bothered to fish it out again (*N'auraient pas repêché*).

The boat that was "Free, steaming, covered with violet fog" (*Livré, fumant, monté de brumes violettes*, with *monté* indicating movement upward as well as covered with), "was making a hole in the reddening sky like a wall" (*Moi qui trouais le ciel rouge-oyant comme un mur*). After this beautiful figure Rimbaud compares the slivers and scraps of clouds outlined by the sun as "sunshine lichens and blue mucus" (*Des lichens de soleil et des morves d'azur*), that is, like mossy growths on the sun or nasal drippings against the blue sky. They are, says Rimbaud, an "exquisite jam for good poets" (*confiture exquise aux bons poètes*). The question is, who are the good poets? In any event, Rimbaud has again managed the "hideously beautiful" in an image that is simultaneously striking and repulsive.

The fourth quatrain of this group began with *Or moi* and continued with *Moi dont*. The fifth included *Moi qui trouais* while the sixth begins *Qui courais* and the seventh *Moi qui tremblais*. The boat was a "mad plank" (*Planche folle*), "spotted with electric crescent-shaped marks" (*taché de lunules électriques*), and "escorted by black sea horses" (*escorté par des hippocampes noirs*), just at the moment when the hot Julys caused "The ultramarine skies" (*Les cieux ultramarins*) to collapse under their cudgel blows (*faisaient crouler à coups de triques*) into "burning funnels" (*aux ardents entonnoirs*).

The boat was trembling because it could feel "the whining fifty leagues away / Of the rutting of Behemoths [another great Biblical monster] and thick Maelstroms" (*sentant geindre à cinquante lieues / Le rut des Béhémoths et des Maelstroms épais*). In contrast to this heavy, animal sexuality the boat was an "Eternal spinner of blue immobilities" (*Fileur éternel des immobilités bleues*), a maker and leaver of wakes in the constantly moving but eternally unchanging blue sea. In spite of its incredible adventures the boat has left no mark upon the sea and thus concludes, "I regret Europe with its ancient parapets" (*Je regrette l'Europe aux anciens parapets*) of solid rock, the symbol of a former and closely knit family and social life, safe from the perils of the raging sea.

The first quatrain of the conclusion returns to the "I have seen" of the preceding group and speaks of "sidereal archipelagoes" (*des archipels sidéraux*), archipelagoes thrown across the sea like stars across the sky, and "islands / whose delirious skies are open to the sailor," to the boat as it drifts along (*des îles / Dont les cieux délirants sont ouverts au vogueur*). The last half of the quatrain is an enigmatic question whose answer constitutes the conclusion of the poem. The boat had spoken of being thrown so high in the sky by the hurricane that it found itself in a "birdless ether." It now asks, "Is it in these bottomless nights that you sleep and are in exile, / Million golden birds, oh future Vigor" (*Est-ce en ces nuits sans fond que tu dors et t'exiles, / Million d'oiseaux d'or, ô future Vigueur*), an expression that recalls the "wine of vigor," the wine of inspiration of "Ma Bohème." Is it in the bottomless depths of the imagination of the poet that can be found those birds that are the vigor and strength of mankind that will see him through future trials and bring him to the happiness of a golden age?

IV *The Song of Home*

The conclusion would seem to be a defeat. After the perfect tense of "I have wept too much" (*j'ai trop pleuré*), the finale to this fantastic voyage is stated in the present: "All Dawns are heartbreaking. / Every moon is atrocious and every sun bitter" (*Les aubes sont navrantes. / Toute lune est atroce et tout soleil amer*). No matter what miracles the imagination can produce, reality is harsh and uncompromising. The boat, moved by an "acrid love" (*L'âcre amour*) that "filled" it "with intoxicating torpors" (*m'a gonflé de torpeurs enivrantes*), wants only to return forever to the magic sea: "Let my keel split! Let me sink into the sea" (*O que ma quille éclate! O que j'aille à la mer*).

If the boat must be denied the wonders of the open sea, if

it must prefer any "European water" (*Si je désire une eau d'Europe*), then it is a little "puddle / Black and cold in which toward a balmy dusk / A squatting child full of sadness launches / A boat frail as a butterfly of May" (*c'est la flache / Noire et froide vers le crépuscule embaumé / Un enfant accroupi plein de tristesses, lâche / Un bateau frêle comme un papillon de mai*). The boat is no longer able, "bathed as it is with the languors of the waves" (*baigné de vos langueurs, ô lames*), "to follow in the wake of cotton carriers" (*Enlever leur sillage aux porteurs de cotons*), nor can it "challenge the flags and pennants" of proud ships (*Ni traverser l'orgueil des drapeaux et des flammes*), nor does it any longer have the courage or desire to "swim under the horrible eyes of old boats" (*Ni nager sous les yeux horribles des pontons*). "The cotton carriers" could very well be the sailing ships of the Hanseatic League of the Middle Ages mentioned earlier, while the ships with their flags and pennants could be warships like the Monitor. The boat does not have the discipline to maintain a regular commercial route nor the courage of flag-flying ships nor even the desire to consort with the old ships converted to other purposes (*pontons*) that are no longer fit for the sea but used in and around ports and for river traffic. With that admission, this fabulous adventure of the poetic imagination comes to an end.

The word *porteurs* ("carriers") takes us back to the second quatrain of the poem while *les yeux horribles* remind us of *l'oeil niais* of the fourth. The *enfant* of the next to the last quatrain recalls *les cerveaux d'enfants* of the third quatrain as well as *Plus douce qu'aux enfants* of the fifth and *montrer aux enfants* of the fifteenth. The uninhibited imagination of childhood combined with the fearless vigor of youth have created a verbal experience that far transcends our prosaic daily life. They have done it by means of poetry that fixes forever what we have seen and alerts us to what we only thought we saw. Poetry must in the end cause us to see what has never been seen. Such was the voyage of "The Drunken Boat."

CHAPTER 5

Songs of a Private Hell

R IMBAUD himself dated *Une Saison en enfer*, the only long
work he published, April–August, 1873. His mother paid the
deposit necessary for the printing of five hundred copies. Shortly
after October 24 Rimbaud distributed six author's copies to
friends and that was the last that was heard of the book until
1901 when a Belgian bibliophile discovered by accident the
remaining copies in the publisher's attic. He destroyed seventy-
five damaged copies but did not reveal his discovery until 1914,
more than forty years after the printing.[1]

In a letter to his friend Ernest Delahaye dated May, 1873,
from his mother's farm at Roche, Rimbaud wrote that he was
composing "some little stories in prose, general title: Pagan
Book, or Negro Book. It is foolish and innocent. Oh innocence!
innocence; innocence, innoc...plague!"[2] Near the end of his
letter he indicated that he already had three such stories written
but would not send them because "*it costs so much*" (p. 268).
The consensus is that he was speaking of three texts that
were used later in or reworked for use in *Une Saison. Nègre*
in the title *Livre nègre* was pejorative in French; the terms
"foolish and innocent" (*bête et innocent*) also interest us, since
Rimbaud went on to exclaim what a plague innocence can be.
In a sense one can say that *Une Saison* is the story of the loss
of innocence and all the anguish that experience entails.

As Rimbaud published it, *Une Saison* is a mixture of nine poems
in prose and seven poems in verse, all of the latter quoted
within the fifth poem in prose, "Délires II: Alchimie du verbe"
(Deliriums II: Alchemy of the Word). The complete text covers
only twenty-four and a half small pages. The individual texts
vary from less than a page to seven pages in length. The best
statement I have found to guide us in our reading of both *Une*

73

Saison en enfer and the *Illuminations* is by one of France's most perceptive critics, Jean-Pierre Richard. If we look at each of Rimbaud's later poems, whether in prose or in verse, we find that it is a landscape, but as Richard says:

. . . his landscape is no longer truly a landscape, but rather an anti-landscape, a pure vision without a witness, a free gathering together of objects each one of which has from now on the right to live its adventure separately and from which we are no longer separated by any film, intellectual, sentimental, or syntactic. The genius of Rimbaud is to spare us all commentary, all proof.[3]

Although Rimbaud speaks in the first person and makes many moral judgments, the reader gets the impression that the other "I" is doing the talking, a disembodied "I" that is not a witness but an assembler of heterogeneous objects that take on a life of their own by the simple fact of naming and by juxtaposition. While great native intelligence is obviously involved, the act is no simple feat of the intellect, no creation of logic. While great emotions are expressed, the goal is not to move the reader by mere sentimentality. While the spontaneous leaps of the imagination are sometimes difficult to follow, the statements are for the most part simple declarations offering none of the tortured syntax of a Mallarmé, for example. The reader does not identify with Rimbaud but rather with the other "I," for whom commentary and proof are superfluous since the reader is participating in the creative act along with that other "I." The reader does not require logic in the disparate sequences of his private stream of consciousness. The sequences have their own logic controlled by the emotional nature of the individual's character and associative experiences. Only in retrospect can the individual create order out of his own stream of consciousness and then only by assembling those elements his intellect chooses to remember.

Nevertheless, *Une Saison* does have a beginning, a middle, and an end. Opening with an introduction, the recollection of what the narrator's situation was "Formerly" (*Jadis*)[4] and continuing with a detailed analysis of the "Bad Blood" (*Mauvais Sang*) of his physical and moral heritage, he passes through his "Night of Hell" (*Nuit de l'enfer*), revealing the "Deliriums"

(*Délires I* and *II*) by which he had hoped to achieve "The Impossible" (*L'Impossible*). With the admission that his goal was impossble comes "The Flash" (of Lightning or of Insight, *L'Eclair*) of intellectual enlightenment followed quickly by the physical light of "Morning" (*Matin*), leaving the narrator with nothing to say but his "Farewell" (*Adieu*). The development within each section is not quite as obvious as this outline would seem to promise.

I A Song of Former Times

If the narrator remembers correctly his life was "Formerly" a veritable feast (*un festin*) in which he enjoyed all the emotional pleasures of love (*tous les coeurs*), all the physical pleasures of the senses (*tous les vins*), all the aesthetic pleasures of beauty (*la Beauté*), all the advantages of social justice (*la justice*). Of these four the last two proved a deception. Beauty was so bitter (*amère*) that he insulted it (*je l'ai injuriée*), justice such a mockery that he armed himself against it (*je me suis armé*) and fled (*Je me suis enfui*). As a result he gave himself up to those magic-working outcasts of society, the Sorceresses (*O Sorcières*) of misery (*ô misère*) and hatred (*ô haine*). He stifled within himself all hope (*toute l'espérance*) and every joy (*toute joie*). For help in his unholy task he called upon the human avengers, the executioners (*les bourreaux*), the natural avengers, the scourges (*les fléaux*), the recourse of the dissatisfied, unhappiness (*Le malheur*), the refuge of the morally corrupt, the mire (*la boue*), the resort of the wicked, crime (*le crime*), and the final retreat of the maladjusted, madness (*la folie*). On the point of croaking (*sur le point de faire le dernier* couac), he thought of searching for the key to his ancient feast (*la clef du festin ancien*). When he found that it was charity (*La Charité*), he knew that he had been dreaming (*Cette inspiration prouve que j'ai rêvé*). A demon (*le démon*) urged him to seek death (*gagne la mort*) by means of all his appetites (*tous tes appétits*) for emotional and physical, mental and moral excesses (*ton égoïsme et tous les péchés capitaux*). He succeeded only too well and to give the Devil (*cher Satan*) his due, he will offer up a few little belated villainies (*quelques petites lachetés en retard*), a few hideous leaves from his notebook of the damned (*quelques hideux feuillets de mon carnet de damné*). In the conclusion to this section Rimbaud himself gives the key to his style which will be neither desciptive nor didactic (*descriptives ou instructives*). He will recount what happened but do not expect the realism of description nor the moralizing of a preacher.

II *A Song of Ancestors*

"Bad Blood"[5] with its eight parts is one of the two longest sections of the poem. In it the narrator claims he inherited from his Gallic ancestors certain physical traits including his blue-white eyes (*l'oeil bleu blanc*), his narrow head (*la cervelle étroite*), and his clumsiness in contests (*la maladresse dans la lutte*). He also inherited certain moral and mental traits, including idolatry (*l'idolâtrie*) and the love of sacrilege (*l'amour du sacrilège*). This remark introduces the problem of religion, which will pervade the poem, as well as all of the vices (*tous les vices*), including anger (*colère*), lust (*luxure*), and, above all, lying (*mensonge*) and laziness (*paresse*). His laziness includes a hatred of all work (*horreur de tous les métiers*), since masters and workers, tied as they are to their job, are no better than peasants (*Maîtres et ouvriers, tous paysans*) tied to their plow. The mention of the plow provokes the rather facile observation that the pen is mightier than the plow (*La main à plume vaut la main à charrue*), but it also occasions the remark, "What a century for hands!—I shall never have my hand" (*Quel siècle à mains!—Je n'aurai jamais ma main*). The nineteenth was the century of the Industrial Revolution when hands were creating new trades on all sides. The narrator feels he will never find his vocation just as Rimbaud seemed never to have found his, just as most men who think they have found theirs, later question their choice. With a job goes domesticity, which is another kind of slavery (*la domesticité mène trop loin*). By way of contrast the narrator detests ironically the straightforwardness and honesty of begging (*L'honnêteté de la mendicité*) as well as criminals (*Les criminels*), who as outcasts in their prison and lacking freedom are like the castrated (*les châtrés*). The nar-

rator is free, whatever his faults, and thus intact (*je suis intact*).
After noting that his lying (*ma langue perfide*) has made his
laziness (*ma paresse*) possible, he goes on to question his freedom. He has observed that all of Europe lives according to the
social justice, already mentioned in "Formerly," guaranteed by
the Rights of Man (*Droits de l'Homme*). He himself is a son of
a family (*J'ai connu chaque fils de famille*), who with his freedom guaranteed, is no freer of his heritage and his society than
the narrator.

The narrator continues to describe his ancestry in the second
paragraph. His forebears included no noteworthy nobles. His
was such an inferior race (*race inférieure*) that it would never
have risen up in revolt (*Je ne puis comprendre la révolte*), to try
to establish a new order. It only rose up in order to pillage
(*piller*) and then was content to return to its lot. If he had
participated in the crusades (*le voyage de terre sainte*), he
would have done it not as a noble but as a peasant (*manant*).
He has visions of Swabian plains (*les plaines souabes*), views of
Byzantium (*vues de Byzance*), the ramparts of Jerusalem (*rem-
parts de Solyme*), but for the peasant the cult of Mary (*le culte
de Marie*) and compassion for Jesus (*l'attendrissement sur le
crucifié*) are no more meaningful than the thousand profane
magic spectacles (*mille féeries profanes*) that are his religion.
Rimbaud then draws the unforgettable portrait of this poor peasant on his magnificent crusade: he has contracted leprosy and
is seated amid broken pots and nettles at the foot of a wall cor-
roded by the sun (*Je suis assis, lépreux, sur les pots cassés et
les orties, au pied d'un mur rongé par le soleil*). So much for
the glorious crusades. Later he would have been an old soldier
bivouaced in the German nights (*reître, j'aurais bivaqué sous
les nuits d'Allemagne*).

He is still a pagan (*Ah! encore: je danse le sabbat*) even if he
can remember nothing beyond his own country and Christianity
(*cette terre-ci et le christianisme*). If he sees himself in the past,
he is always alone, without a family (*toujours seul; sans
famille*), and speaking what language (*quelle langue parlais-je*)?
Certainly he never sees himself among the councils of Christ
(*les conseils du Christ*) nor in the councils of nobles who are
Christ's representatives on earth (*ni dans les conseils des Seig-*

neurs,—représentants du Christ). Today things are quite different. The inferior race (*La race inférieure*) has become the people (*le peuple*). Reason (*la raison*) rather than religion has become our guide. Feudal tribes have become a political entity, the nation (*la nation*), and science (*la science*) is the hope of the world. It has become for body and soul (*Pour le corps et pour l'âme*) a salvation (*le viatique*) with medicine (*la médecine*) for the body and philosophy (*la philosophie*) for the mind, which are perhaps nothing more than old wives' remedies and popular songs somewhat more organized and tidied up (*les remèdes de bonnes femmes et les chansons populaires arrangés*).

What were the pastimes of princes (*les divertissements des princes*), geography, cosmography, mechanics, chemistry (*Géographie, cosmographie, mécanique, chimie*), now belong to all. Science has become the new nobility (*la nouvelle noblesse*), the sign of progress (*Le progrès*), proof that the world moves and turns (*Le monde marche! Pourquoi ne tournerait-il pas?*). The narrator maintains that it is a vision of numbers (*C'est la vision des nombres*), that we are moving toward the spirit (*Nous allons à l'Esprit*), but since he can only express himself in pagan words (*paroles païennes*), ordinary language, he prefers silence. The future holds more than our language can describe or explain.

The third paragraph is one of the most moving, both because of the narrator's never-ending duel with Christianity and because Rimbaud so accurately foretells his own fate. With reason and science as our gods the pagan spirit has returned (*Le sang païen revient*). If the kingdom of the spirit is so close, why has not religion aided us by giving nobility and liberty to our soul (*L'Esprit est proche, pourquoi Christ ne m'aide-t-il pas, en donnant à mon âme noblesse et liberté*)? Because it is already too late, the time of the Gospel has passed (*l'Evangile a passé*), and the narrator still awaits God with greediness (*J'attends Dieu avec gourmandise*). He will always be of an inferior race (*Je suis de race inférieure de toute éternité*).

At first he sees himself on some shore in Brittany (*sur la plage armoricaine*) but that is only his point of departure. He will leave Europe (*je quitte l'Europe*), the sea air will sear his lungs (*L'air marin brûlera mes poumons*), and the out-of-the-way climates will tan his skin like an animal hide (*les climats perdus*

me tanneront). He will revert to the ways of his pagan ancestors. He will return with limbs of iron (*avec des membres de
fer*), a dark skin (*la peau sombre*), a desperate look (*l'oeil
furieux*), and will be mistaken for a member of a strong race
(*une race forte*). He will have money (*j'aurai de l'or*), but, and
here is the irony of Rimbaud's vision, women care for these
fierce invalids returned from hot countries (*Les femmes soignent
ces féroces infirmes retour des pays chauds*) just as Rimbaud
will be attended by nurses in the hospital at Marseilles upon
his last return. He will get involved in politics (*Je serai mêlé
aux affaires politiques*) and be saved (*Sauvé*). For the moment,
however, he is damned (*je suis maudit*) and detests his fatherland (*j'ai horreur de la patrie*). A drunken sleep on the beach
(*un sommeil bien ivre, sur la grève*), which he mentioned at
the beginning of this section, would be preferable to such a fate.

But, says Rimbaud, you never leave home (*On ne part pas*),
because wherever you go you take with you your heavy heritage,
your vices that have tortured you since growing up (*le vice qui a
poussé ses racines de souffrance à mon côté, dès l'âge de raison*).
Innocence has not yet been lost (*La dernière innocence*) nor
timidity (*la dernière timidité*), because he still hesitates to reveal
his disgust and treachery (*mes dégoûts et mes trahisons*) to the
world. Caught between revolt and resignation he can only go
on (*La marche*), dragging his burden (*le fardeau*) through the
desert of life (*le désert*) with its boredom (*l'ennui*) and anger
(*la colère*). What are the alternatives? To whom could he sell
himself (*A qui me louer*)? What idol must he worship (*Quelle
bête faut-il adorer*)? Against what holy image could he revolt
(*Quelle image sainte attaque-t-on*)? What hearts will he break
(*Quels coeurs briserai-je*)? What lie must he maintain (*Quel
mensonge dois-je tenir*)? What crimes must he commit (*Dans
quel sang marcher*)? Again Rimbaud returns to social justice
saying one must protect himself against justice (*se garder de la
justice*). If he were to take up a life of crime and degradation at
least he would not have to worry about old age (*point de vieil-
lesse*). Is he so forlorn that he would offer up to any divine image
his impulses toward perfection (*je suis tellement délaissé que
j'offre à n'importe quelle divine image des élans vers la perfection*)? But at the last minute he remembers that whatever

renunciation (*O mon abnégation*) and whatever charity (*ô ma
charité merveilleuse*) he might want to practice, he must practice here below on earth (*ici-bas, pourtant*). With that realiza-
tion he can only exclaim in resignation, "From what depths,
oh Lord, what a fool I am" (De profundis Domine, *suis-je bête*)!
No matter what your aspirations, you never leave home.

The fifth paragraph is one of the most dramatic of "Bad
Blood." As early as "Le Forgeron" Rimbaud had demonstrated
his sympathy for convicts. He speaks of them here in two con-
nections. One is his attempt to see the world, the blue sky, and
the flowering work of the countryside (*le ciel bleu et le travail
fleuri de la campagne*) through the mind (avec son idée) of a
convict in prison. The larger development, however, is that of
his travels occasioned by his desire to visit the inns and room-
ing houses (*les auberges et les garnis*) consecrated by the convict's visits (*sacrés par son séjour*), to sniff out his fatality in the
cities (*je flairais sa fatalité dans les villes*). The convict is
stronger than a saint (*plus de force qu'un saint*) and has more
good sense than a traveler (*plus de bon sens qu'un voyageur*)
because he alone bears witness to what he feels is his just reward
(*lui seul! pour témoin de sa gloire*), whereas God is the saint's
witness. The court alone judges what is right or wrong (*de sa
raison*), whereas the traveler must conform to the rules of the
road. The narrator recounts his own frightful experiences on
the road during the winter nights, not knowing where he was
going nor why (*ni où tu vas ou pourquoi tu vas*). Like the carcass of "Le Bateau ivre" that the warship and sailing ships
would not have bothered to fish out of the water, no one will
kill this aimless wanderer any more than if he were a cadaver
(*On ne te tuera pas plus que si tu étais cadavre*). When he gets
to the city the mud has turned red and black (*rouge et noire*),
while the city itself is a sea of flames and smoke in the sky
(*une mer de flammes et de fumée au ciel*).

Debauchery and the companionship of women were denied him
(*l'orgie et la camaraderie des femmes m'étaient interdites*), so
that he is a witness without friends (*Pas même un compagnon*)
watching an exasperated crowd facing a firing squad (*une foule
exaspérée, en face du peloton d'exécution*), weeping over a misfortune they could not understand (*pleurant du malheur qu'ils*

n'aient pu comprendre) and forgiving like Jeanne d'Arc (*et pardonnant!—Comme Jeanne d'Arc*). Make no mistake. Our narrator is not of that race of people (*Je n'ai jamais été de ce peuple-ci*). He has never been a Christian (*je n'ai jamais été chrétien*), he doesn't understand the laws (*je ne comprends pas les lois*), he has no moral sense (*je n'ai pas le sens moral*).

The narrator says that he is a beast, a black (*Je suis une bête, un nègre*) but as a true black he can be saved (*Mais je puis être sauvé*). The false blacks are the maniacs, the ferocious, the avaricious (*maniaques, féroces, avares*), the merchant, the magistrate, the general, the emperor, a list that brings to mind Jean Genet's play *Les Nègres*.[6] The emperor with his hierarchical protocol is like an itch (*démangeaison*) we cannot scratch. He has enjoyed tax-free liquor from Satan's distillery (*tu as bu d'une liqueur non taxée, de la frabrique de Satan*) while the people are bowed down with taxes. Such tyrants are inspired by fever and cancer (*inspiré par la fièvre et le cancer*) while the ill and the old are so respectable they ask to be consumed by society (*Infirmes et vieillards sont tellement respectables qu'ils demandent à être bouillis*). The narrator prefers to enter the true kingdom of the children of Ham, the son of Noah and ancestor of the inhabitants of Africa (*J'entre au vrai royaume des enfants de Cham*). Does he really know nature (*Connais-je encore la nature*)? Does he really know himself (*me connais-je*)? Enough talk about knowing (*Plus de mots*). Like the cannibals he buries the dead in his stomach (*J'ensevelis les morts dans mon ventre*). He cannot even foresee the time when he will fall into nothingness as the whites disembark (*Je ne vois même pas l'heure, où, les blancs débarquant, je tomberai au néant*) to kill, to conquer, to convert, and to civilize. Until they do he can only shout with all the frenzy of an African native, hunger, thirst, cries, dance, dance, dance, dance (*Faim, soif, cris, danse, danse, danse, danse*)! Such is Rimbaud's *Livre nègre*, a means of combating the injustice we call justice by joining those who do not know justice, by the refusal of its hypocrisies, by the return to the basic bodily needs, by the return to the expression of self in movement rather than in words, the immediate expression of one's true self rather than by the gloss of reason hiding madness.

III   A Song of Civilization

The whites have arrived (*Les blancs débarquent*) and brought
with them the guns (*Le canon*) of civilization. Everyone must
now accept religion (*Il faut se soumettre au baptême*), put on
clothes (*s'habiller*), and work (*travailler*). The narrator has
received the divine assistance of the Lord (*J'ai reçu au coeur
le coup de grâce*) that comes with repentance. But he does not
need to repent, for he has done no evil (*Je n'ai point fait le mal*).
Spiritually he has not suffered the torments of a soul almost dead
to the idea of good (*les tourments de l'âme presque morte au
bien*). Socially he has not suffered the fate of the dutiful son of
the family (*Le sort du fils de famille*). But just because one
refuses debauchery (*La débauche*) and vice (*le vice*) does not
mean that clocks will no longer continue to count the time of
life by its hours of unrelieved sadness (*l'horloge ne sera pas
arrivée à ne plus sonner que l'heure de la pure douleur*). Will
he become a child of paradise (*un enfant, pour jouer au paradis*)
who has forgotten and is thus innocent of all evil (*dans l'oubli
de tout le malheur*)? Are there perhaps other lives (*Vite, est-il
d'autres vies*)? Are there other possibilities? Wealth is certainly
not the answer (*Le sommeil dans la richesse est impossible*),
since divine love alone bestows the keys to knowledge (*L'amour
divin seul octroie les clefs de la science*). If one accepts religion, nature becomes a spectacle of goodness (*la nature n'est
qu'un spectacle de bonté*) and one can say goodby to the chi-
meras, ideals, and errors (*Adieu chimères, idéals, erreurs*) of the
old ways. The narrator is now faced, as we all are, with two types
of love, divine and earthly (*amour terrestre*). If he has been
elected among the chosen, what becomes of his earthly love
(*ceux qui restent sont-ils pas mes amis*)? They, too, must be saved
(*Sauvez-les*). With this recognition the narrator appears to have
given himself up completely to the Christian religion.

But the boredom of resignation will not suffice (*L'ennui n'est
plus mon amour*). Let us consider the extent of his innocence
(*Apprécions sans vertige l'étendue de mon innocence*). He is not
interested in a religion that gives him Christ for a father-in-law
(*une noce avec Jésus-Christ pour beau-père*). Intellectually he
is not a prisoner of reason (*Je ne suis pas prisonnier de ma*

raison). True, he has pronounced the name of God (*J'ai dit: Dieu*), but he wants freedom in salvation (*Je veux la liberté dans le salut*), not another kind of servitude. Whatever precepts religion offers, every man has his personal idea of reason, scorn, and charity (*Chacun a sa raison, mépris et charité*). The narrator will stick by his common sense (*bon sens*). As for established values, domestic or otherwise (*bonheur établi, domestique ou non*), and work (*le travail*), they are but old truths (*vieille vérité*). Rimbaud then describes the life of the narrator in terms we should remember in discussing the *Illuminations*: my life is not heavy enough, it takes flight and floats far away above action, this dear point of the world (*ma vie n'est pas assez pesante, elle s'envole en flotte loin au-dessus de l'action, ce cher point du monde*). Upon arriving at this dear point of the world the narrator will have realized the detachment necessary to reveal the truth of our life in this world which includes, inevitably, death. Unlike silly old women (*vieille fille*) we must love death as a part of life (*aimer la mort*). The world no longer needs saints, strong men, anchorites, artists (*Les saints! des forts! les anachorètes, des artistes*) who are convinced they are immortal. The narrator can only weep over his own inno-cence (*Mon innocence me ferait pleurer*), since life is a farce that must be played out by all (*La vie est la farce à mener par tous*).

He who accepts this realistic view knows that life is a punish-ment (*voici la punition*). All we can do is push on (*En marche!*), although our lungs burn (*les poumons brûlent*) and our tem-ples throb (*les tempes grondent*). The narrator becomes inco-herent in the enormous struggle, wanting to give up (*je me rends*), to kill himself (*Je me tue*), to throw himself under the horses' hoofs (*Je me jette aux pieds des chevaux*). But (*Ah!*) he will get used to it (*Je m'y habituerai*), for it will be a typical French life, the way of all honor (*Ce serait la vie française, le sentier de l'honneur*). Such bitter irony recalls Flaubert's pitiless conclusion to *Madame Bovary*. The narrator has insisted upon the fundamental innocence of life, refused the "bad blood" of his physical and spiritual heritage, suffered all the temptations of religion, expressed clearly his socialist idealism (*La richesse a toujours été bien public*), denounced the hypocrisies of so-called civilization, rejected accepted values that are good only because accepted, looked death in the face, and resigned himself to the reality in which the only way to fight the establishment is to join it.

IV   *The Song of Hell*

To purge himself of his "bad blood" the narrator must still pass through a "Night in Hell."[7] Although he feels himself as innocent as a savage, he cannot escape his Christian heritage. The famous gulp of poison he has swallowed (*J'ai avalé une fameuse gorgée de poison*) was that of thinking he could free himself for a moment of the world and the past. The venom (*venin*) of such an idea burns his guts (*Les entrailles*), twists his limbs (*mes membres*), leaves him dying of thirst (*soif*), gasping for air (*j'étouffe*), speechless (*je ne puis crier*). Such is the eternal punishment (*l'éternelle peine*) of hell. In contrast, true conversion brings with it righteousness (*bien*), happiness (*bonheur*), and salvation (*salut*), a vision peopled with charming creatures (*créatures charmantes*), filled with strength (*la force*), peace (*la paix*), and noble ambitions (*les nobles ambitions*). Even so, he is damned by his own belief for if one thinks he is in hell, he is (*Je me crois en enfer, donc j'y suis*). The catechism (*catéchisme*), his baptism (*mon baptême*), his parents (*Parents*) have all taught him so. What an innocent pagan he was. He would prefer to fall into that nothingness (*que je tombe au néant*) he mentioned at the arrival of the whites with their civilization (*de par la loi humaine*). Voices haunt and taunt him with their cries of shame (*la honte*), their reproaches (*le reproche*). The Satan of his conscience tells him the fire of damnation he suffers because of his sins is ignoble (*ignoble*), that his anger is foolish (*bête*). The love of magic (*magies*), the false perfumes (*parfums faux*), the childish music (*musiques puériles*), were all mistakes (*Des erreurs*). To claim that he knows what truth (*la vérité*) and justice (*la justice*) are, that his judgment is sound and steady (*sain et arrêté*), is nothing more than pride (*Orgueil*). He is overcome by the nostalgia of childhood, the grass, the rain, the lake, the moonlight when the clock-tower strikes midnight (*l'herbe, la pluie, le lac sur les pierres*, le clair de lune quand le clocher sonnait douze). But that is again the tempting voice of the devil (*le diable*).

Surely there are some honest souls in hell (*Là-bas, ne sont-ce pas des âmes honnêtes*)who wish him well (*qui me veulent du bien*). But he has a pillow over his mouth (*J'ai un oreiller sur la bouche*) and they cannot hear him (*elles ne m'entendent pas*). Besides they are phantoms (*ce sont des fantômes*) of his imagination, since he knows that no one ever thinks of anyone else (*jamais personne ne pense à autrui*). He is roasting in hell (*Je sens le roussi*), an intensification of the observation in the preceding paragraph that the skin of his head is drying up (*La peau de ma tête se dessèche*). The hallucinations are now innumerable (*Les hallucinations sont innombrables*), visions of heaven and hell. In such a state the memory of mankind (*l'histoire*) and all his principles (*principes*) are forgotten, the fantasies of poets and visionaries pale (*poètes et visionnaires*). Time has stopped (*l'horloge de la vie s'est arrêté*), the narrator is no longer of this world (*Je ne suis plus au monde*) but at "that dear point of the world," in ecstasy, experiencing a nightmare, asleep in a nest of flames (*Extase, cauchemar, sommeil dans un nid de flammes*), when all the mysteries become clear, the supernatural mysteries both of Satan, called Ferdinand (*Satan, Ferdinand*) in parts of the Ardennes, who sows his wild seeds (*les graines sauvages*), and of Jesus who walked on the waters (*Jésus marchait sur les eaux irritées*), revealed to us by the lantern of the gospel (*La lanterne nous le montra debout*). Equally clear are the natural mysteries of death, birth, future, past, the birth of the universe and of nothingness (*mort, naissance, avenir, passé, cosmogonie, néant*). Again the narrator is convinced he is the master of all optical illusions (*mâitre en fantasmagories*), of all talents (*tous les talents*). He can produce Negro songs (*chants nègres*), dances by Muslim maidens (*danse de houris*), gold and remedies by alchemy (*de l'or, des remèdes*). Again by contrast, faith assuages, guides, cures (*la foi soulage, guide, guérit*), and consoles (*console*). He admits for a moment that his past life is regrettable (*c'est regrettable*), but again he is out of this world (*hors du monde*), hearing nothing (*Plus aucun son*), feeling nothing (*Mon tact a disparu*). He remembers the chateau, the Saxony, the willow woods (*mon château,*

ma Saxe, mon bois de saules) from the fairyland of his childhood, the days and nights that have passed. He must find a hell
for his anger and his pride (*Je devrais avoir mon enfer pour la
colère, mon enfer pour l'orgueil*), for his lust (*l'enfer de la
caresse*), a whole concert of hells (*un concert d'enfers*). Thus
lured by the voice of Satan, he will die (*C'est le tombeau*), be
eaten by the worms (*je m'en vais aux vers*), dissolve (*dis-
soudre*) into dust. This was the poison (*ce poison*) he swallowed. He begs God for pity (*Mon Dieu, pitié*), but the fire
of hell rises up with the damned (*C'est le feu qui se soulève
avec son damné*). During this "Night in Hell" the narrator vacil-
lates continuously between heaven and hell, having been indoc-
trinated by visions of both. The pagan innocence of some garden
of Eden seems preferable to the burden of guilt religion imposes.
He thinks to escape the world only to find himself condemned
to hell. Sin and salvation cannot be balanced because by living
we sin and are condemned to die.

V   Songs of Delirium

Nowhere has Rimbaud illustrated better his dictum that the
"I is another" than in "Délires I" (Deliriums I).[8] His point of
departure was the parable of the five Wise and five Foolish
Virgins recounted in Matthew 25: 1–13. The parable includes a
bridegroom who is never, however, described as "Infernal."
Scholars long insisted that the "Vierge Folle" (Foolish Virgin)
was Verlaine talking about Rimbaud as "L'Epoux infernal" (Infernal Bridegroom). Finally a scholar came along who demonstrated that Rimbaud was not writing about himself as seen
through the eyes of Verlaine but describing the Infernal Bridegroom he had become through the eyes of the Foolish Virgin
he had been, the same innocent pagan mentioned so frequently
up to this point in *Une Saison*.[9] They are the same but different,
the masculine and feminine poles of Rimbaud's temperament,
innocence and disillusionment, the before and after of the "Night
in Hell," the I of the Other describing the Me.

The poem takes the form of a confession on the part of the
Foolish Virgin who admits that only later will she know the
Divine Bridegroom (***Plus Tard, je connaîtrai le divin Epoux***),

since she is still the slave of the Infernal Bridegroom (*Je suis l'esclave de l'Epoux infernal*), and thus damned and dead to the world (*damnée et morte au monde*). The innocent half of the narrator's character has been subjugated by the Infernal Bridegroom even though he himself is still almost a child (*presque un enfant*). Their life together is not a real life (*La vraie vie est absente*) but a life of the imagination. Or the expression could mean their life is the real life but absent in the sense of imaginary. Like the earlier narrator they are out of this world (*Nous ne sommes pas au monde*). The Foolish Virgin describes her husband's character by revealing first his misogyny. He says that he does not like women (*Je n'aime pas les femmes*) and gives his reasons. It is not so much that he does not like women but rather that the whole concept of love must be reinvented (*L'amour est à réinventer*). In modern society a woman has no choice but to search for security (*Elles ne peuvent plus que vouloir une position assurée*). She can hardly be blamed if, once married, love and beauty are put side (*La position gagnée, coeur et beauté sont mis de côté*), leaving only cold contempt as the food of marriage today (*il ne reste que froid dédain, l'aliment du mariage, aujourd'hui*). Rimbaud also cites the case of women who reveal a real talent for happiness only to be devoured by brutes who are as sensitive as woodpiles (*des femmes, avec des signes du bonheur, ... dévorées tout d'abord par des brutes sensibles comme des bûchers*). Rimbaud later gives another example, that of the woman who devotes her life to an elegant young man (*cet élégant jeune homme*) only to find that he is a malicious idiot (*ce méchant idiot*) and who dies as a result. Rimbaud's so-called misogyny would seem to be based rather closely upon the realities of society as he observed them.

The Infernal Bridegroom also takes the inverted moral view already expressed in *Une Saison*, making glory of infamy, a charm of cruelty (*faisant de l'infamie une gloire, de la cruauté un charme*). This time his heritage, instead of pagan or Negro, is Scandinavian (*mes pères étaient Scandinaves*), barbaric forebears who pierced their side and drank their blood (*ils se perçaient les côtes, buvaient leur sang*). Like them the Bridegroom will cover his body with slashes (*des entailles*) and tattoo marks (*je me tatouerai*). Like his antecedent in *Une Saison* he refuses to work (*Jamais je ne travaillerai*) but can speak in a tender jargon (*patois attendri*) of death that causes repentance (*la mort qui fait repentir*), of the unfortunate (*des malheureux*), of painful toil (*des travaux pénibles*), of departures that rend the heart (*des départs qui déchirent les coeurs*), of people reduced to cattle by their misery (*bétail de la misère*). He could also speak with the sweetness of a young girl learning her catechism (*gentillesses de petite fille au catéchisme*). The foolish Virgin cannot understand why he wanted so much to escape reality (*pourquoi il voulait tant s'évader de la réalité*). Perhaps he has secrets for changing life (*Il a peut-être des secrets pour changer la vie*), but his charity, already mentioned several times in *Une Saison,* is bewitched (*sa charité est ensorcelée*) and thus powerless. Nevertheless, for a certain time the Virgin and the Bridegroom got on well together (*Nous nous accordions*), the two halves of the personality were surprised to find they could work together (*Bien émus, nous travaillions ensemble*). Although the Bridegroom knows he must help others since it is his duty (*il faut que j'en aide d'autres: c'est mon devoir*), the Virgin knows full well that he will never work (*il ne travaillera jamais*), for he wants to live like a sleepwalker (*il veut vivre somnambule*), with his eyes open but with his mind and feelings closed and asleep. Would the goodness and charity of the better half of his personality give him the right to live in the true world (*Seules, sa bonté et sa charité lui donneraient-elles droit dans le monde réel*)? Again Rimbaud foretells his own future when the Virgin says they will travel, hunt in the desert, and sleep on the pavement of unknown cities (*nous voyagerons, nous chasserons dans les déserts, nous dormirons sur les pavés des villes inconnues*). But like the elegant young man become a vicious idiot, the infernal half of the narrator's personality will kill the virgin half, the fate of all charitable hearts (*C'est notre sort, à nous, coeurs charitables*). When he dies the Foolish Virgin wonders if he will ascend, not to heaven but to a heaven (*à un ciel*) which, because of the Bridegroom's character, is obviously not the heaven of the Christian religion but perhaps only the air into which evil spirits disappear. In any case, the pair make an odd couple, (*Drôle de ménage*), the innocent and the infernal make strange bedfellows in one mind and one personality. This conclusion looks forward directly to the conclusion of *Une Saison en enfer*.

"Délires II" (Deliriums II) tells the story of another of the narrator's follies (*L'histoire d'une de mes folies*), his attempt at an "Alchimie du verbe" (Alchemy of the Word).[10] Thinking himself to be in possession of all possible landscapes (*tous les paysages possibles*), he disdained the efforts of well-known painter and poets (*les célébrités de la peinture et de la poésie moderne*). He loved all sorts of quaint and esoteric subjects, dreams of adventures recorded and unrecorded. In his sonnet of the "Vowels" he invented their color (*la couleur des voyelles*). More important, he thought he had discovered a poetic speech accessible, sooner or later, to all the senses (*un verbe poétique accessible, un jour ou l'autre, à tous les sens*). He wrote of silences and nights (*J'écrivais des silences, des nuits*), recorded the inexpressible (*je notais l'inexprimable*), fixed dizziness in words (*Je fixais des vertiges*).

As the first example of his efforts, Rimbaud quotes "Larme" (Tear), but without its title. All but one of the poems quoted in *Une Saison* exist in a form frequently quite different from the form here. I shall use both forms in my study. Like most of the poems quoted "Larme" dates from May, 1872.[11] Its four quatrains of eleven-syllable lines do not rhyme according to a fixed pattern. The scene of the first two quatrains is that of the narrator "Far from the birds, the herds, the village maids" (*Loin des oiseaux, des troupeaux, des villageoises*), "squatting in the heather" (*accroupi dans quelque bruyère*), quenching his thirst (*Je buvais*), that monstrous thirst that has by now become almost metaphysical. Although the narrator is "far from the herds," this scene renders the reply "I shall go drink where the cows drink" of "Comédie de la soif" somewhat more understandable. Rimbaud calls the river "this young Oise" (*cette jeune Oise*), a name he had already used in "Ce qu'on dit au poète." It is a foggy afternoon (*Par un brouillard d'après-midi*) and amid the flowerless silence he is wondering what he can drink. What can he draw from the gourd of the colocasia (*Que tirais-je à la gourde de colocase*)? The colocasia or Egyptian water lily has no gourd, but could Rimbaud mean the flower itself from which he might drink the dew, "Some golden liquor, flat and that

raises sweat" (*Quelque liqueur d'or, fade, et qui fait suer*)?
Does he mean simply beer? Perhaps. In any event, the narrator
in this scene is no advertisement for an inn (*Tel, j'eusse été
mauvaise enseigne d'auberge*). As in "Michel et Christine," a
storm breaks, converting the landscape into "black lands, lakes,
poles, / Colonnades in the blue night, stations" (*des pays noirs,
des lacs, des perches, / Des colonnades sous la nuit bleue, des
gares*). The water disappeared in the dry sand (*L'eau des bois
se perdait sur des sables vierges*) while "The wind from the sky
rained icicles on the ponds" (*Le vent, du ciel, jetait des glaçons
aux mares*). The conclusion is introduced by *Or*, which could
mean the gold of the liquor already mentioned or that of the
fisherman to come, or it could be the conjunction "but" or
"well," meaning "Well! like a fisherman of gold or shells, / To
think that I didn't even bother to drink" (*Or! tel qu'un pêcheur
d'or ou de coquillages, / Dire que je n'ai pas eu souci de boire*),
not even the "tear" of the title. The poem in "Délires II" is reduced to three quatrains plus one line. The awkward reference
to the exotic but gourdless colocasia is eliminated, and the
final line becomes "Weeping, I saw gold—and was unable to
drink" (*Pleurant, je voyais de l'or—et ne pus boire*), perhaps the
gold of the sun reflected on the water, which is more in keeping
with the title and an improvement over the earlier text.

The second poem Rimbaud quoted in "Délires II" is "Bonne
Pensée du matin" (A Good Thought in the Morning), again
without title and again dating probably from May, 1872.[12] Here
I shall follow the earlier text which seems to be more carefully worked out. The first four quatrains, with one exception,
consist of three octosyllables followed by a hemistich. Lines
seven and eight, however, contain eight and four instead of
eight and six syllables if counted as normal speech, or ten and
four syllables if counted according to the rules, thus making a
total of fourteen syllables as do the concluding lines of quatrains one, three, and four. The final quatrain consists of a hemistich, two octosyllables, and concludes with an alexandrine. The
rhyme scheme also reveals variations. The first quatrain rhymes
a b b a while all the rest rhyme *a b a b* except for the two assonances, *Hespérides-s'agitent* and *Bergers-paix,* in the second and

fifth quatrains. Within this relatively free form Rimbaud has given expression to one of his most puzzling flights of fancy.

The first quatrain is deceptively clear. The lovers are still sleeping (*Le sommeil d'amour dure encore*) at four o'clock on this summer morning (*A quatre heures du matin, l'été*) while dawn is clearing away the traces of the previous evening's revelries in a small thicket (*l'aube évapore / L'odeur du soir fêté*). The second quatrain introduces one disconcerting note that wrenches the scene awry. The contrast between the slumbering lovers and the busy carpenters (*les charpentiers /Déjà s'agitent*) is obvious enough. The problem is the location of the workyard (*l'immense chantier / Vers le soleil des Hespérides*). Because Rimbaud wrote in a letter of June, 1872, to his friend Ernest Delahaye of his early morning vigils in his attic room on the Rue Monsieur-le-Prince in Paris during which he watched the workers going off to their jobs,[13] early critics thought that the workyards in this quatrain must be those of Paris. A later critic feels that the workyards are nature itself and the carpenters the insects and animals that stir in the early morning light.[14] The yards are described, however, as being "In the direction of the sun of the Hesperides." The Hesperides were both the nymphs and the legendary garden they guarded, which was located at the western extremity of the world and produced golden apples that afforded immortality. The sun of the lovers rises in the east but the sun of the carpenters is found in the west. The contradiction is more apparent than real, as we shall see later. The introduction of the Hesperides adds four new elements to the poem: the west as opposed to the east; the continuation of the idea of the garden (*les bosquets*), and the heightening of the contrast between the garden and the workyard; the golden apples as symbols of the sun; the apples and the sun as symbols of immortality.

The opening line of the third quatrain would seem to confirm the interpretation of the workyard as nature itself if not a garden (*Dans leur désert de mousse*), but a more puzzling element has been introduced in the form of what the carpenters are constructing. That they are preparing costly ceilings (*les lambris précieux*) on which the wealth of the city is being happily expended (*Où la richesse de la ville / Rira*) is a literal interpretation.

That the figurative wealthy will also be able to enjoy themselves under these literally false skies (*sous de faux cieux*) is
also possible. The rich man is his money. Thus the third quatrain has continued the idea of a garden, while the ambiguity
of the sun in the east and west is emphasized by the reference
to "false skies."

The fourth quatrain brings lovers and workers together. Rimbaud alludes to history by his reference to "a king of Babylon"
(*un roi de Babylone*). From his reference to Nebuchadnezzar
in the *Illuminations* we know that Rimbaud was familiar with
his name as the most famous king and builder of Babylon who
had the Hanging Gardens constructed. Rimbaud describes his
"charming Workers" (*ces Ouvriers charmants*) as "subjects"
(*sujets*) of such a king, who thus becomes the symbol of all
carpenters as well as the builder of "false" gardens in the sky.
The Hesperides were also false gardens in the sense that
they were legendary, lost somewhere beyond the horizon of sea
and sky. But Rimbaud introduces another symbol, this time that
of all lovers in the form of Venus, the mythological goddess of
love. It is only natural that Rimbaud should ask her to forget
for a moment the lovers whose souls are already filled with
pleasure (*Vénus, laisse un peu les Amants*) and turn her attention to the workers (*pour ces Ouvriers*). But Venus is also the
evening star that appears in the western sky and could thus be
the sun of the mythological Hesperides, the sun of the carpenters
thus becoming the sun of the lovers also.

As one might expect, all of the elements of the poem are
gathered together in the concluding quatrain. The reference to
the "Queen of Shepherds" (*O Reine des Bergers*) undoubtedly
led one interpreter to suggest that "Bonne Pensée" was an attempt on Rimbaud's part "to express a modern vision in the
form of which the poets of the eighteenth century were so
fond," more specifically the libretti of Charles-Simon Favart.[15]
But she could also be Venus, the evening star, which is also
called the Shepherd's Star because it lights the lonely nocturnal vigil of the shepherds. She could also be simply the village
maid who brings to the shepherds the water and food (*Porte aux
travailleurs l'eau-de-vie*) that sustain them and make their work
possible. The key word is "laborers," which consolidates the

lovers, carpenters, workers, and shepherds into one group. They all share one thing, activity. They all seek a little immortality, the golden apples of the Hesperides, lovers through their progeny, builders through their constructions. The carpenters were subjects of Nebuchadnezzar and thus historical builders of real structures which, like most of the material creations of man—for example, the "false skies" and Hanging Gardens—are doomed to disappear in the same mists as the mythological Hesperides. The physical pleasures of love are even more evanescent than the structures of man, but lovers and builders both need sustenance, the brandy or eau-de-vie of the poem. That Rimbaud was punning on the double sense of brandy and water of life, I have no doubt. The biblical echo of water and bread of life is clearly heard, as Suzanne Bernard pointed out.[16] This is the water that sustains and soothes, but another kind of water is necessary for life, for lovers as well as carpenters. That is the water that cleanses, physically and spiritually. What better time and place to seek it than in the sea at noon when lovers have at last awakened and workers take their break? What better time to enjoy it than at noon, *midi prompt* as Rimbaud put it in "Mémoire," the moment the immortal sun is at its highest and brightest? That Rimbaud was also punning on *la mer-l'amer* to indicate bitters or curaçao in contrast to the eau-de-vie,[17] I find more difficult to accept.

Almost all of the "Last Songs" of Rimbaud treat the theme of life and death in one way or another. The theme here would seem to be immortality, otherwise there would be no reason for mentioning the sun of the Hesperides. From our mortal viewpoint the sun, the golden apples of the garden, is immortal. If the sun is the source of all energy, the sea was the source of all life. Thus the poem is balanced between the sun of the first quatrain and the sea of the last. The sun and the sea have significance, however, only for us mortals. All of the types mentioned in the poem are engaged in an active physical life of doing, making, and creating. The only activity of the mind is the imagination necessary to create a legendary Hesperides, the idea of immortality. All mortals live in the world, however, whether it be the thicket of the lovers or the mossy desert of the carpenters or the field and stream of the shepherd. This gar-

den of life is our workyard whatever our activity, the garden
and the workyard being one. As mortals we need water to quench
our thirst and cleanse our bodies and souls. We know that our
creations, our "false skies," are as mortal as we are. Still the
hope of immortality lurks in our soul. Caught between the
reality of mortality and the dream of immortality, we search
for peace (*Pour que leurs forces soient en paix*) and are apt
to find it in the mindless and diverting activity of bathing in
the sea. Our hope is the Hesperides. Our reality lies somewhere
between the sun and sea.

CHAPTER 6

More Songs of a Private Hell

B ETWEEN "Bonne Pensée du matin" and "Chanson de la plus haute tour" Rimbaud continues the description of his verbal delirium in a prose that heralds the *Illuminations*. The role of the poetic rubbish (*La vieillerie poétique*) of former times, the traditional rules of French prosody, cannot be over-emphasized. In his hallucinations he saw very clearly a mosque in place of a factory (*je voyais très franchement une mosquée à la place d'une usine*) and a school of drums composed of angels (*une école de tambours faite par des anges*). Continuing the mingling of the high and low, sky and earth, he saw carriages on the roads of the sky (*des calèches sur les routes du ciel*) and a salon at the bottom of a lake (*un salon au fond d'un lac*). His nightmares were filled with monsters and mysteries (*les monstres, les mystéres*), the terrors (*des épouvantes*) of a vaudeville. He confesses that in this life become a vaudeville he found the disorder of his mind holy (*trouver sacré le désordre de mon esprit*). He envied the insects and beasts, the innocence of the limbo (*l'innocence des limbes*) that had been his life, the sleep of virginity (*le sommeil de la virginité*) that had been his former state. He said farewell to that world in some types of romances (*Je disais adieu au monde dans d'espèces de romances*) that include the "Chanson de la plus haute tour."

This poem, that also probably dates from May, 1872,[1] contains six stanzas of six five-syllable lines rhyming *a b a b c c*, the sixth stanza repeating the first. The "Song of the Highest Tower" is the poet's story of how he lost his life. He takes up the theme of his idleness (*Oisive jeunesse*) he had just mentioned (*J'étais oisif*) as a result of which he gave in to all suggestions (*A tout asservie*). Thus by his very willingness (*Par délicatesse*) he wasted his time and lost his life (*J'ai perdu ma vie*). All he can hope is that the time of true love will return (*Que le temps vienne / Où les coeurs s'éprennent*). In the second stanza he describes himself as he was, self-effacing (*qu'on ne te voie*) and undemanding (*sans la promesse / De plus hautes joies*). He wanted nothing to interrupt this worthy withdrawal (*Que rien ne t'arrête / Auguste retraite*). He was so patient (*J'ai tant fait patience*) that he forgot everything (*à jamais j'oublie*). His fears and sufferings (*Craintes et souffrances*) seemed to disappear in thin air (*Aux cieux sont parties*). But an unhealthy thirst (*la soif malsaine*) took possesion of him (*Obscurcit mes veines*) so that he could be compared to a meadow (*Ainsi la prairie*) that has been forgotten (*A l'oubli livrée*) and may grow and flower (*Grandie, et fleurie*) with the good things of life like incense (*d'encens*) and bad things like weeds (*et d'ivraies*) that attract a hundred dirty flies (*cent sales mouches*) with their fierce buzzing (*Au bourdon farouche*). In nine syllables Rimbaud has called upon the sense of smell (*encens*), of touch (*ivraies*), and of hearing (*bourdon* for *bourdonnement*). Alienated as he is from life (*Mille veuvages*) even prayer, the last resort, seems useless (*Est-ce que l'on prie / La Vierge Marie*). This is the sad song of a lost life sung from the isolation of the highest tower, a poem that has to be read aloud to be appreciated.

The poem "Faim" (Hunger) or "Fêtes de la faim" (Celebrations of Hunger) as Rimbaud called it in its earlier form, may have been written around August, 1872.[2] "Faim" contains only three quatrains, whereas "Fêtes de la faim" includes five quatrains and begins and ends with a two-line refrain. Quatrains one, three, and five are composed of seven-syllable lines, whereas two and four alternate seven- and four-syllable lines with irregularities in form and variations in the rhyme scheme. In this hymn to hunger, which begins with a refrain that sounds like a nursery rhyme, Rimbaud asks hunger to go away (*Fuis*). At the moment he has a taste only for earth and rocks (*Si j'ai du goût, ce n'est guères / Que pour la terre et les pierres*). He feeds on air, rock, lands, and iron (*Je pais l'air, / Le roc, les Terres, le fer*). This mineral menu is supplemented in the second quatrain by the bran of the meadow (*Le pré des sons*) and the friendly and vibrant venom of the bindweed (*l'aimable et vibrant venin / Des liserons*). But mostly the food is rock, the pebbles the poor man breaks up (*Les cailloux qu'un pauvre brise*), the old stones of churches (*Les vieilles pierres d'églises*), the boulders left behind by the floods (*Les galets, fils des déluges*) that resemble bread spread out in the gray valleys (*Pains couchés aux vallées grises*). Obviously little of this can be eaten and in the fourth stanza his hunger has become a torment, bits of black air (*les bouts d'air noir*), a blue trumpeter (*L'azur sonneur*) that keeps him awake, his stomach that aches (*l'estomac qui me tire*), a misfortune (*le malheur*). At last leaves have appeared (*Sur terre ont paru les feuilles*) so he could eat ripe fruit (*chairs de fruit blettes*) and gather lamb's lettuce (*je cueille / La doucette*) for the pleasure of his stomach, and the violet (*la violette*) for the pleasure of his eyes. In the end the reader must ask if this is a hunger of the body or of the soul. A hunger that feeds on earth and air and rock would seem to want to possess the world, a sort of monstrous metaphysical hunger that will not stop short of appropriation of the world and spew it out in the form of images that turn the ordinary into the extraordinary, a poetic hunger that will not stop short of appropriation of the world in the word.

I *Song of the Wolf*

The untitled poem that follows without interruption, "Le loup criait sous les feuilles" (The wolf howled under the leaves), was probably written in May or June, 1872.[3] It exists only as published in *Une Saison* and consists of three quatrains of seven-syllable lines, although lines five and twelve have only six, with a variable rhyme scheme. The poem logically follows "Faim," because the wolf is spitting out the feathers (*En crachant les belles plumes*) of his repast of fowl (*De son repas de volailles*). The interesting observation is that like the wolf, the narrator consumes himself (*Comme lui je me consume*), is feeding off his own metaphysical hunger in which he becomes the world and thus consumes himself. The salads and fruits (*Les salades, les fruits*) mentioned in "Fêtes de la faim" only wait to be gathered (*N'attendent que la cueillette*), whereas the spider in the hedge (*l'araignée de la haie*), the spider of our imagination, eats only the violets (*Ne mange que des violettes*)

that were also mentioned in "Fêtes." It is interesting to note that
the *lycène*, a nocturnal butterfly is called a violet in English and
certainly spiders eat butterflies. Otherwise, the only violets we
can eat, aside from the sugared variety, would have to be the
violets of our imagination. Worn out by his efforts the narrator
cries "Let me sleep" (*Que je dorme*), "Let me boil" (*que je
bouille*), whereas we should probably say "Let me roast" on the
altars of Solomon (*Aux autels de Salomon*), let me be sacrificed
to religion so that the broth (*Le bouillon*) of my boiling runs
on the rust (*court sur la rouille*). *Bouillon* can be broth, the
yellow wild flower *bouillon-blanc*, or a bubble. Rust could
indicate that the altars are unused or suggest the red of blood.
The important thing is that the narrator wants to mingle with
the waters of the Kidron (*se mêle au Cédron*) that separates
Jerusalem from the Mount of Olives and disappear forever, become a thing, become one with the world, the ultimate quenching of his metaphysical hunger and thirst.

The effect is heightened as the narrator addresses himself to
happiness and reason (*ô bonheur, ô raison*), claiming that he
has brushed aside the blue of the sky that sometimes appears
black (*j'écarterai du ciel l'azur, qui est du noir*) and become a
part of the world, a thing in nature, a golden spark of pure,
natural light (*étincelle d'or de la lumière* nature). He took on
a facial expression as farcical and bewildered as possible (*je
prenais une expression bouffonne et égarée au possible*). Its
verbal expression is given in "L'Eternité" (Eternity), quoted
without title, which probably dates from May, 1872.[4] The six
quatrains of five-syllable lines reveal a varying rhyme scheme
with the sixth quatrain repeating the first. The claim is that
eternity has been rediscovered at the moment the sea disappears
with the sun (*C'est la mer allée / Avec le soleil*), the moment
when the sun disappears in the sea and the sea disappears in
the fading light of day. Eternity is, after all, made up of an
infinite number of such evanescent moments. With our soul as
witness (*Ame sentinelle*) we must avow (*Murmurons l'aveu*)
that the night into which sea and sun disappeared is nothing
(*la nuit si nulle*), first, because we sleep through it, unaware
that time has passed, and second, because we know nothing of
the final night into which we all disappear which is for us a

nothingness. The day is on fire (*du jour en feu*) with the light of the sun from which no one escapes. The soul wrenches itself free (*Là tu te dégages*) from the emptiness of human praise (*Des humains suffrages*) and the futility of the pitiful bursts of enthusiasm we all share (*Des communs élans*) and soars according to its whim (*Et voles selon*) anywhere out of this world, in eternity for example. Only in the satiny glowing embers (*Puisque de vous seules, / Braises de satin*) of the sun does Duty find an expression (*Le Devoir s'exhale*) without end (*Sans qu'on dise: enfin*), because where the sun is concerned there is no "at last," only a "forever." At that moment there is no hope in life (*Là pas d'espérance*) or in religion (*Nul orietur*). As Malachi 4:2 reads: "But unto you that fear my name shall the Sun of righteousness arise [*orietur*] with healing in his wings." Our only hopes are knowledge and patience (*Science et patience*), reminding us that this poem is the third in the series "Fêtes de la patience." In our human condition and with our knowledge and patience we know that suffering is inevitable (*Le supplice est sûr*) and eternal, our life but the moment the sea disappears with the sun in the day of eternity. The poem is another of Rimbaud's minor miracles.

The prose between "L'Eternité" and "O saisons, ô chateaux" again contains many of Rimbaud's most frequently quoted lines. In the opening sentence he claims he has become a fabulous opera (*Je devins un opéra fabuleux*), which recalls the vaudeville of which he spoke earlier. He himself became a play in which everything was possible. That idea is followed immediately by his famous paradox that all people have a fatality for happiness (*tous les êtres ont une fatalité de bonheur*). Because we are human we have a longing for happiness that becomes a fatality because we spend our life searching for it without finding it. We strive mightily, but action is not life (*l'action n'est pas la vie*), only another way of dissipating our energy, an irritation (*une façon de gâcher quelque force, un énervement*). His conclusion is that morality is a weakness of the brain (*La morale est la faiblesse de la cervelle*), by which he undoubtedly means the Christian morality of which he wrote when he called Christ the eternal thief of energy in "Les Premières Communions."

At the crux of this attempted metamorphosis into an endless,

fabulous opera is the feeling that every being deserves several
other lives (*A chaque être, plusieurs* autres *vies me semblaient
dues*) in which to live out his desires and to realize his happiness.
If you look at the people around you, you find that one man is
unaware of what he is doing and is thus as innocent as an angel
(*Ce monsieur ne sait ce qu'il fait: il est un ange*). If he were
aware of what he was doing, he would probably be doing evil.
Another family is a nest of dogs (*Cette famille est une nichée de
chiens*). No one is what he appears, and thus the narrator spoke
to several men addressing himself to just one moment of one of
their other lives and thus loved a pig who was one of the men
in another incarnation (*je causai tout haut avec un moment d'une
de leurs autres vies.—Ainsi, j'ai aimé un porc*). He experienced
all the sophisms of madness (*des sophismes de la folie*) with the
result that his health was endangered (*Ma santé fut menacée*).
He was haunted by fear (*La terreur venait*), sought escape in
sleep (*Je tombais dans des sommeils de plusieurs jours*), and
awoke only to continue living the saddest of his dreams (*levé,
je continuais les rêves les plus tristes*). He was again on the point
of dying (*J'étais sûr pour le trépas*), of uttering his last croak
as he put it in "Jadis" at the beginning of *Une Saison*. He has
returned to that desperate situation, to the point of his departure, by a route filled with danger (*une route de dangers*) that
leads him to the ends of the earth (*aux confins du monde*) and
even of Cimmeria (*de la Cimmérie*), the land described by
Homer as filled with mist and gloom, with shadow and whirl-
winds (*de l'ombre et des tourbillons*), says Rimbaud.

To recuperate he had to travel (*Je dus voyager*), hoping to
distract the enchantments crowding in on his mind (*distraire les
enchantements assemblés sur mon cerveau*), to find the sea
that he loved as if it could have cleansed him of his stains (*la
mer, que j'aimais comme si elle eût dû me laver d'une souillure*),
an idea Rimbaud expressed in both "Le Coeur volé" and "Le
Bateau ivre." Like the Emperor Constantine he saw the sign of
the consoling cross (*la croix consolatrice*) but he had been
damned by a rainbow (*J'avais été damné par l'arc-en-ciel*). The
promise offered by faith was there, but the laws of pitiless nature
were also operative. Like a refrain the idea of happiness comes
back and back until he must admit that happiness was his

fatality (*Le Bonheur était ma fatalité*), a repetition of the idea just expressed that all people have a fatality for happiness, an idea that will return in the conclusion to this section. It was also for him his remorse, his worm (*mon remords, mon ver*) that ate away at the flesh of life. His life would always be too immense to be devoted exclusively to strength and beauty (*ma vie serait toujours trop immense pour être dévouée à la force et à la beauté*). Elusive happines gnawed at him like a tooth (*Le Bonheur! Sa dent*), became sweet only in death (*douce à la mort*), warned him of the coming of a day of trials at the crowing of the cock (*m'avertissait au chant du coq*), in the morning (ad matutinum), at the coming of Christ (*au* Christus venit). Where now is the consolation of the cross in these most somber cities (*dans les plus sombres villes*)?

II   A Song of Time and Places

The answer is found in "O saisons, ô châteaux!" (Oh seasons, oh châteaus), the last and perhaps the finest of the poems quoted, the conclusion of the "Alchimie du verbe." The three versions that exist have caused a great deal of commentary.[5] In its most complete form it includes eight rhymed couplets of six- and seven-syllable lines plus three repetitions of the first line as a refrain after couplets one, six, and eight. This title or first line has occasioned all sorts of speculation. For me the seasons indicate time, the châteaus place. We all exist in time and space, one of which evolves inexorably and the other of which changes inevitably without moving. Nostalgia is introduced by the question of the second line of the couplet, what soul is without its flaws (*Quelle âme est sans défauts*)? The seasons must thus be seasons past, the life and time spent, misspent, and regretted because of the weakness of our soul. Châteaus are all the places in our lives we now regret also, even the most somber cities just mentioned. Every new place is a potential castle in Spain as well as a potential somber city. The places of our life, like time, have disappeared because time itself has passed and changed all things. Having considered carefully the time and places of his life the narrator can claim that he has made a magic study of happiness (*J'ai fait la magique étude / Du Bonheur*), magic in the sense that he had turned himself into a fabulous opera where everything was possible, every hallucination a reality. Everyone in one way or another makes a study of happiness, makes an effort to find happiness, a study no one can avoid (*que nul n'élude*) since it is part of the human condition.

Interpretation of the third couplet frequently determines one's conclusions about the whole poem. I have not up to this point seen any signs of Verlaine in the poem and find no reason to drag him in now, even if *chaque fois / Que chante son coq gaulois* does mean ejaculation in Ardennes slang. If Rimbaud did mean to introduce Verlaine into the poem, then he must have meant that the tooth of happiness mentioned in the paragraph immediately preceding the poem was Verlaine's penis which awakened him with its cock's crow and which also became sweet at death, soft after ejaculation. Then the pig he loved must have been Verlaine and the somber cities Paris, Brussels, and above all London, and the whole poem is explained, or explained away. I see no reason to violate Rimbaud's syntax by introducing a hypothetical antecedent for the masculine pronoun in the expression "long may he live" (*vive lui*, also *Salut à lui*). While the practice of making a pronoun refer to a noun that is already the object of a preposition may not be grammatically sound, it is done often enough to be acceptable. Thus *lui* refers to *Bonheur* and not to Verlaine, just as *Sa dent* immediately following *Le Bonheur* means happiness's tooth not Verlaine's tooth or whatever. The expression *son coq gaulois* in the earlier version becomes the much more general *le coq gaulois* in *Une Saison*. I feel Rimbaud is saying long may happiness live even with the arrival of day that will awaken us to all our problems.

The fourth couplet offers another masculine pronoun *Il* which again should refer to the preceding happiness or could refer, by anticipation, to the charm (*Ce Charme*) of the following couplet. Either way makes no difference since happiness is the charm. He says he will have no more desires (*je n'aurai plus d'envie*), since happiness has taken charge of his life (*Il s'est chargé de ma vie*). This charm has possessed him body and soul (*Ce Charme! Il prit âme et corps*) and dissipated all his efforts (*dispersa tous efforts*). The happiness that possessed him was that of hallucination and madness, his fatality, so that his question in the sixth couplet—what can be understood from my words (*Que comprendre à ma parole*)—is answered by it, meaning this charm, which has caused them to flee and fly (*Il fait qu'elle fuïe et vole*), has rendered them incomprehensible to others who do not share his enchantment.

Neither the sixth nor the seventh couplet is included in *Une Saison*. The seventh states that if misfortune carries him away (*si le malheur m'entraîne*), its disgrace is certain for him (*Sa disgrâce m'est certain*). The repeated object pronoun *me* is awkward while the possessive adjective *Sa*, although clear, complicates matters. The couplet also obscures the references in the final couplet, making it evident why Rimbaud did not include it in *Une Saison*. If it is included, then *son dédain* becomes the disdain of misfortune that yields him up to the swiftest death (*Me livre au plus prompt trépas*). The *Saison* version is preferable since there the hour of its flight, the departure of this charm (*L'heure de sa fuite*), will be the hour of his death (*Sera l'heure du trépas*). The moment his happiness, his hallucinations, abandon him, he will have returned to reality, which is the death of the imagination. All of that is over and done with (*Cela s'est passé*), and he can conclude that he now knows how to salute beauty (*Je sais aujourd'hui saluer la beauté*), that same beauty he took on his knees in "Jadis" and found ugly. He has lived through his night in hell, survived two kinds of delirium, and is now ready to come to some decision about the experience itself. "O saisons, ô châteaux" disappears into the thin air of the imagination, leaving an undying echo in the mind of the reader.

III   *The Impossible Song*

The drama of *Une Saison* has taken place, leaving four brief sections of conclusion. In the first, "L'Impossible" (The Impossible),[6] Rimbaud again judges his former life, his childhood (*mon enfance*) with its flights (*la grande route par tous les temps*), its unnatural sobriety (*sobre surnaturellement*), its detachment (*désintéressé*), its pride in having neither country nor friends (*fier de n'avoir ni pays, ni amis*), and finds it foolish (*quelle sottise*). He was right, however, in disdaining the "good men" (*ces bonshommes*) who were nothing more than the parasites (*parasites*) of the slavery of women upon whom they depended for cleanliness and health (*de la propreté et de la santé*), particularly now that women are finding their own voice (*aujourd'hui qu'elles sont si peu d'accord avec nous*). He would escape (*je m'évade*) from all that.

He was well acquainted with the damned of this earth (*Je les connais tous*) to whom charity is unknown (*Le charité nous est inconnue*), again that charity of which he spoke in "Jadis." But were the so-called elect (*les élus*) any better, taking such pleasure in their viciousness (*des gens hargneux et joyeux*) they could hardly be called blessers (*des bénisseurs*)?

When he at last came to his senses (*M'étant retrouvé deux sous de raison*), he realized that all these problems arose because we live in the Occident (*nous sommes à l'Occident*). Not that the light is adulterated (*la lumière altérée*) nor form exhausted (*la forme exténuée*) nor movement gone astray (*le mouvement égaré*) simply because we live in the Occident. The narrator's spirit would like to assume all the cruel developments (*tous les développements cruels*) the spirit has undergone (*qu'a subis l'esprit*) since the end of the Orient (*depuis la fin de l'Orient*), since the end of its domination of the known world. We are, nevertheless, condemned to live in the Occident (*il veut que je sois en Occident*) and must judge it for what it is.

He disdains its religion (*les palmes des martyrs*), its art (*les rayons de l'art*), its inventions (*l'orgueil des inventeurs*), its pillaging (*l'ardeur des pillards*), and he would return to the eternal basic wisdom of the Orient (*à l'Orient et à la sagesse première et éternelle*), but that is only an idle dream (*un rêve de paresse grossière*). This opposition between Occident and Orient and the mention of the wisdom of the East have led interpreters to endless extravagant flights of fancy. The first thing to notice is that Rimbaud does not mean the Far East, neither the Hinduism of India nor the Confucianism of China nor the Buddhism of Asia. He means, as he indicates in the following paragraph, the Islamism of the Near East, the Occident of the Orient with its Bible which is the Koran, that part of the world to which Rimbaud traveled later. The narrator intended neither to try to escape the sufferings inflicted on us by modern life (*souffrances modernes*) nor to accept blindly the fatalism of the Koran (*la sagesse bâtarde du Coran*). Nevertheless, since the advent of that special brand of knowledge that calls itself Christianity (*cette déclaration de la science, le christianisme*), men have deceived themselves (*l'homme se joue*) by attempting to discover proofs of its validity (*se prouve les évidences*), a subtle and foolish torture (*Torture subtile, niaise*), the source of the narrator's and everyone else's spiritual meanderings (*mes divagations spirituelles*). The elect, the "good men" like the proverbial Monsieur Prudhomme, are not bothered by any such doubts since they are convinced they were born with Christ Himself (*né avec le Christ*).

Instead of the Eastern sun we in the Occident cultivate fog (*nous cultivons la brume*) and hope to arouse enthusiasm (*la fièvre*) with our watery vegetables (*nos légumes aqueux*). We indulge in drunkenness (*l'ivrognerie*), tobacco (*le tabac*), ignorance (*l'ignorance*), and self-sacrifice (*les dévouements*). All of that is alien to the wisdom of the Orient, our original fatherland (*Tout cela est-il assez loin de la pensée de la sagesse de l'Orient, la patrie primitive*). What is the good of the advantages of modern life if it also invents such poisons (*Pourquoi un monde moderne, si de pareils poisons s'inventent*), a question which reminds us of "the famous gulp of poison" mentioned in "Nuit de l'enfer."

The men of the church would say that this utopia is none other than the dream of Eden (*vous parlez de l'Eden*), that the history of Oriental peoples has nothing to offer (*Rien pour vous dans l'histoire des peuples orientaux*), and they would be right (*C'est vrai*). Philosophers also offer their kind of Eden by maintaining that you may live in the Occident but you are free to live in the Orient of your mind (*Vous êtes en Occident, mais libre d'habiter dans votre Orient*). Such an Eden is a typically Occidental mirage (*Philosophes, vous êtes de votre Occident*). Even so, the spirit must avoid the violent efforts at salvation (*Pas de partis de salut violents*) like the deliriums he has just suffered during his night in hell. Science, too, is not fast enough (*la science ne va pas assez vite*) for the metamorphosis he was trying to effect. But his spirit sleeps (*mon esprit dort*). If it had been sufficiently aware (*bien éveillé*), he would soon be arriving

at the truth (*nous serions bientôt à la vérité*), he would not have
given in to his harmful instincts (*je n'aurais pas cédé aux
instincts délétères*), he would be sailing in total wisdom (*je
voguerais en pleine sagesse*) as one sails on the open sea. The
minute of his awakening revealed to him this purity (*C'est cette
minute d'éveil que m'a donné la vision de la pureté*), but it
lasted only a minute and was gone. It is true that one arrives
at God through the spirit (*Par l'esprit on va à Dieu*) but his
spirit slept, he missed his chance, the dream has proved impossible. What a heartrending misfortune (*Déchirante infor-
tune*)!

After the impossible dream of spiritual purity comes "L'Eclair"
(The Streak of Lightning that can also be The Insight)[7] that
work is our salvation (*Le travail humain*). In opposition to the
biblical judgment in Ecclesiastes that "All is vanity," the modern Ecclesiastes would say that nothing is in vain since we shall
progress inevitably with the aid of science (*Rien n'est vanité: à
la science, et en avant*). Yet we all suffer the death of others
and die ourselves (*pourtant les cadavres des méchants et des
fainéants tombent sur le coeur des autres*). Where then are those
future and eternal recompenses (*ces récompenses futures,
éternelles*) religion promises us?

The narrator has tried work (*Je connais le travail*) and learned
that it is too slow, as is science (*la science est trop lente*), an
idea he had just expressed in "L'Impossible." No matter how
much he prays and how enlightened he thus becomes (*Que la
prière galope et la lumière gronde*), nothing satisfies his press-
ing need. He knows his duty (*J'ai mon devoir*) but like most of
us (*à la façon de plusieurs*) he will put it aside (*en le mettant de
côté*). Let us play a game (*feignons*) and waste time (*fainé-
antons*) by amusing ourselves as we dream up monstrous loves
and fantastic universes (*nous existerons en nous amusant, en
rêvant amours monstres et univers fantastiques*), by pitying ourselves and quarreling with the appearances of the world (*en
nous plaignant et en querellant les apparences du monde*) since
we as a fabulous opera can create unheard of appearances. We
will play all those roles that do not fit the norms of society,
the clown because he is not what he appears, the beggar because
he does not work, the artist whose imagination renders him

different, the bandit because of his crime, the priest because of his vows of poverty and chastity (*saltimbanque, mendiant, artiste, bandit,–prêtre*). As he was about to die (*Sur mon lit d'hopital*), the promise of religion in the form of the incense of the final rites came back to him (*l'odeur de l'encens m'est revenue*) as they were administered by this guardian of the holy herbs (*gardien des aromates sacrés*) who is also a confessor (*confesseur*) and martyr (*martyr*) to his calling, the priest. But that was the religious nonsense of his education (*ma sale éducation d'enfance*). He will live out his twenty years (*Aller mes vingt ans* [Rimbaud had only eighteen to live]) and see what happens. In a sudden about-face, he rebels against death (*je me révolte contre la mort*). Work is no answer (*Le travail paraît trop léger*), and his betrayal to the world (*ma trahison au monde*)–this life we are all condemned to live–would be a too brief punishment (*serait un supplice trop court*), so that he will at the last moment strike out on all sides (*j'attaquerais à droite, à gauche*) to prolong it. But by refusing religion will not he and his soul have lost eternity also (*l'éternité serait-elle pas perdue pour nous*), even the vision of the eternity represented by the disappearance of the sea and sun?

IV A Moving Song

With "Matin" (Morning)[8] comes the regret of never once having had a pleasant, heroic, fabulous childhood (*une jeunesse amiable, héroïque, fabuleuse*) that could have been written down on leaves of gold (*à écrire sur les feuilles d'or*). He asks those who maintain that beasts sob with grief (*des bêtes poussent des sanglots de chagrin*), that the ill despair (*des malades désespèrent*), and that the dead have bad dreams (*des morts rêvent mal*) to tell the story of his fall and sleep (*raconter ma chute et mon sommeil*), for he can no longer speak for himself (Je ne sais plus parler). He thinks he has finished telling his story of hell (*la relation de mon enfer*), which was indeed the hell of olden times, the one whose doors were opened by the Son of Man (*C'était bien l'enfer, l'ancien, celui dont le fils de l'homme ouvrit les portes*). He finds himself in the same desert (*du même désert*), on the same night (*à la même nuit*), when his tired eyes awaken to the guiding silver star (*mes yeux las se réveillent à l'étoile d'argent*), but the Three Kings or Wise Men of life, his heart, soul, and spirit (*les trois mages, le coeur, l'âme, l'esprit*) do not stir. When will we be able to greet the birth of the new work (*saluer la naissance du travail nouveau*), the new wisdom (*la sagesse nouvelle*), that he had been hoping to find and that would eliminate those dictators of our bodies and minds, the tyrants and demons (*la fuite des tyrans et des démons*) as well as superstition (*la fin de la superstition*), so that we can truly for the first time worship Christmas on earth (*adorer—les premiers!—Noël sur la terre*). Although work and religion, philosophy and science are of little assistance, at least the promise of something better can be heard in the song of the heavens (*Le chant des cieux*) and be seen in the progress of mankind (*la marche des peuples*). Therefore, fellow slaves, let us not curse life (*Esclaves, ne maudissons pas la vie*), for it is all we have. That is the morning's message, the "good thought in the morning."

V   A Song of Farewell

The opening words of the conclusion, "Adieu" (Farewell),[9] of *Une Saison en enfer* indicate that the season was, appropriately enough, hot summer since it is now autumn (*L'automne déjà*). The opposition is between the warmth of the life-giving summer sun (*un éternel soleil*) and the cold of winter representing death (*loin des gens qui meurent sur les saisons*). The search had been for divine clarity (*la découverte de la clarté divine*), but autumn (*L'automne*) foretells winter with its impenetrable fogs (*les brumes immobiles*) and its misery (*la misère*) most often observed in the enormous cities whose skies are filled with belching chimneys and muddy rain (*la cité énorme au ciel taché de feu et de boue*). Physical reality includes the rotted rags (*les haillons pourris*), the sodden bread (*le pain trempé de pluie*), and drunkenness (*l'ivresse*), while emotional reality includes all of those thousands of people we have known and loved to whom we have given a bit of ourselves only to discover it was useless for we are inevitably alone in the end (*les mille amours qui m'ont crucifié*). The city becomes a vampire (*cette goule*) who has sucked the blood of millions of dead souls and bodies (*reine de million d'âmes et de corps morts*), all of whom must face the final judgment (qui seront jugés). Physical reality is also represented by the skin eaten away by mud and plague (*la peau rongée*) and the hair and armpits full of lice (*des vers plein les cheveux et les aisselles*), while emotional reality is represented by the worms in the heart (*encore de plus gros vers dans le coeur*). He could have died, stretched out among those nameless, ageless, unfeeling living dead (*étendu parmi les inconnus sans âge, sans sentiment....J'aurais pu y mourir*). He has seen and known misery and detests it (*J'exècre la misère*).

That is one reason why he fears winter (*je redoute l'hiver*) since it is the season when so much effort must be made to keep comfortable (*c'est la saison du comfort*, and Rimbaud uses the English spelling). As a fabulous opera he saw visions in the sky of endless beaches covered with joyous white nations (*au ciel des plages sans fin couvertes de blanches nations en joie*) and sailing above him a great golden vessel, another drunken boat, with its multicolored sails whipping in the morning breezes (*Un grand vaisseau d'or, au-dessus de moi, agite ses pavillons multicolores sous les brises du matin*). He created all the feasts (*toutes les fêtes*), all the triumphs (*tous les triomphes*), all the dramas (*tous les drames*) imaginable. He had tried to invent new flowers, new stars, new flesh, new languages (*de nouvelles fleurs, de nouveaux astres, de nouvelles chairs, de nouvelles langues*). He thought he had acquired supernatural powers (*J'ai cru acquérir des pouvoirs surnaturels*), but it was all a dream. He must bury his imagination and his memories (*mon imagination et mes souvenirs*) and with them all hope for glory as an artist and story teller (*Une belle gloire d'artiste et de conteur emportée*). He had thought himself a wise man and angel (*mage ou ange*) dispensed from all morality (*dispensé de toute morale*) only to find himself back on earth (*rendu au sol*) with a duty for which he must search (*avec un devoir à chercher*) and a reality with which he must come to grips (*la réalité rugueuse à étreindre*). He is, in short, the peasant (*Paysan*) he was destined to be by his "Bad Blood." And the much vaunted charity, could it be the sister of death for him (*la charité serait-elle soeur*

de la mort, pour moi), as he had indicated in "Les Soeurs
de charité?" He has lived on lies (*m'être nourri de mensonge*)
and must seek pardon (*je demanderai pardon*), but is not there
a single helping hand (*pas une main amie*) that will come to
his rescue? Where else can one seek assistance (*où puiser le
secours*)?

This new life without illusions will be difficult (*l'heure
nouvelle est au moins très sévère*). He has won a victory (*je
puis dire que la victoire m'est acquise*) because he has survived
his night in hell and his deliriums with their gnashing of teeth
(*les grincements des dents*), their hissing fire (*les sifflements de
feu*), their stinking sighs (*les soupirs empestés*), and their foul
memories (*les souvenirs immondes*) as well as those who live
with death (*les amis de la mort*) and the backward of all kinds
(*les arriérés de toutes sortes*). To these damned he says, what
if I avenge myself (*Damnés, si je me vengeais*). To do so, one
must be absolutely modern (*Il faut être absolument moderne*),
forget religion (*Point de cantiques*), and hold to the progress
that has been made (*tenir le pas gagné*). He has survived his
night in hell (*Dure nuit*), and, although his face is covered with
blood (*le sang séché fume sur ma face*), there is nothing behind
him except this horrible shrubby tree (*cet horrible arbrisseau*),
which is probably the tree of good and evil of Eden mentioned
by Rimbaud in the *Illuminations*. I am tempted to see in it the
flowering fig tree of Luke that indicates the coming of summer,
since that is the season and thus the tree the narrator has behind him. In any event, the struggle with one's own soul is
as brutal as the physical struggle with others (*Le combat
spirituel est aussi brutal que la bataille d'hommes*), since the
vision of true justice is reserved for God alone (*la vision de la
justice est le plaisir de Dieu seul*). But this is only the eve
(*c'est la veille*) when we need all vigor and true tenderness
possible (*les influx de vigueur et de tendresse réelle*) in order to
be armed at dawn with an ardent and burning patience (*à
l'aurore, armés d'une ardente patience*) for our entrance into
the splendid cities (*nous entrerons aux splendides villes*) of the
future, so different from the enormous city splattered with fire
and mud of today's reality. He then rebukes himself for having
called out for help (*Que parlais-je de main amie*). He has a

great advantage (*Un bel avantage*) because he can laugh at
the old false loves (*rire des vieilles amours mensongères*) of his
former life, the hallucinations and illusions that have proved
empty. He can cover with shame (*frapper de honte*) the lying
couples (*ces couples menteurs*) for he knows that the men live
off the slavery of women (*l'enfer des femmes là-bas*), the slavery
he mentioned in the Seer Letter, repeated in "Les Soeurs de
charité," and emphasized in "L'Impossible." As in "Les Soeurs
de charité," women may be reduced to dependency upon men,
but it is really the men who are helpless without women. Thus
all couples are lying couples. They are also false in another
sense. The famous conclusion of *Une Saison* according to which
it will be possible for him to possess the truth in one soul and
one body (*il me [lui] sera loisible de* posséder la vérité dans une
âme et un corps) indicates that truth is a personal matter that
can only be found within ourselves. A couple thus represents two
truths, both of which cannot be true for both. Another couple is
the body and soul. The moral truth of the soul is in conflict with
the physical truth of the body and until we can reconcile them
into one, we shall suffer our season in hell. The flights of the
imagination and the rigors of reality create a constant struggle
that is the human condition. In *Une Saison en enfer* Rimbaud
gave expression to that conflict in a language that never ceases
to ring in the ears of those who are moved by poetry. If he
repeats himself occasionally in this brief work and if some of the
images seem strained and hyperbolic, *Une Saison en enfer* does,
nevertheless, create the effect of a spontaneous verbal explosion
that sears the soul and scorches the body, roasting them both in
a private hell that we all share in some peculiar and unique way.

CHAPTER 7

Songs of a Private Heaven

THE fate of the manuscript of the *Illuminations* was quite different from that of *Une Saison en enfer*.[1] We know we have the latter in exactly the form and sequence desired by Rimbaud, but we do not even know for sure that the title *Illuminations* was his. We have only Verlaine's word for it who also claimed that Rimbaud intended it in the English sense of "Painted Plates." The problem is compounded by the fact that "Illuminations" does not mean "Painted Plates" in English. After almost a hundred years of tradition and until a definitive manuscript is discovered, we must be content with *Illuminations*. We cannot be completely sure all of the *Illuminations* are by Rimbaud, since they were obviously written at different times in different inks on various kinds of unnumbered sheets of paper and not always in Rimbaud's hand. Nor can we be sure when they were written. Verlaine said between 1873 and 1875, that is, during and after the composition of *Une Saison en enfer*. Other critics claim that some of them must date from 1870 or 1871, but almost none of the dates can be satisfactorily substantiated. The sequence of the *Illuminations* is not by Rimbaud either. The literary critic Félix Fénéon was the first to organize them for publication, by the review *La Vogue* in 1886. Then the editors of *La Vogue* rearranged them for publication in book form that same year. Verlaine had a go at it in 1895, Rimbaud's brother-in-law Paterne Berrichon in 1912, the Rimbaud specialist Bouillane de Lacoste in 1949, Paul Hartmann in 1957, and Albert Py in 1967.

All of which means that nothing can be learned about a specific poem from its position in the sequence of the forty-one poems (or fifty-three if you count subdivisions). Each has to be studied within the context of its own vocabulary and syntax and then in conjunction with the images and ideas it shares with other poems. Like the drawings in an illuminated manuscript these poems each tell a story but when they are put together they do not necessarily tell a new story. The various objects within these antilandscapes exist and coexist, take on a life of their own, constitute a new and different world before the reader's eyes, find a new reality through juxtaposition that requires no explanation or proof. They simply are. We can only marvel at such landscapes when we find ourselves somehow mysteriously in their midst and in the act of experiencing their reality. Our task is to isolate the elements of each landscape and to look at them both separately and together in order to appreciate the full impact of these fleeting visions. Again because of limitations of space, I have had to omit eleven poems in this study.

The title of the first illumination, "Après le déluge" (After the Deluge),[2] immediately suggests two possibilities. The biblical allusion implies judgment, condemnation, and punishment by the flood in order to effect a spiritual renewal. But with the spiritual renewal comes the physical rebirth of the world and all it contains. The physical cleansing is the spiritual rite we have already witnessed in "Le Coeur volé," "Le Bateau ivre," and "Délires II." The first liquid after the deluge is the water of the raindrops in the rainbow (*l'arc-en-ciel*), the natural phenomenon linking the fallen but risen waters of the flood with the waters of the sky, tying earth to heaven, bringing together the physical and the spiritual. The second liquid is the water of the sea, seen this time as rising up in tiers according to the peculiar perspective of primitive paintings (*la mer étagée là-haut comme sur les gravures*). The third liquid is the blood of life, first the human blood shed by Bluebeard (*Le sang coula, chez Barbe-Bleue*); second, the animal blood of the slaughterhouses (*aux abattoirs*). The wives of Bluebeard were sacrificed to his madness. Animals are sacrificed to human hunger. The fourth liquid is milk, another human food and more particularly the food of the young in this young new world (*Le sang et le lait coulèrent*). The linking of blood and milk could indicate that after the blood that flowed as the result of slaughter, blood is now flowing in the veins of the world, while milk is flowing into its system and providing nourishment without slaughter. The fifth liquid is the water of the inland streams, as opposed to the open sea, that is being damned up by the beavers (*Les castors bâtirent*). The sixth is the steaming spiked coffee of adults (*Les "mazagrans" fumèrent*). The use of the idiomatic "mazagrans" reminds us of the language of "Les Douaniers," which also included Arabic expressions. In addition, Mazagran was the area in Algeria heroically and successfully defended by a few French against Abd-el-Kader in 1840. The Arabian emir, who was finally taken prisoner in 1847 and kept in French prisons until 1852, was one of the heroes of Rimbaud's schoolboy poems, "Jugurtha." The seventh is the rain still streaming down the windows of the large house (*la grande maison de vitres encore ruisselante*) after the sudden dazzling downpour (*l'eclatante giboulée*) with its lightning and thunder (*éclairs et tonnerre*). The eighth is by implication the wine of the mass and first communions being celebrated (*La messe et les premières communions se célébrèrent*). We already know Rimbaud's opinion of "Les Premières Communions." The water turns into the ice of dark winter and the polar regions (*le chaos de glaces et de nuit de pôle*). The world is for a moment a desert of thyme (*les déserts de thym*), recalling the "Déserts de mousse" of "Bonne Pensée," but spring follows quickly (*c'était le printemps*). The ice in a tenth metamorphosis becomes the rising waters of the ponds (*Sourds, étang*) and in an eleventh and final transformation becomes the foam (*Ecume*) that will eventually evaporate and disappear into the clouds to descend again as the water (*Eaux*) of the deluge (*les Déluges*) with which the poem began.

The four kinds of animals in this later ark include the pious hare that is saying its prayer to the rainbow (*Un lièvre . . . dit sa prière à l'arc-en-ciel*). The narrator of "Délires II" was damned by a rainbow. There as a natural phenomenon it condemned him to life that includes death as opposed to the eternal life promised by faith in the cross. This eater of grass, the timid rabbit, this creature of nature is praying to a phenomenon of nature, the only connection he knows between heaven and earth. In contrast, to this act of faith that busy predator, the spider, has already spun his web (*la toile de l'araignée*) by which he catches his prey. The industrious beaver has likewise begun the construction of his dam, but it is not meant to catch anything but the water necessary for life. The last animal is the jackal wailing in the desert (*les chacals piaulant par les déserts*), the scavenger that lives off the efforts of others, the carcasses left behind by the lion. The four animals thus represent all of the creatures of nature as they begin life again after the deluge.

The hare stopped amid the sainfoin and moving bellflowers (*les sainfoins et les clochettes mouvantes*), the sainfoin providing forage for animals, the bellflowers offering simply their beauty. But they are not just there. When they are mentioned again by the generic term, they are described as watching (*les fleurs qui regardaient*), mute witnesses to the world. The one herb named is the useful thyme (*thym*), edible by humans as is the fruit of the orchard (*le verger*). The flowering forest that appears dark violet because of its somber shadows (*la futaie violette, bourgeonnante*) is both beautiful and useful, while woods (*les bois*) is again a generic term. At the end of the poem Rimbaud returns to the flowers of the beginning. Here they are open to the world (*les fleurs ouvertes*), receptive, a consolation of nature.

The flowers that display their colorful beauty so freely in nature are contrasted with the precious stones that hide their beauty (*les pierres précieuses qui se cachaient*) deep in the ground and require great labor to be discovered and polished. Flowers and precious stones return at the end of the poem where the latter are described as fleeing (*les pierres précieuses s'enfouissant*) mankind in his search for them. Thus nature is both prodigal and miserly with her beauty.

Man reveals his presence in nature by the structures he builds, great dirty streets for movement (*la grande rue sale*), stands for selling his goods (*les étals*), boats for navigating the seas (*les barques*), slaughterhouses for preparing his food, traveling circuses for his amusement (*les cirques*), houses to live in with windows (*les fenêtres*) and doors (*la porte*), villages with their squares (*la place du hameau*), weather vanes to tell him the direction of the wind (*des girouettes et des coqs des clochers*), a piano to provide music (*un piano*), cathedrals for worship (*la cathédrale*), caravans for travel and trade (*Les caravanes*), hotels for food and lodging (*le Splendide-Hôtel*), bridges for crossing streams and rivers (*le pont*), black cloth to signal his mourning (*draps noirs*), organs for music and worship (*orgues*). Man's structures reveal clearly his double nature, this need for permanence and stability represented by his houses and churches and villages, his restless desire to be elsewhere by his boats and road and bridges.

A landscape without people is a world without consciousness. Impersonal man (*on tira*) appears constructive, but individual man brings with him the terrible destructiveness of his desires and the inevitable sadness of his human condition. The blood and gore of barbarous Bluebeards are coupled with the superstitions of religion that hinder us from seeing clearly (*le sceau de Dieu blêmit les fenêtres*). Or Rimbaud could mean by this last expression that God controls the seasons and brings winter that covers our windows with frost. The big house shelters children in mourning (*les enfants en deuil*), the same children as those in Rimbaud's first poem, "Les Etrennes des orphelins." These children are looking at the same religious pictures (*les merveilleuses images*) Rimbaud mentioned in "Les Premières Communions." One child (*l'enfant*), who reappears in "Aube," went out into the village square and turned around and around with his arms out (*tourna ses bras*) as children will. The weather vanes understood him (*compris*) because they, too, turn eternally in the same place, telling the direction of the wind and thus foretelling the weather and the future, just as the boy foretells the man. Eccentric Madame *** had a piano placed high in the Alps (*Madame *** établit un piano dans les Alpes*) while mass and first communions were being celebrated on a hundred thousand altars (*cent mille autels*), numerical hyperbole that contrasts strongly with the single piano. But man is a roving animal, departing in his caravans (*Les caravanes partirent*). The moon (*la Lune*), an element of nature on high, hears the destructive jackals howling down below as well as the clumsy, rustic poetry of creative man that growls in the orchard (*les églogues en sabots grognant*).

Whether man remains in one place or travels widely, life is a voyage and a search for the father, for our origins, through the seasons of time. The Telemachus of Fénelon in his *Télémachus* of 1699–1717 suffered even more trials in his search for his father Ulysses than Ulysses himself. One of them was his passionate love affair with Eucharis, a companion of the nymph Calypso who welcomed the shipwrecked Ulysses to her island and then detained him ten years. Thus it is Eucharis who announces spring (*Eucharis me dit que c'était le printemps*), the time of love and renewal which is only one stage of the journey, however. Life is a storm that brings with it mourning (*draps noirs*) and sadness (*tristesses*). Once settled in his life after the excitement of the deluge and the pleasures of travel, man finds only boredom (*un ennui*), for no matter how long he lives, how far he travels, how strong his faith, the sorceress and guardian of the ultimate secrets of life and death with her intimate knowledge of earth (*le pot de terre*) will never be willing to reveal to us what she knows (*la Reine, la Sorcière ... ne voudra jamais nous raconter ce qu'elle sait*) and what we shall never know (*que nous ignorons*). We survived the deluge, "We had the experience but missed the meaning," as T. S. Eliot put it. That is the human condition even after the deluge with its promise of rebirth and renewal.

The beauty of the poem results from its diaphanous images, the unexpected juxtapositions, the terror and sadness, the sound and the silence, the movement and the stillness, the human and the inhuman, the ordinary vocabulary and the exotic terminology. We have participated in this kaleidoscopic cataclysm and our vision of the world can never be quite the same.

I Songs of Childhood

The second illumination, "Enfance" (Childhood),[3] is divided into five sections filled with the fantasies and memories of childhood. Section I is composed of three apparently unrelated paragraphs plus one sentence of conclusion. Each paragraph takes place in a different locality, but they are all near or associated with the life-giving sea: the beach (*des plages nommées*), the edge of a forest (*A la lisière de la forêt*) not so far from the sea, as will be evident, the terraces next to the sea (*les terrasses voisines de la mer*). The first paragraph presents an idol, giving us his physical description, his heritage and character, and finally the nature of his domain. He has black eyes and yellow hair (*yeux noirs et crin jaune*), which makes us think of a

grotesque Oriental idol. He has neither parents nor a court (*sans
parents ni cour*), which makes him sound more like the Christian
God. He is more noble than a Mexican or Flemish fable. This
mixture of lands, one just across the border from Charleville
and the other far across the sea, reveals the freedom of association of the child's imagination. The sea and land of his domain
(*son domaine*) are described as unexpectedly blue and green
(*azur et verdure insolents*). The strange thing about this domain
is that while its beaches are called by names that are ferociously
Greek, Slavic, and Celtic (*de noms férocement grecs, slaves,
celtiques*), its waves are without boats (*des vagues sans vais-
seaux*). This idol who came from nowhere except the child's
imagination is going nowhere except in the child's imagination.

The elements of the second paragraph that takes place on the
edge of the forest are flowers, a girl, and the deluge. Like the
flowers of "Après le déluge," these are dream flowers (*les fleurs
de rêve*), but, instead of being simply open and looking on,
these flowers ring like bells (*tintent*)—recalling, even so, the
bellflowers of the previous illumination—burst (*éclatent*), and
give light (*éclairent*), a mixture of attributes that takes us back
to the synesthesia of "Voyelles." A girl with orange lips (*la fille
à lèvre d'orange*) is seated with her knees crossed (*les genoux
croisés*) while the limpid flood (*le clair déluge*) wells up from
the meadows below (*sourd des prés*). Up above, rainbows (*les
arcs-en-ciel*), the flora (*la flore*), and the sea (*la mer*), shade
(*ombrent*), pass over (*traversent*), and clothe (*habillent*) her
nudity (*nudité*). The extraordinary flowers of the beginning
of the paragraph return in the colors of the rainbow but accompanied this time by all the plants and trees of the forest that
protect and provide for this dryadlike girl, this wood nymph
who is one with nature. The evanescent rainbow of "Après le
déluge" reminds us of our mortality while still carrying within
itself those drops of water that will descend again in life-giving
rain to form a new flood that will well up from the earth in the
form of flowers.

The third paragraph is an enumeration of all the different
types of women to be found on the terraces near the sea: the
strolling ladies (*Dames qui tournoient*), the proud black female
children and giants (*enfantes et géantes, superbes noires*) who

stand out in the verdigris moss (*dans la mousse vert-de-gris*) like jet jewels on the thick soil of the thickets and thawed little gardens (*bijoux debout sur le sol gras des bosquets et des jardinets dégelés*), young mothers and big sisters with eyes full of pious pilgrimages (*jeunes mères et grandes soeurs aux regards pleins de pèlerinages*), the exotic sultanas and princesses with their tyrannical gaits and costumes (*sultanes, princesses de démarche et de costume tyranniques*), and finally, the little strangers and gently unhappy ones (*petites étrangères et personnes doucement malheureuses*).

Thus Rimbaud has run the gamut of the objects of love, the idol of sacred love who is ineffective in his insularity, nature herself with all her beauties who represents an abstract and all-embracing love of the world that only reminds us of our transitoriness, and profane love in the form of women both familiar and strange, high and low, near and far. One eventually tires of all three loves and reverts to the boredom of surfeit of the physical love of the "dear body" and the sentimental love of the "dear heart" (*Quel ennui, l'heure du "cher corps" et "cher coeur"*), the ultimate ennui of a Baudelaire but without his morbid foreboding.

"Enfance II" is composed of four brief paragraphs and might be called the poem of absence. The first paragraph mentions all the people who are absent but strangely so in specific places, the dead girl buried behind the rosebushes (*la petite morte, derrière les rosiers*), the dead young mother seen in a dream descending a flight of stairs (*la jeune maman trépassée descend le perron*), a cousin's coach that screeches on the sand (*La calèche du cousin crie sur la sable*), the little brother who is far away in India watching the setting sun in a field of carnations (*La petit frère [il est aux Indes!] là, devant le couchant, sur le pré d'oeillets*), the old people buried upright in the ramparts covered with gillyflowers (*Les vieux qu'on a enterrés tout droits dans le rempart aux giroflées*). The old and the young, the sister and mother and cousin and brother, the grandparents, have all disappeared.

The second paragraph enumerates all the places that have been abandoned: the general's house with its swarm of golden leaves that his family has left for the South (*L'essaim des feuilles* d'or entoure la maison du général. Ils sont dans le midi), the empty inn (l'auberge vide), the chateau for sale (Le château à vendre), the locked and abandoned church (Le curé aura emporté la clef de l'église), the uninhabited garden lodges (les loges des gardes sont inhabitées), the palisades so high one can see only their rustling tops but there is nothing to be seen there anyway (Les palissades sont si hautes qu'on ne voit que les cimes bruissantes. D'ailleurs il n'y a rien à voir là-dedans). Defense represented by the general, trade represented by the travelers, government represented by the local lord, religion represented by the curate, growth represented by the gardeners, have all been abandoned leaving empty silence behind them.

The villages themselves show no signs of life. There are no roosters (sans coqs), symbolizing food and the continuation of life, and no anvils (sans enclumes), symbolizing the constructive life. The sluicegates are standing idly open (L'écluse est levée), and water is flowing uselessly while the wayside crosses and mills, the islands and millstones have become a desert in this peopleless world (O les Calvaires et les moulins du désert, les îles et les meules).

To fill this empty silence the child's imagination created magic flowers that buzzed (Des fleurs magiques bourdonnaient), slopes that cradled him (Les talus le berçaient), fabulously elegant beasts that moved about (Des bêtes d'une élégance fabuleuse circulaient), thick storm clouds that piled up on the high sea (Les nuées s'amassaient sur la haute mer). The vigorous movement of the verbs bourdonnaient, berçaient, circulaient, and s'amassaient contrasts strongly with the silence and stillness of the preceding paragraphs. But note that the high sea of the child's imagination is composed of an eternity of hot tears (faite d'une éternité de chaudes larmes), the sad regret for all the people and places disappeared and abandoned in one short life for which even an active imagination has difficulty in creating replacements. If "Enfance I" revealed the boredom experienced as the result of relations with too many people, "Enfance II" draws just the opposite picture, the sadness of the child left to people the world with the creatures of his imagination. He can only fill it with the things of nature that console us but that pass away as inevitably as childhood and our fellow mortals.

"Enfance III" is composed of a series of seven simple sentences all introduced by *il y a* ("there is"). The statements are deceptively simple, however. The first is that there is a bird in the woods whose song stops you in your tracks and makes you blush (*Au bois, il y a un oiseau, son chant vous arrête et vous fait rougir*), a birdsong so beautiful it makes you pause to catch your breath. Contrasted with the sound of the song is the silence of the clock that no longer strikes the hours (*Il y a une horloge qui ne sonne plus*). Time as well as movement has stopped. Opposed to the bird and clock on high there is down below a bog with a nest of white beasts (*Il y a une fondrière avec un nid de bêtes blanches*), nature with its threatening creatures. Between high and low there is a cathedral that sinks and a lake that rises. (*Il y a une cathédrale qui descend et un lac qui monte*). The structures of man are eventually drowned by the forces of nature. We have already seen "the sea rising up in tiers" in "Après le déluge." Rimbaud has just spoken of "the high sea" in "Enfance II" and will speak of it again in "Enfance IV." Water as a necessity of life constantly threatens to sweep life away while offering man his greatest adventures. There is also a small beribboned baby carriage that has been abandoned in a copse and is free to rush down the path like "La Bateau ivre" going down its river (*Il y a une petite voiture abandonée dans le taillis, ou qui descend le sentier en courant, enrubannée*). *Enrubannée* echoes *abandonée* phonetically while offering the contrast of the time and care of tying up cutely and uselessly with the indifference of abandonment. The landscaps is suddenly peopled by a troupe of little actors in costumes glimpsed on the road through the edge of the forest (*Il y a une troupe de petits comédiens en costumes, aperçus sur la route à travers la lisière du bois*), but these are people who are not what they seem and disappear quickly. There is finally, just when you are suffering most from hunger and thirst, someone who is hunting you down (*Il y a enfin, quand l'on a faim et soif, quelqu'un qui vous chasse*). Just when you need help most, you are not only denied and disdained but stalked like an animal. Song and time cannot save us anymore than nature with her threatening waters and her hidden beasts. Religion in the form of the cathedral eludes us. The baby carriage of childhood so carefully decorated by an adoring mother must eventually be abandoned and then life begins its blind rush downhill. The diversion of the traveling players lasts only a minute while the reality of hunger and thirst stalks us like a hunter. The boredom of "Enfance I" and the sadness of "Enfance II" have become the terror of "Enfance III."

"Enfance IV" offers us all the roles the child plays in his imagination. Three of the paragraphs begin with "I am" (*Je suis*), the fourth with "I should be" (*Je serais*), while the fifth draws the conclusion. The narrator says he is the saint in prayer on the terrace (*Je suis le saint, en prière sur la terrasse*) and compares himself to the peaceful beasts that graze right down to the sea of Palestine (*comme les bêtes pacifiques paissent jusqu'à la mer de Palestine*). We are back on the terrace by the sea of "Enfance I," the sea of the Holy Land of religion. If a child can be a saint in his imagination, he can also be a scholar in his somber armchair (*Je suis le savant au fauteuil sombre*), snug in his library where the branches and rain beat against the windows (*Les branches et la pluie se jettent à la croisée de la bibliothèque*). If one cannot take refuge in religion or knowledge, then there is also travel (*Je suis le piéton de la grand'route*) through the stunted forests (*par les bois nains*) on land. The sound of the open sluicegate mentioned in "Enfance II" will cover the sound of his footsteps (*la rumeur des écluses couvre mes pas*), while he watches for a long time, like the little brother in India, the melancholy clouds turned by the setting sun to a golden wash hanging on the line (*Je vois longtemps la mélancolique lessive d'or du couchant*). Even better, he would be the child abandoned on the jetty that has sailed away for the high sea (*Je serais bien l'enfant abandonné sur la jetée partie à la haute mer*), the sea of adventure, or he could be the little groom doing nothing more exciting than following a country lane (*le petit valet suivant l'allée*). Whether it is the forehead of the little valet that touches the sky (*dont le front touche le ciel*) or his path that will touch the sky makes no difference. He is either looking up with high hopes or following a path that can only lead him onward and upward. These are the "several other lives" that are due everyone in "Délires II." Whether we choose to be a saint or a savant, a wanderer by land or by sea, old or young, the paths are rough (*Les sentiers sont âpres*) and the hillocks are overgrown with broom (*les monticules se couvrent de genêts*), making the going difficult. The air becomes still (*L'air est immobile*) and the birds and springs seem so far away (*Que les oiseaux et les sources sont loin*) one becomes convinced that it can only be the end of the world lying ahead of us (*Ce ne peut être que la fin du monde, en avançant*). Every child believes that the end of the world will come, presaged by a magic moment. But that is the I who is another dreaming. The real me, an object in the world like other objects, lives out its allotted time in boredom, sadness, terror, and trial.

"Enfance V," like its predecessor, contains five short paragraphs but its claustrophobic atmosphere differs radically from that of the other parts of "Enfance." The settings of the first three paragraphs are a tomb, a table, and an underground living room. Paragraph four describes in greater detail the surroundings of the living room and offers a paradox that is reconciled in the conclusion.

The atmosphere is established in the first paragraph by the request that a tomb be rented (*Qu'on me loue enfin ce tombeau*). "This" tomb is whitewashed, so that the lines in the cement stand out in relief (*blanchi à la chaux avec les lignes du ciment en relief*). In addition, the tomb is far below the surface of the earth (*très loin sous terre*).

Without transition the narrator is seated at a lamp-lit table (*Je m'accoude à la table, la lampe éclaire très vivement*) where he has come to the conclusion that further reading would be pointless (*ces journaux que je suis idiot de relire, ces livres sans intérêt*). The wisdom of the past and present are of no use to him in his unusual situation.

Only then do we learn that the table is in the living room of his house and that the houses of others are firmly rooted at an enormous distance above his subterranean living room (*A une distance énorme au-dessus de mon salon souterrain, les maisons s'implantent*), there where the mists gather (*les brumes s'assemblent*) and the mud is red or black (*La boue est rouge ou noire*). We recognize immediately that we are again in the monstrous city of "Adieu," the city of endless night. That the

city Rimbaud had in mind was or was not London is of no interest. If Rimbaud had meant to specify London, he would have
done so. Obviously he means all great cities that dehumanize
man and rob him of the sun while smothering him in a psychological as well as physical night. The important fact is that his
living room and "this tomb" are one and the same.

Beneath the houses but still above his living room are located
the drains and sewers of the city (*Moins haut, sont des égouts*),
leaving one with the uncomfortable fear of imminent seepage.
His living room is surrounded by the heavy earth of this globe
(*Aux côtés, rien que l'épaisseur du globe*) and perhaps by gulfs
of azure and wells of fire (*Peut-être des gouffres d'azur, des pits
de feu*). The pits or whirlpools of azure suggest the sea or the
sky while the wells of fire suggest the bowels of the earth. The
implied paradox is strengthened by the declaration that it is
perhaps on these levels that moons and comets, seas and fables
meet (*C'est peut-être sur ces plans que se rencontrent lunes et
comètes, mers et fables*). Moons and comets could collide in the
sky of the gulfs of azure within the sight of man. The storied
seas that tempt man with adventure as well as the fables of man
that rise like the oracles of Delphi within his psyche are both
tied to the earth. The water that fills the seas is constantly rising
from the seas to the heavens and returning as rain to replenish
the seas. The fables of man that rise from the pits of fire are
almost always attempts by man to transcend his earthbound
condition, to secure knowledge of the unknowable future and
an unattainable heaven.

The ambiguity of high and low, heaven and earth, is resolved
in the final paragraph, To divert his mind during his hours of
bitterness, the narrator imagines balls of sapphire and metal
(*Aux heures d'amertume je m'imagine des boules de saphir, de
métal*), blue crystal balls like the dome of heaven in which
one hopes to read the future, heavy leaden balls like the globe
of the earth from which one hopes to learn of the past. Caught
between his aspirations for the one and the reality of the other,
imprisoned in his earthly home that will prove to be a stifling
tomb, the narrator is master only of silence (*Je suis maître du
silence*). If he were to cry out, who would hear him? Thus he
wonders why an appearance of a ventilator would grow pale

at the corner of the vault (*Pourquoi une apparence de soupirail blêmirait-elle au coin de la voûte*). This cellar window, this vent would offer the promise of light and air, of freedom and life, but it grows pale as his hopes pale within the whitewashed tomb that is life on earth, the ultimate fate of all youth, a grim and pessimistic conclusion to the lyric fantasies of childhood.

That Rimbaud may have found some of the vocabulary and images of "Parade" (Parade)[4] in the accounts of Captain Cook or the poems of an obscure German Romantic or the description of a religious procession in the square of the cathedral of Milan is interesting but not much help in interpreting the poem. The poem is a vivid description of a frightening parade of sinister characters. Who are they? Rimbaud tells us in the first three sentences and reiterates the idea in the last two sentences of the poem. The characters are first described in general terms as robust rogues (*Des drôles très solides*), several of whom have exploited your worlds (*Plusieurs ont exploité vos mondes*). The key words are "your" and "worlds." Rimbaud is addressing his readers and saying that rogues like these do not exist simply in this poem; they are not figments of his imagination but have invaded and taken advantage of the readers' worlds. Which worlds? Readers exist in two worlds, that of reality and that of fantasy, the imagination, and dreams. These rogues are solid, so that one is tempted first to think of reality, but when Rimbaud says they have no needs (*Sans besoins*) and are in no hurry to put to work their brilliant faculties (*peu pressés de mettre en oeuvre leurs brillantes facultés*) or their knowledge of your consciousness (*et leur expérience de vos consciences*), the apparent nature of the rogues begins to change. If they are solid but have no needs, they appear so solid perhaps as to seem real, but if they have no needs and take their good time to invade our consciences as well as that of the poet, then perhaps they are not real but the poetic fiction of dreams, particularly since they also have knowledge of our consciences. Most translators into English adopt the moralistic approach to *consciences*, which also means, of course, physical and mental consciousness. Whether these demons are the creatures of our bad conscience or the inhabitants of mental consciousness that remains awake while we are physically asleep makes little difference. In both cases they haunt our worlds, our conscience as well as our consciousness, our real and our dream worlds. The rogues of dreams become our solid reality.

Rimbaud then describes their physical condition, their eyes, facial features, voice, walk, and costumes. He says they are mature (*Quels hommes mûrs*), which repeats the idea of *solides*, and that their eyes are dazed like a summer night, red and black, in fact tricolor, blue but with the white sclera streaked with red, such a pale blue they are like steel flecked with golden stars (*Des yeux hébétés à la façon de la nuit d'été, rouges et noires, tricolores, d'acier piqué d'étoiles d'or*). Their facial features are deformed, leaden, sallow, burned (*des faciès déformés, plombés, blêmis, incendiés*), their hoarse voices lively (*des enrouements folâtres*), and their walk cruel in their tawdry clothes (*La démarche cruelle des oripeaux*).

Some of them are young (*Il y a quelques jeunes*), and Rimbaud wonders what they would think of the naive Cherubino (*comment regarderaient-ils Chérubin*) of Beaumarchais' play *Le Mariage de Figaro*. In his innocence Cherubino was just awakening to the sweet language of love while these demons have frightening voices (*voix effrayantes*) and dangerous resources (*quelques ressources dangereuses*) unknown to a simple Cherubino. They are sent into towns as male prostitutes (*On les envoie prendre du dos en ville*), all decked out in disgusting luxury (*affublés d'un luxe dégoûtant*). Such characters would have little in common with the gentle Cherubino.

In the second paragraph Rimbaud describes where and what his revolting players perform. Their theater is the most violent Paradise of mad sham (*O le plus violent Paradis de la grimace enragée*). They are not to be compared with Fakirs, the Hindu wonder-workers, or other theatrical buffooneries (*Pas de comparaison avec vos Fakirs et les autres bouffonneries scéniques*). Note that Rimbaud again uses *vos* and for the last time. The creatures of the reader's imagination pale in comparison with those of the poet. In their costumes that look as if they had been gotten up in a bad dream (*Dans des costumes improvisés avec le goût du mauvais rêve*), they perform plaintive ballads (*complaintes*), tragedies about bandits and spiritual half-gods such as never existed in history or religion (*des tragédies de ma-*

landrins et de demi-dieux spirituels comme l'histoire ou les religions ne l'ont jamais été). As Chinese (*Chinois*), Hottentots (*Hottentots*), bohemians (*bohémiens*), simpletons (*niais*), hyenas (*hyènes*), Molochs (*Molochs*), old madnesses (*vieilles démences*), and sinister demons (*démons sinistres*), they mix popular, maternal tricks with beastly poses and caresses (*ils mêlent les tours populaires, maternels avec les poses et les tendresses bestiales*). They interpret new plays (*pièces nouvelles*) and "sentimental" songs (*chansons "bonnes filles"*). Master jugglers (*Maîtres jongleurs*) transform the place and the people (*le lieu et les personnes*) by means of their magnetic and thus hypnotic plays (*la comédie magnétique*). In the excitement eyes flame (*Les yeux flambent*), blood sings (*le sang chante*), bones swell (*les os s'élargissent*), while tears and red streaks stream down (*les larmes et des filets rouges ruissellent*). Like a bad dream, their raillery or their terror may seem to last a minute or entire months (*Leur raillerie ou leur terreur dure une minute, ou des mois entiers*). Since this is the poet's dream, he alone has the key to this savage parade (*J'ai seul la clef de cette parade sauvage*). But the reader cannot forget that such demons are ready and able to take over his dreams at any moment and then only he will have the key to his savage parade.

The fifth illumination, "Antique" (Antique), is brief but baffling.[5] This gracious son of Pan (*Gracieux fils de Pan*)—who was the Greek god of forests, pastures, flocks, and shepherds and represented as having the legs and sometimes the ears and horns of a goat—is described by Rimbaud as having a forehead crowned with flowers and berries (*ton front couronné de fleurettes et de baies*), while his eyes roll like precious balls (*tes yeux, des boules précieuses, remuent*). His cheeks, like the lips of the faun of "Tête de faune," are spotted with brown dregs of wine (*Tachées de lies brunes*) and hollow (*tes joues se creusent*). His big teeth gleam (*Tes crocs luisent*). His chest resembles a zither (*Ta poitrine ressemble à une cithare*), while ringing music circulates in his blond arms (*des tintements circulent dans tes bras blonds*). His heart beats in his stomach where his double sex sleeps (*Ton coeur bat dans ce ventre où dort le double sexe*). The poet asks this hermaphroditic satyr to walk at night (*Promène-toi, la nuit*), just as statues seem to move in the eery light of night. He asks him to move gently this thigh, this second thigh, and this left leg (*en mouvant doucement cette cuisse, cette seconde cuisse et cette jambe de gauche*). The poem tells no story but the description mingles the literary, musical, and plastic arts in such a way that the reader sees before him this ambiguous and double sexed creature moving with the musical grace of an ancient classical vision. Perhaps the most effective interpretation of this poem is a good performance of Benjamin Britten's *Les Illuminations*, opus 18, for tenor and string orchestra.

II   A Song of Beauty

Another brief vision carries the English title "Being Beauteous"[6] and is composed of one long and one short paragraph. The long paragraph describes a tall Beautiful Being outlined against the snow (*Devant une neige un Etre de Beauté de haute taille*). From there on the description becomes more and more ambiguous. This adored body has been conjured up by the sounds of both death and music, the whistlings of the former and the muffled circles of the latter (*Des sifflements de mort et des cercles de musique sourde font monter . . . ce corps adoré*). Threatened by death and sustained only by the sounds of music, fragile Beauty seems to grow larger and tremble like a ghost (*s'élargir et trembler comme un spectre*). The scarlet and black wounds in this proud flesh (*des blessures écarlates et noires éclatent dans les chairs superbes*) have been identified as its mouth and its eyes, its nipples and its sex, but Rimbaud has just spoken of death. A Beautiful Being, human or sculpted, is threatened by the ravages of time and ultimate death while creating the passing effect of muffled music. Thus the colors natural to life deepen, dance, and disengage themselves around this Vision (*Les couleurs propres de la vie se foncent, dansent, et se dégagent autour de la Vision*) that is still taking shape in the sculptor's outdoor studio (*sur le chantier*). As the thrilling shivers caused by its beauty rise and rumble (*les frissons s'élèvent et grondent*), the frantic flavor of these effects (*la saveur forcenée de ces effets*) becomes loaded again with the combination of death and music, the whistlings, and, this time, a raucous music (*se chargent avec les sifflements mortels et les rauques musiques*). Notice should be taken of the contrast between *écarlates-éclatent*, which is raucous, and *frissons-forcenée*, which suggests the whistling sounds. These are the deadly effects that the world, far behind us, hurls at nature, the mother of beauty (*le monde, loin derrière nous, lance sur notre mère de beauté*), so that she recoils (*elle recule*) but nevertheless rises up (*elle se dresse*) as the Being of Beauty of the opening line. When she does so, she provides our bones with the new and amorous body that is beauty (*nos os sont revêtus d'un nouveau corps amoureux*), this beauty of which death is an integral part.

In the brief paragraph of conclusion the Being Beauteous is described as having an ashen face, an escutcheon of hair which some critics see as the sex, and arms of crystal (*la face cendrée, l'écusson de crin, les bras de cristal*), a being so beautiful that the poet can only, again according to some critics, masturbate (*Le canon sur lequel je dois m'abattre*) while contemplating it through the tangle of trees and light air (*à travers la mêlée des arbres et de l'air léger*). I see the poem as another of Rimbaud's attempts to define artistic beauty. Beauty mingles death and music, the ghostly and the all too human, the natural and the supernatural, the eternal and the ephemeral, color and sound. We recognize beauty by the shivers, the involuntary reaction it creates within us, caused in part by our knowledge that beauty inevitably includes death in the sense that beauty is a thing that does not have human life but lives nevertheless. Every artist, every poet must feel, when he aims at anything as fragile as beauty, that his attempt is as subtle as a cannon shot and all too apt to destroy beauty rather than create it. Nature is the mother of beauty and through its tangible and intangible elements, the trees and the air, the artist may succeed. And he may not.

CHAPTER 8

Songs of a Private Heaven
(continued)

THE tenth illumination, "A une raison" (To a Reason),[1] contains five brief, enigmatic declarations. A close look reveals that the first has to do with a tap of the finger (*Un coup de ton doigt*), the second with a step of the foot (*Un pas de toi*), the third with a turn of the head (*Ta tête se détourne*). The fourth reveals the reasons for these actions, while the fifth constitutes the conclusion. We need look no further than the eighteenth century to find Reason as a religon and the cause for revolution. A host of Utopian and Illuminist writers of the nineteenth century expatiated at length on the idea. Rimbaud is saying that just one tap of the finger of Reason is sufficient to create the new harmony (*commence la nouvelle harmonie*) of races and creeds, man and woman. He is saying that just one step forward by Reason is necessary to enlist the new men and set them in motion (*la levée des nouveaux hommes et leur en-marche*) in the cause of new harmony. He is saying that just a turn of the head of Reason will reveal the new love on all sides (*le nouvel amour! Ta tête se retourne,—le nouvel amour*). The youth, the future of the world (*les enfants*), beg Reason to change their lot (*Change nos lots*)—just as Rimbaud declared that life must be changed—and to eliminate plagues (*crible les fléaux*) beginning with time (*à commencer par le temps*), the one thing Reason cannot change but can help us to utilize more efficiently. Youth asks Reason with its new harmony and new love to raise up the substance of its fortunes and prayers (*Elève n'importe où la substance de nos fortunes et de nos voeux*), its material and moral welfare, anywhere and everywhere. The conclusion is that Reason has come from always (*Arrivée de tou-*

130

jours), has always been a necessity, and will spread everywhere (*qui t'en iras partout*), as it inevitably must.

"Matinée d'ivresse" (Morning Drunk)[2] is quite probably Rimbaud's poetic transcription of a trip on hashish. His hope was to discover his own concept of the good and the beautiful (*O mon Bien! O mon Beau!*) through drugs. He contrasts the beginning of the trip three times with its end, referring to children twice. Although it began with a big bang (*Fanfare atroce*), he did not stumble (*je ne trébuche point*). It was an enchanted torture rack (*Chevalet féerique*) he mounted with a big hurrah (*Hourra*) for this unprecedented experience (*pour l'oeuvre inouïe*) that would result in a marvelous body (*pour le corps merveilleux*), a psychological and physiological experiment he was trying for the first time (*pour la première fois*). Later he says it began with some distaste (*par quelques dégoûts*) and all possible boorishness (*par toute la rustrerie*), again physical and psychological reactions.

Rimbaud then enumerates all the promised effects, the superhuman promise made to the created body and soul (*cette promesse surhumaine faite à notre corps et à notre âme créés*) that they would experience madness (*démence*), elegance (*L'élégance*), knowledge (*la science*), violence (*la violence*), the overshadowing of the idea of good and evil (*enterrer dans l'ombre l'arbre du bien et du mal*), the end of tyrannical niceties (*deporter les honnêtetés tyranniques*). He experienced the laughter of children (*Rire des enfants*), the discretion of slaves (*discrétion des esclaves*), the austerity of virgins (*l'austérité des vierges*), the horror of faces and objects from here (*horreur des figures et des objets d'ici*). He hopes that all of them may be consecrated by the memory of this vigil (*sacrés soyez-vous par le souvenir de cette veille*).

If the children laughed nervously when he began his experiment, a fact he remembered during the experience (*Cela commença sous les rires des enfants*), they will laugh when it is over (*cela finira par eux*) upon seeing its aftereffects. Rimbaud maintains that the drug will remain in his veins even after the trip, after the music has died down, and he has returned to the old unharmonious life (*Ce poison va rester dans toutes nos veines même quand, la fanfare tournant, nous serons rendus à l'ancienne inharmonie*). One desired effect was to bring about a very pure love (*afin que nous amenions notre très pur amour*), but, since the human mind is incapable of seizing immediately this eternity (*ne pouvant nous saisir sur-le-champ de cette éternité*), the trip ends in nothing more substantial than a stampede of perfumes (*cela finit par une débandade de parfums*), leaving the lout who began it feeling he is an angel of flame and ice (*cela finit par des anges de flamme et de glace*).

In spite of the disappointment the poet finds his little drunken vigil holy (*Petite veille d'ivresse, sainte*) if only because of the mask against reality it afforded him (*quand ce ne serait que pour le masque dont tu nous as gratifié*). He affirms it as a method (*Nous t'affirmons, méthode*), because yesterday it rendered bigger than life each of the stages of his life (*Nous n'oublions pas que tu as glorifié hier chacun de nos âges*). He has faith that by means of this drug (*Nous avons foi au poison*) he can arrive at a vision of the good and the beautiful because he has learned to give up his entire life every day (*Nous savons donner notre vie tout entière tous les jours*), and it is only by offering up one's whole life every day that he will arrive at the ultimate good and beautiful. For this is the time of the assassins (*Voici le temps des Assassins*), the word *assassins* coming from the Arabic *hashshashin*, those addicted to hashish. Such are the effects promised by hashish, such are the results of the experiment that fit in well with Rimbaud's poetic methods as outlined in the Seer Letters. The reader has difficulty distinguishing those illuminations that may have been written under the influence of drugs from those that were not. The conclusion that this is the time of the assassins reinforces Rimbaud's concept that modern times cannot be compared with olden times, an idea expressed as early as "Soleil et chair." Poetically the echo *gratifié-glorifié* heightens the seventeen other uses of fricative *f*'s that fill this fleeting experience.

The poem we call "Phrases" (Sentences)[3] is undoubtedly two poems, the first composed of three short parts, the second of five. A woman speaks in the first part, either a man or woman could be speaking in the second, and a man speaks in the third. Taken together they offer a complete picture of the necessary and inevitable relationships between the sexes, of love, in short.

The woman notes that when the world is reduced to a single dark woods, the frightening Black Forest of childhood fairy-tales in which the children's astonished eyes shine (*Quand le monde sera réduit en un seul bois noir pour nos quatre yeux étonnés*), turned into one beach just for two faithful children (*en une plage pour deux enfants fidèles*), into one musical house for their mutual understanding (*en une maison musicale pour notre claire sympathie*), then she will find him (*je vous trouverai*). Let there be only one man left on earth, old, alone, calm, and handsome, surrounded by an "unprecedented luxury" (*Qu'il n'y ait ici-bas qu'un vieillard seul, calme et beau, entouré d'un "luxe inouï"*), she would be at his knees (*je suis à vos genoux*). Her declarations that follow are among those most frequently quoted to demonstrate Rimbaud's antifeminism. Within the context of the poem I find their meaning quite opposite. She says that since she is the one who realized all of his memories (*Que j'aie réalisé tous vos souvenirs*), since she is the one he loved and with whom he lived, she has helped to create all those recollections that are for him his memory of the past. While sharing together means fulfillment of one kind, it also sometimes means limiting the other in what he can do or say, frustrating his wishes and desires, strangling some of his impulses (*que je sois celle qui sais vous garrotter*) precisely by means of his love for her. In that sense she will stifle him (*je vous étoufferai*). The echo *je vous trouverai-je vous étoufferai* rings in our ears.

This interpretation is substantiated by the battle of the sexes recounted in the second. When lovers are united by their love and thus very strong (*Quand nous sommes très forts*), who recoils (*qui recule*) in the face of difficulties? When they are very happy (*très gais*), who worries about ridicule (*qui tombe de ridicule*)? And when they are being very bad (*Quand nous serons très méchants*), what could anyone do about them (*que ferait-on de nous*), since they are so united in love? The conclusion is a happy one. Get all decked out, dance, and laugh (*Parez-vous, dansez, riez*), because no one will ever be able to live without love (*Je ne pourrai jamais envoyer l'Amour par la fenêtre*). Another echo, *recule-ridicule*, resounds in our ears.

The cry of the man is desperate. He calls his companion (*Ma camarade*) a beggar (*mendiante*), since she must live off the money he earns, a child-monster (*enfant monstre*) in her dependency that becomes demanding. Secure in her home, she is indifferent to the unhappy women and the machinations and even the troubles (*comme ça t'est égal, ces malheureuses et ces manoeuvres, et mes embarras*) he encounters in the world. He asks her to cling to him and his difficulties (*Attache-toi à nous*) with her impossible voice (*avec ta voix impossible*) that is his only hope in his vile despair (*unique flatteur de ce vil désespoir*). The nasal *m's* of *Ma camarade, mendiante, monstre, comme, malheureuses, manoeuvres, mes embarras, impossible,* lend substance to this anguished cry from the supposedly strong male who is in the end so dependent upon woman. I should call it a strange kind of antifeminism, if that's what it is.

The second half of "Phrases," more descriptive than emotive, takes place on a cloudy July morning (*Une matinée couverte, en Juillet*). A taste of ashes floats in the air (*Un goût de cendres vole dans l'air*) while the odor of wood rises from the fireplace (*une odeur de bois suant dans l'âtre*). The flowers are water-soaked (*les fleurs rouies*), the promenades in disorder (*le saccage des promenades*), the drizzle of the canals covers the fields (*la bruine des canaux par les champs*). The weather is so miserable one is tempted to think of the toys and incense of Christmas (*pourquoi pas déjà les joujoux et l'encens*).

Rimbaud suddenly interrupts this gloomy description with a spark of gold. No matter what the weather, he has stretched cords from belltower to belltower, garlands from window to window, chains of gold from star to star and he dances (*J'ai tendu des cordes de clocher à clocher; des guirlandes de fenêtre à fenêtre; des chaînes d'or d'étoile à etoile, et je danse*). The power of poetry transforms the landscape of reality into a seascape where one is free to dance with happiness.

Nevertheless, as the mist continues to rise up from the deep pool (*Le haut étang fume continuellement*), he wonders what sorceress will rise up in the misty sunset (*Quelle sorcière va se dresser sur le couchant blanc*), counterbalanced by the violet foliage of the darkened clouds of evening that will be descending (*Quelles violettes frondaisons vont descendre*). This contrary movement continues in the next sentence with the observation

that the public funds are melting away in celebrations of fraternity (*Pendant que les fonds publics s'écoulent en fêtes de
fraternité*) that suggest Bastille Day in the form of exploding
skyrockets like the sound of a bell the color of rosy fire in the
clouds (*il sonne une cloche de feu rose dans les nuages*). In
addition to the sense of taste evoked by the cinders and the sense
of smell by the wood in the fireplace, Rimbaud has added the
sense of sound with the bell and the sense of sight with colors.
The taste of cinders in the first sentence becomes in the last a
dark powder with the agreeable taste of India ink that rains
down softly on his vigil (*Avivant un agréable goût d'encre de
Chine une poudre noire pleut doucement sur ma veillée*), a
sentence that comes closest to Verlaine's quotation from Rimbaud in epigraph to his poem "Il pleure dans mon coeur," *Il
pleut doucement sur la ville,* a statement that has not yet been
found in Rimbaud's works. In any event, the poet has obviously
been watching the fireworks from his window, for we are now
back in the room of the opening lines. He turns out the light
(*Je baisse le feu du lustre*), throws himself on the bed (*je me
jette sur le lit*), turns to the wall (*tourné du côté de l'ombre*),
and conjures up girls and queens (*mes filles, mes reines*) in his
sexual fantasy.

I A Song of Bridges

With "Les Ponts" (Bridges)[4] Rimbaud gives us the first of his
descriptions of imaginary cities that will constitute an important
part of the *Illuminations* later. The perspective of this evoca-
tion extends from the gray crystal skies (*Des ciels gris de cristal*)
of the beginning to the blue-gray water (*L'eau est grise et bleue*)
of the conclusion. Between the two the bizarre sketch (*Un bizarre
dessin*) with its maze of bridges, shimmering domes, masts and
parapets comes to life, peopled with musicians in red uniforms
and filled with the sounds of their music. Just at the moment we
accept the reality of this curious apparition, a white ray of sunshine, falling from high in the sky, reduces to nothing this
theatrical scene (*Un rayon blanc, tombant du haut du ciel,
anéantit cette comédie*). We have had the illumination. As suddenly as it came, it disappears, leaving us with the knowledge

that we cannot always believe what we see just because we see what we believe.

If quaint architecture was the point of departure in "Les Ponts," with people added to give it life, the subject of the first of three poems on cities, "Ville" (City),[5] is the physical and moral condition of the millions of inhabitants of a modern industrial metropolis. The lack of taste inside and out as well as in the plan of the city itself, the lack of churches and temples (*aucun monument de superstition*), morality and language reduced to their simplest level, the lack of communication, the distressing similarity of everyone's education, work, and old age, have reduced its citizens to specters engulfed in thick clouds of coal smoke, specters become new Erinyes, the avenging spirits of the Greeks who pursued evildoers and inflicted madness. Here death without tears, despairing love, and crime stalk the streets. The narrator, as a passing observer, draws a comparison between this life and that of the shadow of the woods and summer nights as well as with life on the continent (*les peuples du continent*) and speaks of his cottage (*cottage*), so that one is tempted to think of Rimbaud's experiences in London. But again Rimbaud has drawn an accurate picture of the misery of urban life in all cities, a scene to haunt the mind like a nightmare.

The circus of "Enfance III," glimpsed on the road through the edge of the forest, returns in "Ornières" (Ruts).[6] From the title one might expect the circus to be mired down in muddy ruts but these ruts turn out to be a thousand rapid ruts of the humid road (*les mille rapides ornières de la route humide*) through which this procession of fairies (*Défilé de féeries*) has passed at a great gallop (*au grand galop*) on a summer morning (*l'aube d'été*). The elaborately decorated wagons are filled with children decked out for a suburban pastoral (*pleins d'enfants attifés pour une pastorale suburbaine*). The actors of the circus of "Enfance III" were described as little, suggesting children. Circuses are designed for the amusement of children, and yet there is something enormously sad about them. The brilliant movement of the poem is both continued and brought to a halt by the concluding lines. There we learn that even coffins under their canopy of night with ebony plumes (*Même des cercueils sous leur dais de nuit dressant les panaches d'ébène*) are speeding along to the trot of the great blue and black mares (*filant au trot des grandes juments bleues et noires*). This sudden apparition of the symbols of death indicates to me that creations of the imagination like this fairy circus, this false and fragile world, die just as all real and human things die but that, as creatures of the imagination, they also continue their voyage through time and the mind, ready for rebirth at the touch of the magic wand of the poet.

II *A Song of Cities*

Since Rimbaud indicates clearly at both the beginning and end of "Villes" (Cities)[7] that he is describing a dream, I see no reason to find in this fantastic oneiric vision anything other than the product of a vivid imagination. Cities of the future they may well be, but cities of the past they certainly are. They are located in the mountains, the Alleghenys and Lebanons of our dreams (*ces Alleghanys et ces Libans de rêve*), the East and the West, the New World with its exotic Indian names and the Old World with its historical and biblical names. The only city mentioned by name is the Bagdad of fable and fantasy. The movement from *montés* at the beginning of the poem across summits (*cimes*), rooftops of inns (*les toits des auberges*), high mountain fields (*les champs des hauteurs*), avalanches (*les avalanches*), above crests (*Au-dessus du niveau des plus hautes crêtes*), and belfries (*beffrois*), and back to *monts* at the end emphasizes the circularity of this dream.

The noteworthy phonetic element of the opening descriptive passage that sets the swirling sonorous scene is the number of contrasts between the sibilant and hard *k* sounds: *chalets-cristal, cratères-ceint-colosses-cuivre-rugissent, sonnet-sur-canaux-chalets, chasse-carillons-crie-corporations-chanteurs-accourent-éclatants-comme-cimes.* The constant clash between the two sounds reinforces the visual impact of this chaotic scene.

With the corporation of giant singers (*Des corporations de chanteurs géants*), Rimbaud introduces literary allusions, this first in the form of the Mastersingers, guilds established for the cultivation of poetry and music in Germany during the late Middle Ages and early Renaissance. Rimbaud adds bravery to the

sound of music by his reference to Roland and his valiant horn
of Medieval French literature (*les Rolands sonnent leur
bravoure*). Venus, the goddess of love and symbol of the sea;
Diana, the goddess of the hunt and symbol of the forests; the
half-woman, half-horse centauresses of the mountains of Thessaly;
and the Bacchantes, the female attendants of Bacchus, the god
of wine, are all drawn from Greek literature and legend. Mab,
the fairy queen held to govern men's dreams, is drawn from
Shakespeare in English literature. As Rimbaud says, all legends
change and evolve in the cities (*Toutes les légendes évoluent...
dans les bourgs*) of our dreams. Such allusions people this dream
with creatures from the dreams of others, enriching its texture
and enlarging its affective scope.

Almost everyone agrees that the chalets of crystal and wood
that move on rails and invisible pulleys (*Des chalets de cristal
et de bois qui se meuvent sur des rails et des poulies invisibles*)
are cable cars. To this vision is added a chaos of sounds: craters
that roar melodiously (*Les vieux cratères...rugissent mélodi-
eusement*), amorous celebrations that ring out (*Des fêtes
amoureuses sonnent*), a pack of chimes that clamors (*La chasse
de carillons crie*), horns that blare (*les Rolands sonnent leur
bravoure*), fleets with male choruses (*flottes orphéoniques*).
the murmur of pearls and precious shells (*la rumeur des perles
et des conques précieuses*), the flowers that low like cattle (*des
moissons de fleurs...mugissent*), the suburban Bacchantes who
sob (*Les Bacchantes des banlieues sanglotent*), the moon that
burns and howls (*la lune brûle et hurle*), the groups of belfries
that sing (*Des groupes de beffrois chantent*), the unknown music
that issues from châteaus of bone (*Des châteaux bâtis en os
sort une musique inconnue*), and the group that sang the joy
of the new work (*des compagnies ont chanté la joie due travail
nouveau*). Again as Rimbaud says, enthusiasms rush through
these cities (*les élans se ruent dan les bourgs*) of our dreams.

Poetic effects crowded into one sentence like *Bacchantes-ban-
lieues-sanglotent* and *lune-brûle-hurle* reveal the extreme con-
centration realized by Rimbaud. The constant shifting of perspective from high (*chalets, colosses*) to low (*cratères, canaux*),
the incessant rising up (*rejoint les champs des hauteurs, mon-
tent*) and settling down (*écroulement, s'effondre*), keep the

mental eye of the reader on the move. Such are just some of the elements of Rimbaud's prodigious vision. In his conclusion he wonders what helping hands (*Quels bons bras*) and what time (*quelle belle heure*) will restore to him this region from which come his sleep and his slightest movements (*me rendront cette région d'où viennent mes sommeils et mes moindres mouvements*). The reader gets the impression that these anti-landscapes are the result of awakened dreams, possible only in dreams recounted by a totally alert consciousness.

I find perhaps too much schizophrenia in Rimbaud's poetry. Nevertheless, in view of the Prince and the Genie of "Conte," who are explicitly one personality, and the king and queen of "Royauté," who could form one character, I am tempted to find in the eighteenth illumination, "Vagabonds" (Vagabonds),[8] not Verlaine and Rimbaud but Rimbaud and the "I" of the "I is another," the two sides, the timid and the adventurous, of any character, particularly since the conclusion of this poem refers directly to the place and the formula (*le lieu et la formule*) of Rimbaud's method outlined in the Seer Letters.

The "I" observed is the pitiful brother (*Pitoyable frère*) to whom the "I" observer owed so many atrocious sleepless nights (*Que d'atroces veillées je lui dus*). The "I" observer confesses he did not seize hold fervently enough of his undertaking of the seer (*Je ne saisissais pas fervemment de cette entreprise*). He had made fun of the other's weakness (*Je m'étais joué de son infirmité*), and thus through his own fault they would both find themselves in exile and in slavery (*Par ma faute nous retournerions en exil, en esclavage*), since they had failed to attain the vision of the seer. The "I" observed attributed to the "I" observer a very strange bad luck and innocence and added disquieting reasons for them (*Il me supposait un guignon et une innocence très bizarres, et il ajoutait des raisons inquiétantes*).

The "I" observer replied by snickering at this satanic doctor (*Je répondais en ricanant à ce satanique docteur*), satanic because they were both held back by his weakness. He ended up by slipping out the window (*et finissais par gagner la fenêtre*). Once free and separated from his other self by a countryside crossed by bands of rare music (*par delà la campagne traversée par des bandes de musique rare*), he was able to create (*Je créais*) phantoms of a future nocturnal luxury (*les fantômes du futur luxe nocturne*), the visions of *Une Saison en enfer* and the peopled landscapes of the *Illuminations* themselves, for example. Certainly this act of creation was at least a vaguely hygienic distraction (*Après cette distraction vaguement hygiénique*), sufficiently distracting psychologically so that he could lie down to sleep (*je m'étendais sur une paillasse*). Almost every night just after he had gotten to sleep (*presque chaque nuit, aussitôt endormi*), the poor uncomprehending brother would get up (*le pauvre frère se levait*), his mouth rotted (*la bouche pourrie*) so that he could not put his visions into words, his eyes torn out (*les yeux arrachés*) so that he could not see his own visions, the way he imagined himself in his own dreams (*tel qu'il se rêvait*), and dragged the other "I" into the room while howling out his dreams of idiot grief (*se tirant dans la salle en hurlant son songe de chagrin idiot*) at not being able to put his visions into words.

The "I" observer had in all sincerity (*J'avais en effet, en toute sincérité d'esprit*) undertaken the task of returning him to his primitive state of son of the sun (*pris l'engagement de le rendre à son état primitif de fils du Soleil*), to that state when he, too, could capture and translate immediately and instinctively the emanations from people and places and things into illuminations for the human mind. Once reconciled they would wander (*nous errions*), nourished by spring water (*nourris du vin des cavernes, cavernes* being an Ardennes expression for springs) and the bread of the road (*du biscuit de la route*), the simplest of necessities, while the "I" observer was still hard pressed to find the place and the formula for further illuminations (*moi pressé de trouver le lieu et la formule*).

While the city of "Les Ponts" is picturesque and remains somewhat two-dimensional as in an old engraving, that of "Ville" is modern and a point of departure for moral judgments on urban life. The cities of the first "Villes" are utopian creations of literary legend, whereas those of the second "Villes"[9] are fantastic visions of the future based upon a past tradition of classical architecture (*les merveilles classiques de l'architecture*) but with allusions to Cardinal Wolsey's Hampton Court outside London, the Sainte-Chapelle in Paris, and to London and Paris themselves. Their most striking aspect is their enormity with an official acropolis that exceeds the most colossal conception of modern barbarity (*L'acropole officielle outre les conceptions de la barbarie moderne les plus colossales*), buildings done in an unusual taste for enormity (*dans un goût d'énormité singulier*), art galleries twenty times larger than Hampton Court (*vingt fois plus vastes qu'Hampton-Court*), street lamps like giant candelabra (*quais chargés de candélabras géants*), a dome about fifteen thousand feet in diameter (*Ce dôme est... quinze mille pieds de diamètre environ*), whereas the largest dome in the world, that of the Hagia Sophia in Istanbul, is just over one hundred feet in diameter. The atmosphere is a strange contrast between the dull light caused by the immutably gray sky (*le jour mat produit par ce ciel immuablement gris*), the imperial brilliance of the buildings (*l'éclat impérial des bâtisses*), and the eternal snow on the ground (*la neige éternelle du sol*). A Norwegian Nebuchadnezzar (*Un Nabuchodonosor norwégien*) built the stairways of the ministries (*a fait construire des escaliers des ministères*), where even the subordinates are haughty (*les subalternes... sont déjà plus fiers que des..*, word indecipherable) and the guardians and officers cause one to tremble (*j'ai tremblé à l'aspect des gardiens de colosses et officiers de constructions*). The streets resemble today's malls that eliminate traffic (*Par le groupement des bâtiments en squares, cours et terrasses fermées, on a évincé les cochers*). Amid all these gigantic structures the parks take the form of primitive nature cultivated by a proud art (*Les parcs représentent la nature primitive travaillée par un art superbe*) like the "natural" Romantic English gardens.

The view across footbridges of brass (*des passerelles de cuivre*), platforms (*plates-formes*), and stairways (*des escaliers*), through the markets (*les halles*) and around pillars (*les piliers*) creates the sensation of a perspective in depth (*la profondeur de la ville*). The observer can only wonder at the other possible levels of this fabulous city (*quels sont les niveaux des autres quartiers sur ou sous l'acropole*). He goes on to describe the commercial section of the city with its galleries and arcades (*avec galeries à arcades*). Suddenly Rimbaud introduces Eastern details into this snowy northern city by the mention of Indian nabobs (*nababs*) with their coaches of diamonds (*une diligence de diamants*), red velvet seats (*Quelques divans de velours rogue*), and polar drinks costing great amounts of rupees (*des boissons polaires dont le prix varie de huit cents à huit mille roupies*). Police must exist (*Je pense qu'il y a une police*), but the law is so peculiar (*Mais la loi doit être tellement étrange*) that he gives up trying to form an idea of what the adventurers are like in this place (*je renonce à me faire une idée des aventuriers d'ici*). This absence of moral judgment contrasts strongly with the condemnations of "Ville" but is qualified in the final paragraph.

The suburbs of the conclusion are a bizarre conglomeration of Paris streets (*une belle rue de Paris*), a democracy (*L'élément démocratique*), English counties (*le "Comté"*), and an eternal west of forests and great plantations (*l'occident éternel des forêts et des plantations prodigieuses*) where savage gentlemen (*les gentilshommes sauvages*) hunt out their news in the light that has been created (*chassent leurs chroniques sous la lumière qu'on a créée*). The poem loses itself in fantasy as the suburbs of these cities disappear strangely into the countryside (*le faubourg se perd bizarrement dans la campagne*). When Rimbaud said we must be absolutely modern, he created cities to show us what he meant, visions of cities so close to contemporary reality as to be frightening. This is the way it will be with all of us "civilized" gentlemen who are still savage enough to kill one another and who read our papers not in the natural light of the sun but in the artificial light we have created.

III *A Song of Vigils*

The twentieth illumination, "Veillées" (Vigils),[10] has three parts. Part I resembles "Départ" somewhat, since it, too, is composed of a series of statements based on one grammatical formula. According to the poem a vigil is that moment of enlightened repose, neither feverish nor languorous, on a bed or on a meadow (*C'est le repos éclairé, ni fièvre, ni langueur, sur le lit ou sur le pré*). That is the first step, the physiological and psychological state conducive to hallucination. The second and third steps are the emotional ones of friendship and love. The friend must be neither ardent nor feeble (*C'est l'ami ni ardent ni faible. L'ami*) and the loved one neither tormenting nor tormented (*C'est l'aimée ni tourmentante ni tourmentée. L'aimée*). In this moment of total relaxation and suspended animation, all ambition dissolves, air and the world are not even sought (*L'air et le monde point cherchés*). It is, quite simply, life (*La vie*). It is so simple one can only ask, was this it (*Etait-ce donc ceci*), and it is so fragile that merely asking the question causes the dream to cool (*Et le rêve fraîchit*) and disappear. Just as the moment is caught between waking and sleeping, so the poem is caught between verse and prose. The assonances *pré-aimée* and *ami-vie-ceci-fraîchit* heighten the poetic effect of this fragile moment.

Part II is a brief paragraph that draws in swift strokes the visions of this vigil. First there is the light that illuminates the scene (*L'éclairage*), picking out the building beam (*l'arbre de bâtisse*) that supports this dream structure. At the two ends of the room (*Des deux extrémités de la salle*) with its rather ordinary decor (*décors quelconques*), harmonious elevations come together (*des élévations harmoniques se joignent*). Such is the physical setting for the vigil. The wall facing the watcher (*La muraille en face du veilleur*) offers three types of subjects, a succession of psychological impressions (*une succession psychologique*) including parts of friezes (*de coupes de frises*) that are solid, in three dimensions, and representing movement, strips in two dimensions and perhaps in colors that create the atmospheric effect (*de bandes atmosphériques*), and geological conditions that give the appearance of possible accidents in nature (*d'accidences géologiques,* with *accidences* a rare word indicating the condition necessary for an accident). This physical setting for an intense and rapid hallucination (*Rêve intense et rapide*) is peopled with sentimental groups (*de groupes sentimentaux*) of beings of all types of characters and all types of appearances (*des êtres de tous les caractères parmi toutes les apparances*). Dreams have no limits. Such is the second vigil which with its exact material description differs greatly from the first with its enumeration of psychological affinities.

Vigil I took place primarily in the mind while Vigil II took place in a room. Vigil III takes place aboard a boat where

the lamps swing and the carpets seem to creak with the action
of the waves (*Les lampes et les tapis de la veillée font le bruit
des vagues*) at night as they pass along the hull and around the
steerage (*la nuit, le long de la coque et autour du steerage*).
The sea in this hallucination swells up like the breasts of Amelia
(*La mer de la veillée, telle que les seins d'Amélie*). Inside the
cabin the tapestries reach halfway up the wall (*Les tapisseries,
jusqu'à mi-hauteur*) and picture thickets of lace (*des taillis de
dentelle*) tinged with emerald green (*teinte d'émeraude*) into
which dive the turtledoves of dreams (*où se jettent les tourterelles de la veillée*). The many sharp dental sounds of *tapisseries,
hauteur, des taillis de dentelle, teinte d'émeraude, jettent,* and
tourterelles de sharpen the keenness of perception in this hallucination. In the conclusion all of these visions seem to have
risen from a stretch of black hearth (*La plaque du foyer noir*)
like genuine suns over the shores (*de réels soleils des grèves*).
The trip is over, the dreamer has returned to the shores of
reality to find that his hallucinations came from wells of magic
(*puits des magies*). As day breaks and his dream dissipates,
he is left with a single view of dawn this time (*seule vue
d'aurore, cette fois*). Other times may leave him with other
visions.

"Mystique" (Mystic)[11] is one of the more enigmatic of the
Illuminations and thus has provoked much commentary. Its
four brief paragraphs describe an antilandscape filled with
disparate objects that lead a life of their own, a landscape that
slowly evolves into a skyscape as in "Phrases." The reader is
presented with a band of angels dancing in their woolen robes
on the slope of a bank (*Sur la pente du talus les anges tournent
leurs robes de laine*). That the slope is covered with grass the
Surrealist color of steel and emerald (*dans les herbages d'acier
et d'émeraude*) no longer surprises us in a Rimbaud poem.
This pastoral scene is disturbed by flames that leap up to the
summit of the knoll (*Des prés de flammes bondissent jusqu'au
sommet du mamelon*). Since the angels are dancing on the
slope of the hill, the reader must now see them through a
threatening film of flame. Situated on either side of this ridge
are evil and good, just where one would expect them to be with
evil on the left and good on the right. Evil includes all the

homicides and battles (*tous les homicides et toutes les batailles*) as well as all the disastrous sounds that make their rounds (*tous les bruits désastreux filent leur courbe*). On the right is the horizon of the orients (*la ligne des orients*), the eternal source of light and enlightenment for Rimbaud, as well as the promise of progress (*des progrès*).

The moral landscape is again filled with a group at the top of the picture (*la bande en haut du tableau*), a sight that becomes a sound composed of the turning and the bounding murmur of shells of the sea and human nights (*la rumeur tournante et bondissante des conques des mers et des nuits humaines*), the murmurs of the beauties of nature and the ecstasy of people. For the first time Rimbaud ends a paragraph with a comma, so that the sound of this paragraph is metamorphosed back into the sights of the last paragraph, the flowered softness of the stars, the sky, and all the rest (*La douceur fleurie des étoiles et du ciel et du reste*) that descends opposite the bank like a basket (*descend en face du talus, comme un panier*) and creates a blue and flowering abyss below (*fait l'abîme fleurant et bleu là-dessous*), the flowers of the sky that are the stars as well as the grass starred with flowers, the blue of the sea as well as the sky, the night of nature that engulfs us with the dark of sleep, eliminating sight and putting an end to our visions.

IV   A Song of Flowers

The twenty-third illumination, "Fleurs" (Flowers),[12] is a vision in which flowers are and are not flowers. The only two flowers mentioned are the digitalis or foxglove with its sprig of dotted white or purple flowers, which is used as a medicine, and the rose. The setting of the narrator who is looking at the digitalis is spectacular: a golden tier amid silken cords, gray gauzes, green velvets, and crystal disks that darken like bronze in the sun (*D'un gradin d'or,—parmi les cordons de soie, les gazes grises, les velours verts et les disques de cristal qui noircissent comme du bronze au soleil*). He is in a theater but is it a theater of nature or of man? Both, I think. The golden tier could be the golden beach, cords of silk could be the sun's rays, the green velvet could be grass, the crystal disks of the lights that seem to turn brown when the lights are dimmed could be patches of light on the sea that suddenly disappear with the passing of clouds, or sparkling flowers that turn brown from too much sunlight. He sees the digitalis opening up on a carpet whose design is made up of a silver filigree dotted with eyes and as fine as hair (*un tapis de filigranes d'argent, d'yeux et de chevelures*), much like a medieval tapestry with flowers that appear to be eyes.

These eyes and flowers become in the second paragraph pieces of yellow gold sown on agate (*Des pièces d'or jaune semées sur l'agate*). Agate is variegated with its colors in stripes, clouds, or mosslike forms. Thus it could symbolize the multiple colors of nature or the marble floor of the theater. The mahogany pillars (*des piliers d'acajou*) could be trees supporting the emerald dome of the sky (*supportant un dôme d'émeraudes*), while bouquets of white satin and slender rods of rubies (*des bouquets de satin blanc et de fines verges de rubis*) could be the white and red flowers surrounding the water rose (*entourent la rose d'eau*). They could also be stage decor. There is no water rose but Rimbaud used the expression "the roses of the reeds" (*roses des roseaux*) in "Mémoire" to indicate a water flower. Here he would seem to be saying water lily.

The sea and the sky are like a god with enormous blue eyes and a snowy figure (*Tels qu'un dieu aux énormes yeux bleus et aux formes de neige*) that attracts to the marble terraces a host of young and strong roses (*attirent aux terrasses de marbre la foule des jeunes et fortes roses*). Strangely enough we are again, as in "Michel et Christine," left with the blue, white, and red of the tricolor. Is the blue of the sea and sky the blue of, and thus the eyes of, this god? If so, Rimbaud has just called the dome of the sky emerald green. Are the snowy forms the marble terraces or mounds of white flowers? Are the strong young roses the youthful blood this god of nature attracts to its pure altars? We have seen flowers, but reality has been so transformed that the vision must depend upon the imagination the reader brings to it. Aside from one digitalis and a host of roses he may see no flowers at all.

"Nocturne vulgaire" (Common Nocturne)[13] indicates by its

title that it is a night song common to us all. In it we are witness to the fantastic possibilities of the "fabulous opera" Rimbaud's imagination became in "Délires II." A breath of air suffices to open operatic breaches in the walls (*Un souffle ouvre des brèches dans les cloisons*) of this house where the rotted roofs pivot (*le pivotement des toits rongés*), the hearth expands to infinity (*disperse les limites des foyers*), and the windows darken (*éclipse les croisées*). Descending a vine (*Le long de la vigne*) from the rooftop where he had supported his foot on a gargoyle (*m'étant appuyé du pied à une gargouille*), an omen of the beasts to come, the narrator enters a coach of another period (*ce carrosse dont l'époque est assez indiquée*), which becomes the hearse of his sleep (*Corbillard de mon sommeil*), a sort of shepherd's caravan of his foolishness (*maison de berger de ma niaiserie*), which veers wildly on the grass of an obliterated road (*vire sur le gazon de la grande route effacée*), indicating that in a dream all ways are lost. In a flaw in the glass (*dans un défaut en haut de la glace de droite*) swirl white lunar faces, leaves, and breasts (*tournoient les blêmes figures lunaires, feuilles, seins*). The vision turns dark green and blue (*Un vert et un bleu très foncés*) just as the wagon is unhitched near a spot of gravel (*Dételage aux environs d'une tache de gravier*).

The real nightmare begins with a whistle calling forth a storm, the accursed biblical city of Sodom (*siffler pour l'orage et les Sodomes*), beleaguered Jerusalem (*les Solymes*), wild beasts, and invading armies (*les bêtes féroces et les armées*). Will the phantom coachmen and beasts of his nightmare (*Postillons et bêtes de songe*) come back to life in the most suffocating forests (*reprendront-ils sous les plus suffocantes futaies*) in order to bury him up to his eyes in a silken spring (*pour m'enfoncer jusqu'aux yeux dans la source de soie*) and send them off (*Et nous envoyer*), whipped across the thrashing waters (*fouttés à travers les eaux clapotantes*) and the spilled drinks (*les boissons répandues*), to roll on the barking of mastiffs (*rouler sur l'aboi des dogues*). The vision of an old shepherd's caravan careening through the air, supported by the sound waves of the yapping of dogs is perhaps one of the most unusual sights of literature, rendering this nocturne less common than its title indicates. As Rimbaud says in his conclusion that takes us back to the beginning, all that is needed is the slightest breath of air to expand the limits of the hearth of our imagination (*Un souffle disperse les limites du foyer*).

"Marine" (Seascape)[14] is one of two illuminations in the form of free verse. Its ten lines vary from four to thirteen syllables with no rhymes and only echoes of assonances like *argent-lands, écume-reflux,* and *l'est-forêt.* The comparison, which is neither stated nor implied but which simply exists, is between the plows of the sea and the prows of the land. In a crossing of the term silver they are described as chariots of silver and copper (*Les chars d'argent et de cuivre*) and prows of steel and silver (*Les roues d'acier et d'argent*), silver only in appearance because of the sunlight. *Char* is the general term for chariot and certain kinds of wagons, whereas *charrue* translates "plow," but since they beat the foam (*Battent l'écume*) and uproot the bramble stumps (*Soulèvent les souches des ronces*), Rimbaud obviously intends plow. Opening with chariots immediately raises the whole poem to the level of fantasy. Rimbaud then speaks of the currents of the moor (*Les courants de la lande*) and the immense ruts of the ebb tide (*Et les ornières immenses du reflux*) that flow in a circular movement (*Filent circulairement*) toward three destinations, with the repetition of *vers* the important poetic device: eastward (*vers l'est*), toward the pillars of the forest (*Vers les piliers de la forêt*), and toward the shafts of the pier (*Vers les fûts de la jetée*). *Fûts* can mean both the trunk of a tree and the shaft or column of a piling used to support a pier. The vision disappears in a burst of illumination when its angle is struck by whirlpools of light (*Dont l'angle est heurté par des tourbillons de lumière*), almost as if the chariot of the sun had blinded us temporarily. *Dont* generally refers to an immediately preceding noun or pronoun but given the structure of this poem, it could refer to every noun, wiping them all out as a conclusion. Thus this sea-piece disappears from the reader's view like a ship over the horizon.

CHAPTER 9

Songs of a Private Heaven
(concluded)

THE twenty-seventh illumination, "Angoisse" (Anguish),[1] is composed of five brief but dense paragraphs and begins with the enigmatic pronoun "She" (*Elle*) without antecedent. Only in the fourth paragraph does the Vampire (*la Vampire*), also capitalized, supply the missing antecedent. The vampire would seem to be time that sucks our life blood, turning youth into old age. The anguish of the title is, as the narrator says, that of the lost youth of this being, myself (*Jeunesse de cet être-ci: moi*). He asks that time pardon the crushed ambitions (*pardonner les ambitions continuellement écrasées*), that a comfortable end make up for the years of want (*une fin aisée répare les âges d'indigence*), that just one successful day hide from us the shame of our fatal lack of skill (*un jour de succès nous endorme sur la honte de notre inhabileté fatale*).

The parenthetical expressions of the second paragraph enumerate all the visions of youth, the accolades (*O palmes*) to be earned, the riches (*diamant*) to be gained, the love and strength (*Amour, force*) of which it is capable. Youth is at the same time a demon and a god (*démon, dieu*) to be prized above all joy and fame (*plus haut que toutes joies et gloires*) in every way everywhere (*de toutes façons, partout*).

He asks that scientific (*des accidents de féerie scientifique*) and social (*des mouvements de fraternité sociale*) advances be cherished as the progressive restitution of that first freedom (*soient chéris comme restitution progressive de la franchise première*) we all receive at birth promising us a better life and the brotherhood of man. But the vampire of time renders us docile with age (*Mais la Vampire qui nous rend gentils*), forcing us to be content with what she has left us (*commande que nous nous amu-*

sions avec ce qu'elle nous laisse) To attempt anything more in old age would only make us look silly (*ou qu'autrement nous soyons plus drôles*). The conclusion lists the things time has left to us: our wounds (*aux blessures*), our agony (*aux supplices*), and our torture (*aux tortures*). We can only continue (*Rouler*), crippled as we are, with the necessities of life, air and water, but we become weary of breathing (*l'air lassant et la mer*), while these necessary elements maintain the silence of nature and finally kill us (*le silence des eaux et de l'air meurtriers*) through time. Our tortures laugh at us in their silence that swells atrociously like the sea (*qui rient, dans leur silence atrocement houleux*). The anguish of our failed ambitions, ideals dissipated, and opportunities irrevocably lost, fills old age with the bitter fruit of defeat at the hands of time.

I *The Song of the Barbarian*

"Barbare" (Barbarian)[2] offers another antilandscape but one with a complex structure. Instead of a linear succession of visions the form is fugal with one theme set against another. The first set of variations on a theme is introduced by expressions of time, *Bien après* (Long after), of condition, *Remis* (Freed), and of distance, *Loin* (Far from). Each expression introduces in turn a series of the realities of life: time, people, and places in the first (*Bien après les jours et les saisons, et les êtres et les pays*); in the second, the moral characteristic of pride in our acts that were heroic (*Remis des vieilles fanfares d'héroïsme*) but which still seduce our heart and head (*qui nous attaquent encore le coeur et la tête*) because of our pride rather than our heroism; the third theme is suggested in the second by the use of *loin,* far from the former assassins (*loin des anciens assassins*), but continues on the moral plane of those failures of our character that stifle our impulses toward the good. In the third theme we are far from the old retreats (*Loin des vieilles retraites*), that is, the excuses and alibis we used as a haven for our inadequacies but which were thereby, in the double meaning of the French word *retraites*—which contrasts vividly with the earlier *fanfares d'héroïsme*—a withdrawal and a defeat; we are also far from the old flames (*des vieilles flammes*) of desires which attracted us because we heard and felt them (*qu'on entend, qu'on sent*) in our very being. The word *vieilles* is used three times like a haunting musical figure.

Set off against the first theme of the realities of life is a second, that of the extravagant and ominous visions of the mind like a pavilion of meat bleeding on the silk of seas and arctic flowers (*Le pavillon en viande saignante sur la soie des mers et des fleurs arctiques*). Visions, like arctic flowers, do not exist (*elles n'existent pas*), but they are, nevertheless, the intangible half of reality, its countertheme and counterpart. This pavilion reminds us of the butchers' stalls that were erected in "Après le déluge," particularly since they were followed immediately by an allusion to the blood that flowed at Bluebeard's and in the slaughterhouses. The contrast is not only between the raw meat dripping blood on seas as smooth as silk but also between the two life liquids: the blood that burns in our veins and is expended in the sea of life, and the calm, cool water from which life emerged and which sustains life. The beauty of the imagination is indicated by the arctic flowers that do not exist. The exclamation *Oh!* introduces a louder and more emphatic repetition of this theme.

The third theme is introduced by a soft, sweet refrain of delights (*Douceurs*) that appears four times and as it does, summarizes the themes of reality (*O monde*) and creative imagination (*La musique*). A musical coda usually begins after the repetition of the first subject. Rimbaud's begins after the repetition of the second subject but still serves as a winding-up of the main subjects that develop into the conclusion. The four elements of this theme are the fire, water, air and earth of the ancient Greeks: the glowing coals of braziers (*Les brasiers*) that rain down in gusts of frost (*pleuvant aux rafales de givre*); the fires in the rain that sparkles like diamonds as it is buffeted by the wind (*les feux à la pluie du vent de diamants*), a rain that is hurled down by the earthly heart eternally carbonized for us (*jetée par le coeur terrestre éternellement carbonisé pour nous*), the endless cycles of the seasons. Such are the material realities of the world (*O monde*).

The braziers return (*Les brasiers*), associated this time with the foaming waters of the sea (*et les écumes*). Attached to, and deriving from, these realities is the music (*La musique*) created by our imagination in imitation of the sounds of nature, a veering of abysses (*virement des gouffres*) and the clash of hunks of ice with the stars (*choc des glaçons aux astres*). The coda begins with the recapitulation of delights, world, and music (*O Douceurs, ô monde, ô musique*) and tells us that in them we find the forms of life (*Et là, les formes*), water in the form of the sweat (*les sueurs*) of our efforts, the living beauty of hair (*les chevelures*), and our eyes (*les yeux*) with which we witness our visions. All of them float (*flottant*) in the water of our sweat and of the boiling white tears (*les larmes blanches, bouillantes*) of our grief that is assuaged by the delights (*ô douceurs*) of life like the music of a feminine voice (*la voix féminine*) that seems to reach down to the very depths of the volcanoes, the braziers of nature, and the freezing arctic grottoes (*arrivée au fond des volcans et des grottes arctiques*) that shelter the nonexistent arctic flowers of our imagination. We are left in the end with the pavilion (*le pavillon*) of our imagination, ready to repeat the endless musical round of life. We are all barbarians as we intrude on the beautiful realities of the world with the creations of our imagination that are not separate and distinct from reality but an integral part of it, that is, poetry.

"Solde" (Sale)[3] contains eight short paragraphs, six of which begin with *A vendre* ("For sale"). The second and seventh offer examples for the preceding paragraph, whereas the eighth serves as conclusion. In this liquidation everything is for sale that the Jews have not sold (*ce que les Juifs n'ont pas vendu*), that is, items that cannot be bought in the ordinary market. The first two paragraphs include the moral and immaterial aspects of life. The third offers the material things, the fourth social relations, the fifth places in space and time, the sixth and seventh the creations of the mind.

The moral and immaterial aspects of life include our actions that lie between nobility and crime (*ce que noblesse ni crime n'ont goûté*), that is, almost all of them; everything of which accursed love and the infernal honesty of the masses are unaware (*ce qu'ignorent l'amour maudit et la probité infernale des masses*), that is, all the beautiful and productive phases of true love that an accursed love cannot know and all the subtle nuances of relationships that the masses cannot experience because of their narrow concept of honesty, an honesty that is either rigidly moral through lack of education or morally lax because of their social condition; all of those aspects of life which are beyond time and knowledge (*ce que le temps ni la science n'ont pas à reconnaître*) like voices restored (*Les Vox reconstituées*), the fraternal awakening of all choral and orchestral energies and their immediate application (*l'éveil fraternel de toutes les énergies chorales et orchestrales et leurs applications instantanées*), the choral representing the human expression of fraternity, the orchestral representing the mechanical but musical expression; the unique occasion for freeing our senses (*l'occasion, unique, de dégager nos sens*). This last item recalls the aspirations of the Seer Letters and would seem to suggest that Rimbaud is proclaiming their failure. We need not go outside the poem for the explanation, however. This freeing of the senses can mean simply their refinement and elevation that render us sensitive to the beauty and possibilities of life.

The material aspects include the bodies that are priceless (*les Corps sans prix*) because of their beauty or because we cannot live without them; outside any race (*hors de toute race*), because the concept of race is so often a limiting discrimination; beyond every world (*de tout monde*), because we live only in the world; beyond all sex (*de tout sexe*), because it, too, is a reason for discrimination; beyond all lineage (*de toute descendance*), the physical heritage that can limit capacity and encourage contempt. Material aspects include the riches that seem to spring up with every step forward (*Les richesses jaillissant à chaque démarche*) like the hardness, clarity, purity, and beauty of diamonds (*Solde de diamants sans contrôle*).

Among political relations anarchy for the masses is for sale (*l'anarchie pour les masses*), since through it one had hoped to improve their condition; irrepressible satisfaction for the superior amateurs (*la satisfaction irrépressible pour les amateurs supérieurs*), since mankind progresses as often through profound love as through genius; atrocious death for the faithful and lovers (*la mort atroce pour les fidèles et les amants*), since death is doubly painful for those who truly love.

Place and space are for sale in the form of houses and migrations (*les habitations et les migrations*), since a home can be both a refuge and a prison, a migration a flight to freedom or to want; diversions like sports (*sports*) and fairylands (*féeries*) that prove nothing or exist only in the imagination; perfect comforts (*comforts parfaits*, and again Rimbaud uses the English spelling) on which we expend so much effort; all the noise and movement that indicate a possible future progress (*le bruit, le mouvement et l'avenir qu'ils font*).

The operations of the mind are for sale including the applications of calculations (*les applications de calcul*) for which our intelligence is not prepared; the unprecedented leaps of harmony (*les sauts d'harmonie inouïs*) to which our ears are not yet accustomed; the lucky discoveries (*Les trouvailles*) and the unexpected terms (*les termes non soupçonnés*) we find for expressing them for which we could not have hoped; immediate possession (*possession immédiate*) of the mad and endless impetus toward invisible splendors (*Elan insensé et infini aux splendeurs invisibles*) and unperceived delights (*aux délices insensibles*), with its bewildering secrets for every vice (*ses secrets affolants pour chaque vice*), since such aspirations seem to be realized only through evil, and its frightening gaiety for the crowd (*sa gaîté effrayante pour la foule*) that is happy without comprehending the consequences.

In conclusion the material things (*les Corps*), the immaterial means of communication and revelation (*les voix*), the immense and unquestionable opulence (*l'immense opulence inquestionable*, with Rimbaud misspelling the English word) are for sale but will never be sold (*ce qu'on ne vendra jamais*), because they represent our being (*les Corps*), our means of sharing (*les voix*), and our aspirations (*l'opulence*). In spite of that fact the salesmen have not completed their task (*Les vendeurs ne sont pas à bout de solde*) and travelers, the seekers, need not turn in their accounts just yet (*Les voyageurs n'ont pas à rendre leur commission de si tôt*). This sale of all the positive aspects of life will go on as long as men live, but humanity will not buy because of its lack of vision and comprehension. The aspirations of the Seer Letters are for sale to the lowest bidder, but they will remain on the shelves and in the showcases of literature as impossible possibilities.

II   *The Song of the Fairy*

The thirty-first illumination, "Fairy,"[4] is the second of three with titles in English and is divided into two parts, "Fairy I" and "II Guerre" (II War). The unidentified Helen in "Fairy I" joins the ranks of Rimbaud's mysterious women, Madame ° ° ° of "Après le déluge," Henrika of "Ouvriers," Amelia of "Veillées III," the *Elle* of "Angoisse" and "Métropolitain," with more to come. The poem is an enumeration of all the things that have conspired to make Helen what she is. I do not believe, as English translators would have it,[5] that the saps conspired in the shadows, the lights in the silence. Because of the structure of the poem, I believe the saps and lights conspired together in the shadows and silence, thus setting up a whole complex of relationships. Saps are interior and thus not exterior and ornamental (*les sèves ornamentales*, with *ornamentales* an Anglicism for *ornementales*). Since they are interior, they can be considered as moving in the shadows (*dans les ombres*), but the feminine beauty and natural impulses they create are opposed to the idea of virgin (*vierges*). The shadows in which the saps circulate are virgin because they are still unexplored and unexploited. Interior and unseen saps moving in the shadows contrast with the exterior and witnessed lights (*les clartés*) that are impassive (*impassibles*), physically and emotionally incapable of feeling, motionless as opposed to rising sap. What guiding lights there are are as beautiful, as far removed, and as silent as the stars (*le silence astral*). Virgin and silence can be human, whereas shadows and astral belong to nature and thus to things.

In the second half of the first paragraph the ardor of summer (*L'ardeur de l'été*) continues the movement of the sap, while the necessary indolence (*l'indolence requise*) echoes the impassiveness of the lights. Just as the ardor was entrusted to the birds (*confiée à des oiseaux*), so the indolence was entrusted to a boat (*à une barque*). The birds were silent (*muets*) like the stars, whereas the boat was in mourning (*de deuils*) for the losses of the past. The boat is also unusual since it is priceless (*sans prix*), one's past being his only past. Indolence in the form of the boat was moving slowly and silently through coves of dead loves and dispirited perfumes (*par des anses d'amours morts et de parfums affaissés*). The prepositional phrase *par des anses* will be joined by *sous la ruine* ("amid the ruins") in the following paragraph. The birds are living and the boat is a thing, but the former are silent and the latter was in mourning. A cove is a refuge but its loves were dead and its perfumes discouraged. The senses of sight, sound, and smell are all awakened by this melancholy paragraph.

The prepositional phrase that opens the first paragraph, *Pour Hélène*, is joined by the opening of the second, *Après le moment* ("After the moment"), which has to do with time like that of the third, *Pour l'enfance d'Hélène* ("For the childhood of Helen"). The fourth paragraph is a continuation of the enumerations of the third. The second paragraph is composed of two prepositional phrases (from-to) plus an incomplete third. All three involve sound, a song (*de l'air*), bells (*de la sonnerie*), and cries (*des cris*). The song is that of the woodcutters' wives (*des bûcheronnes*), which helps explain the ruin of the woods; the bells are those of cattle (*des bestiaux*); and the cries come from the steppes (*des steppes*). Thus the sounds are caused by humans, animals, and places and constitute a happy song, the sound of bells to indicate location, and the screech (of the wind?) from the steppes. We go from the human sound of the song to the natural sound of the torrent in the ruin of the woods (*à la rumeur du torrent sous la ruine des bois*), from the sound of the cowbells to their echo in the valleys (*à l'écho des vals*). The sound of rushing water and of echoes is repeated and reassuring. The ominous cries from the steppes find no such echo.

For the childhood of Helen two sets of two things shivered, bestirred themselves; furs (*les fourrures*) to keep her physically warm and the shadows (*les ombres*), either those of the dead who have joined the things of nature or those of nature herself, who have stirred in order to keep her mentally and emotionally alert; the bosom of the poor (*le sein des pauvres*) who provided compassion and work for her physical comfort, the legends of heaven (*les légendes du ciel*) that offered diversion. With heaven we are back to the stars of the first paragraph, those extraterrestrial influences on all our lives.

As a result both her eyes and her dance (*Et ses yeux et sa danse*), the means by which she sees and interprets the world and the means by which she expresses herself, are still superior (*supérieurs encore*) to three things: to the precious gleams (*aux éclats précieux*) of material objects that take us back to the lights and stars of the first paragraph; to the cold influences (*aux influences froides*), the lack of enthusiasm and the indifference we all experience; and to the pleasure (*au plaisir*) of the decor and the hour (*au décor et de l'heure*), the place and time in which we live which are unique (*uniques*), because even Helen can live only in one place and one time. Thus her attributes are priceless, superior, and unique, leaving the reader with a strange but strong impression of this eternal woman who is every woman, the "Fairy" of the title who is both natural and supernatural.

Part II, "War," differs widely from "Fairy." It contains only one paragraph plus one sentence of conclusion. The paragraph is divided into three sections: the then of childhood (*Enfant*), the now of the present (*A présent*), and the results of the experiences of the two periods. As a child the experience of certain skies (*certains ciels*), the places where he found himself, refined his vision (*ont affiné mon optique*), his way of seeing the world and others. During that time all the characters of others (*tous les caractères*) exerted an influence on the features of his physiognomy (*nuancèrent ma physionomie*), shaped the outward expression of his character as he is seen by others. All of the usual natural phenomena took place (*Les Phénomènes s'émurent*) which for the child are extraordinary because he is seeing them for the first time. The adult becomes aware of the inevitable passing of time (*l'inflexion éternelle des moments*), a physical phenomenon, just as he learns of the frightening and endless infinity of mathematics (*l'infini des mathématiques*), the things of the mind, with the development *éternelle-moments-infini* heightening the contrast between the times of the body and the mind. These two ideas haunt him in this world (*me chassent par ce monde*) where he suffered (*où je subis*) rather than enjoyed all civil success (*tous les succès civils*), the esteem of his fellowmen as well as the respect of strange children (*respecté de l'enfance étrange*) and enormous affections (*des affections énormes*). For adults the ideas of children are unexpected and thus strange while all of us live through enormous affections that end but leave us changed. As a result of these experiences he dreams of a war of right or of might (*Je songe à une Guerre de droit ou de force*) based on an entirely unexpected logic (*de logique bien imprévue*). Rimbaud may well have had the aspirations of his Seer Letters in mind, the desire to change life, or he may simply be expressing his hopes for progress in general that can only be realized by the "War" of the title but which also, if all men made the effort to join in the fraternal harmony, would be as easy and simple as a musical phrase (*C'est aussi simple qu'une phrase musicale*). Great music seems to be easy and natural, almost inevitable, although we know the enormous effort the composer must exert in order to produce it. In that sense this war will be as simple as a musical phrase and in that sense it will resemble music.

The thirty-fourth illumination, "Scènes" (Scenes), is composed of eight paragraphs,[6] the first and last of which serve as introduction and conclusion and are linked in a circular movement by the verb *divise-se divise*. The opening paragraph reveals that the ancient comedy pursues its harmonies (*L'ancienne Comédie pursuit ses accords*), for this is comic opera as we learn later. It also divides up its idylls (*et divise ses Idylles*) for presentation on the stage that is described in the next six paragraphs. Paragraphs two and three, divided in some editions by a period and in others by a comma, describe the stage itself and the audience; four, the wings; five, actors and their settings; six, musical scenes and their settings; and seven, the play, its setting, and its audience.

Whether paragraphs two and three are separated by a period or a comma is unimportant, because I am convinced they are the same, the third being an amplification of the second. The opening clauses of paragraphs two, four, five, and six—*Des boulevards, Dans des corridors, Des oiseaux,* and *Des scènes*—reinforce this impression. Rimbaud is playing on the word *tréteau* in the sentence, *Des boulevards de tréteaux,* because it means both the sawhorses we see in the streets and the supports used in the early theater to elevate the stage so the actors could be seen by the audience. In the plural it has come to mean the "boards" or the stage itself. Thus this lengthy outdoor stage has the appearance of a long wooden pier (*Un long pier en bois; pier* is an Anglicism) running from one end to the other of a rocky field (*d'un bout à l'autre d'un champ rocailleux*) where a barbarous crowd, the audience, mills around under the denuded trees (*où la foule barbare évolue sous les arbres dépouillés*).

Paragraph four is incomplete grammatically and could thus serve as an introductory clause to the following paragraph, again divided as they are by a period in some editions and a comma in others. Rimbaud speaks of corridors of black gauze (*Dans des corridors de gaze noire*), and although *coulisses* is the French for backstage or wings, the black gauze leads me to believe these corridors are the stage wings where, following the lead of guides with lanterns and leaves (*suivant le pas des promeneurs aux lanternes et aux feuilles*), actors in bird costumes from the medieval mystery plays swoop down on a pontoon (*Des oiseaux des mystères s'abattent sur un ponton; ponton* is the word Rimbaud used in the conclusion of "Le Bateau ivre"). Actors and audience are difficult to distinguish at this point since the *promeneurs* could be strollers in the promenade gallery or ushers leading the audience to their seats with lanterns and programs. The situation gets more complicated, because the stage, first described as a marine pier in a rocky field, has now become a pontoon of masonry (*un ponton de maçonnerie*), moved by the archipelago covered with the spectators' boats (*mû par l'archipel couvert des embarcations des spectateurs*). The stage retains its reality of wood and stone, but what takes place on it is another matter. An archipelago is both the expanse of water containing a chain of islands and the group of islands itself. The mysterious actor-birds swoop down on their stage that rises up like a pontoon in the water of the archipelago and is thus surrounded by the spectators like a pontoon surrounded by boats in a harbor or the pontoon faces the shore of the island covered by the spectators and to which their boats are tied.

On the stage the lyric scenes accompanied by flute and drum (*Des scènes lyriques accompagnées de flûte et de tambour*) slope down in spaces created under the ceilings (*s'inclinent dans des réduits ménagés sous les plafonds*) around the lounges of modern clubs or the halls of the ancient Orient (*autour des salons de clubs modernes ou des salles de l'Orient ancien*). What was a public and outdoor theater has become private and indoor. What was Western has become Eastern. The stage knows no limits of place or country.

The magic spectacle, and every play is a magic spectacle, takes place on the summit of an amphitheater crowned by thickets (*La féerie manoeuvre au sommet d'un amphithéâtre couronné par les taillis*). Or it moves and modulates (*On s'agite et module pour les Béotians*), that is, musically as in an opera, for the Boetians, the barbarians of paragraph three, in the shade of moving forests on the ridge of cultivated lands (*dans l'ombre des futaies mouvantes sur l'arête des cultures*).

This comic opera divides up on our stage (*L'opéra-comique se divise sur notre scène*) at the point of intersection of ten partitions erected from the gallery to the footlights (*à l'arête d'intersection de dix cloisons dressées de la galerie aux feux*), that is, the ten stalls or sections in which the spectators are seated and whose partitions stretch from the rear heights of the hall down to the edge of the footlights and seem to and do converge on the stage. Reading this poem is like attending a mystery play which one may or may not have understood completely. When it is over the reality of the hall imposes itself on our consciousness while the mysterious birds still flit through our mind.

III   A Song of History

The five paragraphs of "Soir historique" (Historic Evening)[7] offer three visions. The first occupies two paragraphs and is the personal vision of the naive tourist (*le touriste naïf*) we all are in this life. In paragraph three the second vision is a broader one of the whole world that goes beyond the naive tourist's enslaved vision (*A sa vision esclave*). The fourth paragraph recounts the failure of such visions, and the final paragraph promises a third vision that will be witnessed by the serious being (*l'être sérieux*) with quite different results.

On some evening, for example (*En quelque soir, par exemple*), when the naive tourist finds that he has managed to escape from our economic horrors (*que se trouve le touriste naïf, retiré de nos horreurs économiques*), a master's hand will play on the harpsichord of the meadows (*la main d'un maître anime le clavecin des prés*). Aroused by this music of the earth the naive vision includes a card game being played at the bottom of a pond (*on joue aux cartes au fond de l'étang*) whose surface is a mirror evoking queens and their pretty ladies (*miroir évocateur des reines et des mignonnes*). Note that the scene from ordinary life takes place on a level inferior to that of the queens who represent exalted political power. In addition, there are the female saints of religion with their veils of modesty (*on a les saintes, les voiles*), the threads of harmony, and the legendary chromaticisms (*et les fils d'harmonie, et les chromatismes légendaires*). These visions of religion and artistic creations are witnessed high above daily life and politics in the glow of the setting sun (*sur le couchant*).

The tourist shudders at the passage of the hunts (*Il frissonne au passage des chasses*) that have killing as their goal and of the hordes (*et des hordes*) of unthinking marauders. Instead of being active and creative, this vision that is a comedy drips on the grassy stage (*La comédie goutte sur les tréteaux de gazon*). Such stupid plots only confuse the poor and the weak (*Et l'embarras des pauvres et des faibles sur ces plans stupides*).

But there is a vision broader than this slavish one which sees Germany rising up on scaffolds toward the moons (*l'Allemagne s'échafaude vers des lunes*). Farther away, the Tartar wildernesses light up (*les déserts tartares s'éclairent*) and ancient revolts rumble in the center of the Celestial Empire over stairways and the thrones of kings (*les révoltes anciennes grouillent dans le centre du Céleste Empire, par les escaliers et les fauteuils de rois*). These visions of national aggrandizement, far-off awakenings, and ancient revolts are nothing more than a small, pale, and flat world, Africa and the countries of the Occident, that is going to be erected (*un petit monde blême et plat, Afrique et Occidents, va s'édifier*). It is interesting to note that Rimbaud does not include his favored Orient in this latter group of nations, and for good reason. This ballet of known seas and nights (*Puis un ballet de mers et de nuits connues*) is nothing more than worthless chemistry (*une chimie sans valeur*) and impossible melodies (*et des mélodies impossibles*).

They are the result of the same bourgeois magic (*La même magie bourgeoise*) we find everywhere the mailcoach drops us off (*à tous les points où la malle nous déposera*). Even the most elementary physicist (*Le plus élémentaire physicien*), that is, one who might at least be acquainted with the basics of the chemistry of change, feels that it is no longer possible to submit to this personal atmosphere (*sent qu'il n'est plus possible de se soumettre à cette atmosphère personnelle*) that is nothing but a fog of physical remorse (*brume de remords physiques*), which is an affliction even to acknowledge (*dont la constation est déjà une affliction*).

The revolutions Rimbaud has in mind will be much more earthshaking than that, including the moment of the sweatingroom (*Non!—Le moment de l'étuve*) when we really sweat it out, of seas swept away (*des mers enlevées*), of subterranean conflagrations (*des embrasements souterrains*), of the whole planet carried away (*de la planète emportée*), and of all the resulting exterminations (*et des exterminations conséquentes*). These revolutions that take place on three levels—on the surface of the earth, underground, and in the atmosphere—are certainties indicated in the Bible with so little malice (*certitudes si peu malignement indiquées dans la Bible*) and by the Norns (*et par les Nornes*), the three Norse goddesses of fate, an allusion Rimbaud could have found in Leconte de Lisle[8] but, since he frequently refers to Norway, he may well have encountered them elsewhere in his reading. The important thing is that these revolutions are promised both by religion and legend and will be witnessed only by the serious (*qu'il sera donné à l'être sérieux de surveiller*). But they will not be merely the effect of legend (*Cependant ce ne sera point un effet de légende*) but a change of life that will transform the world, the goal of Rimbaud's "Alchemy of the Word."

Obviously the thirty-sixth illumination takes its name from the character "Bottom"[9] of Shakespeare's *A Midsummer-Night's Dream*. Rimbaud's hero undergoes three transformations instead of one. Finding reality too prickly for his great character (*La réalité étant trop épineuse pour mon grand caractère*), he changes first into a bird, which is not surprising when we remember Bottom's song about the blackbird, thrush, wren, finch, sparrow, lark, and gray cuckoo (III. 1). Rimbaud's Bottom found himself in Madame's, that is, Titania's house (*je me trouvai néanmoins chez Madame*) in the form of a big blue-gray bird (*en gros oiseau bleu*), soaring toward the moldings of the ceiling while dragging his wing through the shadows of evening (*s'essorant vers les moulures du plafond et traînant l'aile dans les ombres de la soirée*).

He stood at the foot of the canopy of the bed, for this is after all a dream, that supported adored jewels and physical masterpieces (*Je fus, au pied du baldaquin supportant ses bijoux adorés et ses chefs-d'oeuvre*), only to find himself turned into a big bear (*un gros ours*). Again the transformation is not surprising since Oberon mentions a bear twice (II. 1, 2) when plotting to pour the magic juice in the sleeping Titania's eyes that will cause her to love the first thing she sees on waking. Hippolyta talks at length of a bear (IV. 1) and Theseus mentions one in noting how easy "is a bush suppos'd a bear" in the night (V. 1). Rimbaud's bear has violet gums and a coat whitened with sorrow (*aux gencives violettes et au poil chenu de chagrin*) as well as eyes of the crystal and silver of consoles (*les yeux aux cristaux et aux argents des consoles*).

Suddenly all became shadow and a burning aquarium (*Tout ce fit ombre et aquarium ardent*). Shakespeare speaks of "hot ice" (V. 1). In the morning (*Au matin*), at this quarrelsome June dawn (*aube de juin batailleuse*) in midsummer, Rimbaud's Bottom finally found himself turned into the ass of Shakespeare's play. In that guise he ran through the fields (*je courus champs, âne*), trumpeting and brandishing his grievance (*claironnant et brandissant mon grief*) until the suburban Sabine women came to throw themselves on his breast (*jusqu'à ce que les Sabines de la banlieue vinrent se jeter à mon poitrail*). Shakespeare's Bottom, upon waking to find himself an ass, threatens to sing his dream-ballad at the end of their play, perhaps the dream-ballad Rimbaud has given us. Shakespeare's lone Titania has become a horde of Sabine women famous in legend for having been tricked and carried off by the early Romans just as Titania was tricked. What can one say except all's well that ends well.

The illumination "H"[10] joins "Le Coeur volé" as an erotic enigma. The Hortense of "H" remains unexplained unless we adopt the method of one interpreter of "Le Coeur volé" and find in the letter the outstretched arms and legs of the body in ecstasy or lassitude. Nevertheless, the message seems clear enough. The givens are all the abominations that violate the atrocious actions of Hortense (*Toutes les monstruosités violent les gestes atroces d'Hortense*). These monstrous and atrocious gestures are performed in a solitude composed of three elements: erotic technique, lassitude, and amorous drive (*Sa solitude est la mécanique érotique, sa lassitude, la dynamique amoureuse*). The antecedent for *elle* is ambiguous. It could be solitude, technique, lassitude, or drive, or—in retrospect or anticipation—Hortense. I take it to be the last preceding feminine singular noun *dynamique*. This drive that generally constitutes the individual's awakening to sexuality begins to exert itself in childhood (*Sous la surveillance d'une enfance*) and has been, at numerous times in the past (*elle a été, à des époques nombreuses*), the passionate hygiene of the races (*l'ardente hygiène des races*), the harmless release of frustrated feelings, the calming of passionate desires, an expression of sexuality that can suffice until the relations sanctified by marriage. But it can also lead to unhappiness (*Sa porte est ouverte à la misère*), for like the practice of any excess, the morality of actual beings (*Là, la moralité des êtres actuels*) can lose itself in the passion or action of this solitary practice (*se décorpore en sa passion ou en son action*), which is the terrible shudder of newly discovered love (*O terrible frisson des amours novices*). An intimate part of female sexuality is menstruation (*sur le sol sanglant*), which Rimbaud mentioned in "Le Juste restait...," but what can we make of the clear hydrogen (*par l'hydrogène clarteux*, in which *clarteux* is colloquial for *clair*)? The symbol of hydrogen is of course the

H of the title while the element is also odorless and colorless (*clarteux*). Although a gas it may well symbolize the seminal fluid, as one critic suggests.[11]

In answer to the exhortation to find Hortense (*trouvez Hortense*), I can only point out that she exists in every sentence. The phonetically nonexistent H of her name is supplied by the title. Also, the letters of her name can be found as follows:

t*O*utes les monst*R*uosi*TE*s viole*N*t le*S* g*E*stes atroces d'hortense.
sa s*O*litude est la mécanique e*R*o*T*iqu*E*, sa lassitude, la dy*N*amique amoureu*SE*.
s*O*us la su*R*veillance d'une enfance elle a é*T*é, à d*E*s époques *N*ombreu*SE*s l'ardente hygiène des races.
sa p*OR TE* est ouverte à la *Mi SE*re [provided *em* is pronounced as in *temps,* an exception that does not by any means prove the rule].
Là, la m*OR*ali*T*é d*E*s êtres actuels se décorpore e*N* *S*a passion ou *E*n son action.
O te*R*rible frisson des amours novices sure le sol sanglan*T* Et par l'hydrogè*N*e clarteux! trouvez horten*SE*.

If this is not what Rimbaud means, then he has simply supplied a description of female masturbation in a peculiarly apt language.

"Mouvement " (Movement) is the second of two illuminations in free verse and contains four stanzas, three of eight lines and one of four as conclusion.[12] The number of syllables varies from three to twenty-one. The reader gets the impression from the first stanza that he is making another extravagant voyage like that of "Le Bateau ivre." The hairpin turns on the steep banks of the river's cataracts (*Le mouvement de lacet sur la berge des chutes du fleuve*), the abyss that exists at the stern (*Le gouffre à l'étambot*), the speed of the descent (*La célérité de la rampe*), and the enormous caprice of the current (*L'énorme passade du courant*) recall the earlier poem, but this boat has its voyagers. These details of the passage conduct, through unheard-of lights (*Mènent par les lumières inouïes*) and chemical invention (*la nouveauté chimique*), the voyagers surrounded by the waterspouts of the valley (*Les voyageurs entourés des trombes du val*) and of the river (*Et*

166   ARTHUR RIMBAUD

du strom). Rimbaud seems to associate the German language
with water and the sea for we found *wasserfall* in "Aube."
   These voyagers are the conquerors of the world (*Ce sont
les conquérants du monde*) who are hunting for a personal
chemical fortune (*Cherchant la fortune chimique personnelle*).
Sport and comfort travel with them (*Le sport et le comfort
voyagent avec eux*), which recalls the *sports, féeries et comforts
parfaits* of "Solde." They may take away with them the education of races, classes, and beasts (*Ils emmènent l'éducation /
Des races, des classes et des bêtes*) on this boat (*sur ce
Vaisseau*). They find repose mingled with dizziness (*Repos
et vertige*) in the torrential light (*A la lumière diluvienne*)
during their terrible evenings of study (*Aux terribles soirs
d'étude*).
   The conclusion is introduced in the third stanza by *Car*
("For"). From their talk and their apparatus (*Car de la
causerie parmi les appareils*) comes blood (*le sang*). But
flowers, fire, jewels (*les fleurs, le feu, les bijoux*), and agitated
accounts are also to be found on this fugitive deck (*Des
comptes agités à ce bord fuyard*). Blood symbolizes the human
sacrifice necessary for progress, flowers the natural beauty,
fire the transformation of matter into energy, the jewels natural
resources, the accounts the written stories as opposed to the
earlier talk (*la causerie*). One can see (*On voit*) their stock
of studies (*leur stock d'études*) rolling like a dyke beyond the
hydraulic power road (*roulant comme une digue au delà de la
route hydraulique motrice*) that is monstrous and endlessly
lighting up (*Monstrueux, s'éclairant sans fin*), which would
almost seem to be the description of a railway. Their innova-
tions have driven them into harmonic ecstasy (*Eux chassés
dans l'extase harmonique*) and the heroism of discovery (*Et
l'héroïsme de la découverte*).
   In the four lines of conclusion a young couple stands out
(*Un couple de jeunesse s'isole*) in contrast to these conquerors
of the world in ecstasy over their discoveries and so-called
progress. The couple, almost in spite of or in the face of the
most surprising atmospheric accidents (*Aux accidents atmosphériques les plus surprenants*), isolate themselves on the
ark (*sur l'arche*) and sing and take up their positions (*Et*

chante et se poste). Is it the ancient savagery of the human race that is being forgiven (*Est-ce ancienne sauvagerie qu'on pardonne*) in the form of this young couple? Does humanity remain unchanged in spite of its material (*chimique*) progress? Does this couple represent that little group who, whatever the odds (*accidents atmosphériques*), does its job (*se poste*), finds happiness (*chante*), and works for the perpetuation of all that is human and humane in the face of mechanized, material progress? Those are a few of the questions Rimbaud seems to be asking.

IV   A Song of Devotion

Rimbaud's last enigmatic ladies appear in "Dévotion" (Devotion) and it is in part to them that this worship is addressed.[13] The eight short paragraphs begin with the preposition *A* ("To") except six and seven which begin with an adverbial phrase followed by the preposition, *Aussi bien à* and *Ce soir à*. The first three are dedicated to women, the fourth to childhood and old age, the fifth to the poor, the sixth to all religions, the seventh to a mysterious Circeto, while the eighth serves as a conclusion with a play on the preposition *A*.

The first two are addressed to the narrator's sisters but whether they are blood sisters or nuns is not revealed. All three women's names begin with *L*, a change from Hélène, Henrika, and Hortense. The first two names are exotic—Louise Vanaen de Voringhem, apparently Flemish, and Léonie Aubois d'Ashby, a hybrid Franco-English name. Louise has her blue trumpet turned toward the North Sea (*Sa cornette bleue tournée à la mer du Nord*), obviously as a directional signal for the shipwrecked (*Pour les naufragés*). Louise thus represents a sort of saint for tavelers.

Léonie is connected with the strange syllable *Baou*. I see no reason why Rimbaud with his knowledge of English would give us the phonetic transcription of "bow" as in to bow one's head unless he intended the word as a Franco-English hybrid like Léonie's name. I am attracted to the explanation that it is a Malay word meaning to smell bad, since it is followed immediately by the buzzing and stinking summer herb (*l'herbe d'été bourdonnante et puante*) that is used for curing the fever of mothers and children (*Pour la fièvre des mères et des enfants*). Léonie thus represents another savior of mankind, the nurse with her medicine.

Lulu, on the other hand, is a demon (*démon*) who has retained a taste for the chapels of the time of her childhood friends and of her incomplete education (*qui a conservé un goût pour les oratoires du temps des Amies et de son éducation incomplète*). I fail to see any lesbians lurking here but rather an Emma Bovary. All schoolgirl chums are Friends, with a capital F. Although Lulu is the demon of the eternal female and her education is incomplete, she has cut her education short for men (*Pour les hommes*). Thus education is added to the list. The paragraph is also dedicated to the Madame *** we encountered in "Après le déluge," she who had the piano hoisted up the Alps. Lulu and Madame *** obviously represent two aspects of feminine character.

The fourth paragraph is dedicated to the adolescent the narrator was (*A l'adolescent que je fus*), to the formative years of one's life so influenced by the holy old man (*A ce saint vieillard*) from either a hermitage or a mission (*ermitage ou mission*) who reminds us of the *brahmane* of "Vies I." The fifth is devoted to the spirit of the poor (*A l'esprit des pauvres*) and to a very high clergy (*Et à un très haut clergé*) who may or may not have helped relieve the condition of the poor. Rimbaud's irony is deceptive, particularly when we recall the *chaste robe noire* of Tartuffe, the sentiments expressed in "Accroupissements" and "Les Pauvres à l'église," and the *noir grotesque* of "Les Premières Communions."

The sixth paragraph is devoted to every cult (*à tout culte*) in such a place of memorial worship (*en telle place de culte mémoriale*), an expression which certainly sounds more like a translation from English than good French, and amid such events which one must attend (*parmi les événements qu'il faille se rendre*) either because he is following the aspirations of the moment (*suivant les aspirations du moment*) or because of his own serious vice (*ou bien notre propre vice sérieux*). These are not, then, organized religions but the groups to which we gravitate because of our character or temperament or because of events.

The seventh paragraph is the most enigmatic of all. It is dedicated to a still unidentified Circeto with tall mirrors (*à Circeto des hautes glaces*) which could also be enormous icebergs as we shall see. She is fat as a fish (*grasse comme le poisson*) and lit up like the ten months of the red night (*et enluminée comme les dix mois de la nuit rouge*), the polar night. The sibilants of *Ce soir, Circeto, glaces, grasse,* and *poisson* highlight this ominous character. Her heart is of amber, which is reddish like the night, and of spunk (*son coeur ambre et spunk*), the Anglicism indicating tinder that gives off a spark to light a fire as well as the moral characteristic of courage. All of this for his lone prayer mute like these regions of night (*pour ma seule prière muette comme ces régions de nuit*) and preceding acts of bravery more violent than this polar chaos (*et précédant des bravoures plus violentes que ce chaos polaire*). Rimbaud has already spoken of *le chaos de glaces et de nuit du pôle* in "Après le déluge," the *soleil des pôles* in "Métropolitain," and *fleurs* and *grottes arctiques* in "Barbare." This cold and lifeless region must have held some attraction for him, or some revulsion. I see Circeto as an enchantress, rather than a prostitute, with tall mirrors to reflect her mysterious appearance and confuse the visitor or with great icebegs that chill the blood of the worshipper. She may well be a combination of Homer's Circe and Hesiod's Ceto,[14] the latter name linking her to the cetaceans or whales, which would explain why she appears as fat as a fish. Rimbaud could also have found the Boetians of "Scènes," the Prometheus of the Seer Letters, and many another allusion in Hesiod. Circeto's surroundings are as dimly lit as the polar nights in the center of which she glows like amber and spunk. She represents the mysterious in life which attracts us and causes us to commit violent acts for reasons we cannot explain.

In the conclusion the narrator's devotion will be realized at any cost (*A tout prix*) or will be dedicated to all the costs (*A tout prix*) necessary and will be accompanied by all the songs (*et avec tous les airs*), even on metaphysical voyages (*même dans des voyages métaphysiques*). In the latter case there will be even more (*Mais plus alors*) than all the costs and all the songs since metaphysics takes us beyond the material and the earthly. Such is the poet's devotion to all things of heaven and earth, seen and unseen, known and unknown. All he has to do is put it into words, which Rimbaud did.

V A Song of Genius

The forty-first and last illumination, "Génie" (Genie), recapitulates Rimbaud's aspirations for progress and undoubtedly owes something to Michelet.[15] The poem can be divided into three parts: the first includes the first four paragraphs, all but the third of which begin with *Il* ("He"); the second contains eight short paragraphs, of which the first and last two begin with the exclamation *O* and the central four begin with the possessive adjective "his"; the thirteenth paragraph serves as a conclusion.

This genie or genius, since *génie* means both, is the embodiment of the ideal of progress. As such, he is a man for all seasons, winter and summer, present and future. The first paragraph lists his accomplishments in two sentences under two headings: affection and the present (*l'affection et le présent*), affection and the future (*l'affection et l'avenir*). Each heading is followed by three pairs of deeds, the first three dealing with the material aspects of life: time, food, and place. He has caused the house to be opened to foamy winter and to the murmur of summer (*il a fait la maison ouverte à l'hiver écumeux et à la rumeur de l'été*), that is, the snowy weather of winter that covers the dormant landscape like foam and the sweet sounds of bourgeoning summer, since we must live in time; he has purified drink and food (*qui a purifié les boissons et les aliments*), since we must eat to live; he is both the charm of those places we only pass through (*le charme des lieux fuyants*) and the superhuman delight of those places where we pause (*le délice surhumain des stations*), since we must live in space. The three pairs under the heading affection and the future deal with the emotions: he is the strength, moral and physical, and the love (*la force et l'amour*) that we, in our anger and boredom (*dans les rages et les ennuis*), see passing high above our mortal plane in the stormy sky (*dans le ciel de tempête*) which symbolizes our rage, and the flags of ecstasy (*les drapeaux d'extase*), symbol of our love and enthusiasms. The second paragraph is divided into two groups of four, the first continuing the list of the genie's qualities, the second enumerating our benefits from those qualities. He is again love (*l'amour*) but also perfect and reinvented moderation (*mesure parfaite et réinventée*), marvelous and unforseen reason (*raison merveilleuse et imprévue*), and eternity (*l'éternité*). These four attributes are incorporated into a beloved machine of fatal qualities (*machine aimée des qualités fatales*), fatal because we must die. Fatality is paired with the terror we have all had (*Nous avons tous eu l'épouvante*) at his concession and at ours (*de sa concession et de la nôtre*). Thanks to him we have experienced four things, the pleasure of physical good health (*la jouissance de notre santé*), the thrust of our mental faculties (*l'élan de nos facultés*), the egoistic love of self (*affection égoïste*) combined with passion for him (*passion pour lui*). Just as eternity summed up the first four qualities, so he loves us for his endless life (*lui qui nous aime pour sa vie infinie*).

Paragraphs three and four delineate our relations with him and his ultimate goal. We recall him (*nous nous le rappelons*) and he seems to go off (*il voyage*), but if our adoration disappears (*si l'Adoration s'en va*), it still rings (*sonne*) because his promise still rings (*sa promesse sonne*) in our ears: away with superstitions (*Arrière ces superstitions*) of which we are the victim, these old bodies (*ces anciens corps*) of which we are the slaves, these households of which we become the servants, and these ages (*ces âges*) to which we are tied, for it is this epoch that has foundered (*C'est cette époque-ci qui a sombré*).

Unlike the Christ of Christianity he will not go away (*Il ne s'en ira pas*) and thus will not have to come down again from some heaven (*il ne redescendra pas d'un ciel*). He will not redeem us (*il n'accomplira pas la rédemption*) for the anger of women and the follies of men (*des colères des femmes et des gaîtés des hommes*) nor for all our sins (*de tout ce péché*). There will be no need, for it will already be an accomplished fact (*car c'est fait*) simply because he is (*lui étant*) and because he is loved (*et étant aimé*).

The first two exclamations, like the last two, enumerate mainly mental and moral abstract qualities, whereas the four paragraphs that separate them list physical characteristics. The first exclamation includes his breathing, his heads or his brains, and his journeys or races (*ses souffles, ses têtes, ses courses*) that account for the terrible swiftness of the perfection of forms and action (*la terrible célérité de la perfection des formes et de l'action*) in nature; for the fecundity of the spirit and the immensity of the universe (*fécondité d l'esprit de immensité de l'univers*).

The four physical elements include his body (*Son corps*), his sight (*Sa vue*), his day (*Son jour*), and his step (*Son pas*), each of which is accompanied by details in pairs. His body is the dreamed of detachment (*Le dégagement rêvé*) and the breaking up of grace coupled with the new violence (*le brisement de la grâce croisée de violence nouvelle*). His sight sees all of the ancient genuflections and penalties (*tous les agenouillages anciens et pienes*) eliminated by his passing (*relevées à sa suite*). His day will bring the abolition of all sonorous and moving sufferings in a more intense music (*l'abolition de toutes souffrances sonores et mouvantes dans la musique plus intense*). His step will lead migrations greater than the ancient invasions (*les migrations plus énormes que les anciennes invasions*).

The last two exclamations include him and us (*lui et nous*), who together form a pride that is more benevolent than lost charities (*l'orgueil plus bienveillant que les charités perdues*). The mention of charity takes us back to the beginning of *Une Saison en enfer* where charity was described as the key to that feast. But that idea was only a dream because charity had already been lost. The last exclamation includes the world and the clear song of new misfortunes (*monde! et le chant clair des malheurs nouveaux*). In these last six paragraphs the *violence nouvelle* and *malheurs nouveaux* are pitted against the *agenouillages anciens* and *anciennes invasions* with the knowledge that change cannot be effected without violence and suffering that will be new because it will be different but hopefully less harmful than the old.

The final paragraph concludes with a series of pairs that recapitulate the poem. The genie has known us all and loved us

all (*Il nous a connus tous et nous a tous aimés*), a combination
of knowledge and emotion. In a return to the time of the beginning of the poem, the narrator says that we must know that
this winter night (*cette nuit d'hiver*) of the soul that stretches
from cape to cape (*de cap en cap*), from tumultuous pole to
the château (*du pôle tumultueux au château*), the house of the
first sentence of the poem, from the crowd to the beach (*de la
foule à la plage*), and from look to look (*de regards en regards*),
leaves our strengths and sentiments weary (*forces et sentiments
las*). We must know how to hail him and see him (*le héler et le
voir*) and send him back (*le renvoyer*), and how to follow him
beneath the tides and to the top of the deserts of snow (*sous
les marées et au haut des déserts de neige*), and how to follow
his views, his breathing, his body, and his day (*suivre ses vues,
ses souffles, son corps, son jour*)—an enumeration that gathers
together all of the physical attributes that must be attained if
we are going to realize the spiritual goals of the new religion
of this genie who is all of us in his aspirations and none of us in
all of his accomplishments.

Obviously Rimbaud expected too much of himself, of literature, of mankind, and of the world, but only those who go too
far, go far enough. If he did not achieve his ambitions as a seer,
he did leave to posterity, like Villon before him, a Little and
Great Testament in the form of *Une Saison en enfer* and the
Illuminations that are still being read a hundred years after they
were written and that promise to be read, again like Villon, five
hundred years from now. These antilandscapes, these visions,
these aspirations exist only in the imagination of the writer
and his reader, but just as reality is inseparable from the dream,
so reason is inseparable from the imagination. The fiction of
these seemingly antipoetic poems becomes a part of the fact of
our lives. To that extent Rimbaud realized his goal almost in
spite of himself and frequently in spite of us, his readers.

CHAPTER 10

Conclusion: This Absurd Undertaking

WHATEVER one may think of Rimbaud's poetry, its perva-
sive influence in almost all areas of modern critical and
creative thought can hardly be denied. The how and why of its
influence are much more difficult to explain.

If one picks up a volume on the critical theory of literature
he finds Rimbaud's *illumination* defined as "the pure but transient vision, the aesthetic or timeless moment."[1] I agree that
his vision was pure because uncluttered and uninhibited and
transient by its very nature. I also agree that the poetic moment
is timeless precisely because it is aesthetic. If Rimbaud's experience was preternatural, as an inquiry into some varieties of
such experiences would have us believe, it was beyond the ordinary only because of his extraordinary poetic abilities. I cannot
agree that *Une Saison en enfer* represents his "final judgment on
his excursion into the realms beyond space and time."[2] We are
no longer so convinced that *Une Saison* was any kind of final
statement while his "excursion" took place in a specific space
and at a definte time, an excursion into the realm of the imagination which is never really free of the here and now.

If one delves into a study of existential philosophy, he finds
"Rimbaud's unconditional break with Western civilization—the
civilization of the white man," described as "the sign of a break
within the civilization. Rimbaud was thus among the first of the
creative artists to announce primitivism as one of the goals of
his art and life"[3]; he was also the Nietzsche of poetry (p. 133).
The great structural anthropologist Lévi-Strauss emphasized
"the significance of Rimbaud's intuition that metaphor can change
the world,"[4] since after reading his poetry the reader can never
experience reality in quite the same way again.

Whether one chooses a study of Symbolist art[5] or of the re-

174

lations between criticism and modern art,[6] he will find Rimbaud mentioned in one connection or another. If he chooses a study of tradition and revolution in Romantic literature[7] or a study of modern fiction according to which Rimbaud desired "not communication but communion" in "a language that is not conventional but natural,"[8] or a study of the structure of discourse in poetry as well as fiction, he will find Rimbaud cited as an example. In this last case the author claims that Rimbaud's ambition in the sonnet of the "Vowels" was "to cause us *to live*, in the *text*, the myth of poetry which is to create myths (and sometimes to denounce them at the same time)."[9]

Rimbaud's influence on modern French music has been noted[10] while a popular contemporary novelist could not resist adapting Rimbaud's famous statement about "a long, immense, and reasoned deranging of all the senses" to his own purposes.[11] Nor could a young novelist resist noting in his autobiography that his maternal grandfather had once been the employer of Rimbaud in Cairo.[12] Nor can novelists,[13] film makers,[14] dramatists,[15] and choreographers[16] resist the temptation of trying to recreate Rimbaud's life in fiction, on film, in plays, or in dance, with more and sometimes less success.

Scholars have long been trying to evaluate Rimbaud's influence and to offer instructive comparative studies of Rimbaud and, for example, in French literature, Cros,[17] Char,[18] Claudel,[19] Lautréamont,[20] and Baudelaire,[21] Rimbaud and Hart Crane in American literature,[22] Rimbaud and Georg Trakl in German literature,[23] Rimbaud and Emanuele Sella in Italian literature,[24] and, more recently, Rimbaud and William Blake in English literature,[25] to note only a few. By way of contrast, a recent critic has managed to produce a 646-page tome[26] purporting to study the revolution in poetic language at the time of Lautréamont and Mallarmé near the end of the nineteenth century. She mentions Rimbaud only seven times, twice on the same page with reference to his inability to find a place for himself in the bourgeois Third Republic and to his disappearance (p. 366) and twice with reference to his flight (pp. 400, 442). She quotes Delahaye quoting something Rimbaud may have said (p. 510, n. 2) and speaks of his "exotic voyage" (p. 526). Only in the conclusion does she give her reasons for excluding those "summits" of

French literature, Baudelaire, Nerval, and Rimbaud from her study: "...they still remain too close to the esthetic exigency and their negativity appears to be an anarchic and individual revolt rather than an attempt at social intervention" (p. 617). Although I respect the author's desire and need to limit her subject, I am not sure how definitive such a work can claim to be in spite of its length and its attempts at "social relevance" if Rimbaud's effect on language is totally ignored. It seems to me that a much stronger case can be made for the poetry of both Baudelaire and Rimbaud as attempts at social intervention when contrasted with that of Mallarmé, for example.

All the more so because a respected critic wrote almost twenty years ago that "the unique prestige of Rimbaud's poetry results from the marriage it brings about, and which will never again be realized after it, between a pouring forth and a form, from the mingling it effects...between a 'grace' and a 'violence,' the simultaneous possession it makes possible of an 'elegance,' a 'knowledge,' and a 'vigor.' "[27] And because an excellent poet wrote that "the greatness of Rimbaud will endure for having refused the bit of liberty he could have made his in his century and his milieu, in order to serve as witness to the alienation of man and for calling upon man to go beyond his moral misery to the tragic confrontation of the absolute."[28] His social relevance could hardly be more profound.

To effect such a change Rimbaud must have been "one of the great discoverers of the irrational regions of the human psyche," as one scholar put it.[29] Thanks to his poetry "we live the adventure of a consciousness that through its impetus causes the world to exist or rather to become under its amazed look."[30] Another critic maintains that Rimbaud's greatest achievement was "to render actively manifest one of the most important laws of textuality: to oblige the reader to be conscious of the operation it is in the process of effecting and that defines it as a detour and supplement to the text—like active writing filling in the gaps in the reading of a text constantly carried forward."[31]

Rimbaud will still be read in the year 2000, according to another critic, because "he embodies the universal adolescent, tormented and in revolt, the fallen angel who, remembering a 'former life,' rebels against his destiny. In the space of a metaphysical morning, in a tragic suspension between heaven and hell, Rimbaud embodied the human condition in all its dimensions."[32] But that revolt was "the first example of a true rebellion, that is, a rebellion that does not wish to found anything, that does not wish to impose any image of man different from that which is current but which simply denounces the scandal of existence."[33]

In contrast, the great Mexican poet Octavio Paz maintains that Rimbaud's works are "a criticism of reality and of the 'values' that support it or justify it: Christianity, morality, beauty."[34] He goes on to say:

... modern poetry is an attempt to do away with all conventional meanings because poetry itself becomes the ultimate meaning of life and of man; therefore, it is at once words and meanings, the realm of silence, but at the same time, words in search of the Word. Those who dismiss this quest as "utter madness" are legion. Nonetheless, for more than a century a few solitary spirits, among them the noblest and most gifted human beings who have ever trod this earth, have unhesitatingly devoted their entire lives to this absurd undertaking. (p. 5)

"This absurd undertaking" has forever influenced the way in which we apprehend and comprehend the world. The aspirations and defeats of this teenager are those of every man and no man. His private hell and private heaven have become a public domain by means of which we see ourselves and the world a bit more clearly. If we see ourselves a bit more clearly, perhaps we understand ourselves a bit better. If we do, then "this absurd undertaking" was worth all it cost Rimbaud, and it cost him everything. Who now is willing to pay so dearly?

Notes and References

To conserve space, references to the revised Pléiade edition of the *Œuvres complètes* of 1972 are indicated by OC, to the Garnier edition by Suzanne Bernard of 1960 by B. Complete references are given only for those works not included in the bibliography. For works in the bibliography, sufficient information is given to identify them there. All translations are the present author's unless otherwise indicated.

Chapter One

1. Biographical details have been taken from OC xxxix–lii; B v–xiv; Matarasso and Petitfils, *Album Rimbaud*.
2. OC 1028.
3. André Breton, *Manifestes du surréalisme*, Collection Idées (Paris: Gallimard, 1963), p. 39.
4. Pierre Gascar, *Rimbaud et la Commune*, p. 167, n. 1.
5. W. H. Auden, "Rimbaud," in *Selected Poetry* (New York: Random House, 1958), p. 50.

Chapter Two

1. For the dates of manuscripts and a Rimbaud chronology, see the articles by Pierre Petitfils, Marcel A. Ruff, and Nicole Boulestreau.
2. OC 21–22, 858–60; B 59–60, 372–73.
3. OC 36–38, 875–77; B 83–84, 385–87.
4. OC 42–43, 884–85; B 93–94, 392–93.
5. OC 60–65, 910–13; B 121–26, 418–21.
6. OC 22, 860–62; B 61, 373–74.
7. OC 46–47, 888–91; B 100–101, 397–99. See also the article by A. R. Chisholm.
8. Yves Bonnefoy, *Rimbaud par lui-même*, p. 42.
9. OC xxii–xxvii, 248–54, 1073–78; B 343–50, 544–53.
10. Pierre Daix, "La grille de Rimbaud," in *Nouvelle critique et art moderne, essai* (Paris: Seuil, 1968), p. 25.
11. Pierre Gascar, *Rimbaud et la Commune*, p. 179.

Chapter Three

1. OC 39, 880–81; B 87, 389.
2. OC 43–45, 885–87; B 95–97, 393–96.
3. B 394.
4. OC 51–52, 897–98; B 108–9, 403–5.
5. B 404.
6. OC 898.
7. OC 53, 898–903; B 110, 405–10.
8. René Etiemble, *Le sonnet des voyelles,* p. 214.
9. Robert Faurisson, "A-t-on LU Rimbaud?" *Bizarre.* See also articles by Theodore E. D. Braun and Claudine Hunting.
10. Etiemble, *Le sonnet des voyelles,* p. 233.
11. OC 55–60, 906–10; B 115–20, 414–18.
12. E.T.A. Hoffmann, *Tales,* ed. Christophe Lazare (New York: A. A. Wyn, 1946), p. 217.
13. Yves Bonnefoy, *Rimbaud par lui-même,* p. 54.
14. OC 65–66, 913–14; B 127, 421.

Chapter Four

1. OC 66–69, 915–24; B 128–31, 422–29. See also articles by René Etiemble in *Hygiène des lettres,* IV, and Robert Faurisson.
2. Bernard Weinberg, *The Limits of Symbolism,* pp. 89–126.
3. B 424.
4. OC 920–21.

Chapter Five

1. OC 949–52.
2. OC 267.
3. Jean-Pierre Richard, *Poésie et profondeur,* pp. 240–41.
4. OC 93, 952–54; B 211–12, 455–57.
5. OC 94–99, 954–59; B 213–19, 457–62.
6. See the article by Abigail Israel on Rimbaud-Genet relations.
7. OC 99–102, 959–62; B 220–22, 462–64.
8. OC 102–6, 962–65; B 223–27, 465–68.
9. M.-A. Ruff, *Rimbaud.* pp. 171–76.
10. OC 106–12, 965–67; B 228–34, 468–73.
11. OC 72, 106–07, 926–28; B 148, 228–29.
12. OC 76, 108, 931–32; B 155, 434–35. See also the articles by Margaret Davies, Yves Denis, and Claude Zilberberg.
13. OC 265–66.
14. OC 931–32.

15. Jules Mouquet, in Arthur Rimbaud, *Œuvres complètes,* Text edited and annotated by Rolland de Renéville and Jules Mouquet, Bibliothèque de la Pléiade (Paris: Gallimard, 1946), p. 679.

16. B 435.

17. See the article by Yves Denis.

Chapter Six

1. OC 77–78, 108, 933–34; B 158–59, 229–30, 436–37.
2. OC 83–84, 109, 939–40; B 169–70, 231, 441–42.
3. OC 89, 109–10, 949; B 181, 232, 449.
4. OC 79, 110, 934–35; B 160, 232–33, 437–38. See also the article by Hans-Jost Frey.
5. OC 88–89, 111–12, 946–48; B 179–80, 234, 448–49.
6. OC 112–14, 967–68; B 235–37, 473–75.
7. OC 114–15, 969–70; B 238, 475.
8. OC 115, 970; B 239, 476.
9. OC 115–17, 970–72; B 240–41, 477–79.

Chapter Seven

1. OC 972–77. See also articles by Jean-Claude Coquet, Renée Riese Hubert, and Louis S. Nielsen.
2. OC 121–22, 978–79; B 253–54, 479–81. See also articles by Margaret Davies and Yves Denis.
3. OC 122–25, 980–81; B 255–58, 481–85..
4. OC 126, 982–84; B 261, 486–88. See also the article by Nathaniel Wing.
5. OC 127, 984; B 262, 488.
6. OC 127, 985; B 263, 488–90.

Chapter Eight

1. OC 130, 988; B 268, 492–94.
2. OC 130–31, 988–89; B 169, 494–96.
3. OC 131–32, 989–90; B 270–71, 496–98.
4. OC 133–34, 991–92; B 273, 498–99. See also the article by Nathaniel Wing.
5. OC 134, 992; B 274, 499–500. See also the article by C. A. Hackett.
6. OC 135, 993; B 275, 500–501.
7. OC 135–36, 993–94; B 276–77, 501–2.
8. OC 136–37, 994; B 278, 502–4.

9. OC 137–38, 995–96; B 279–80, 504–5.

10. OC 138–39, 996–98; B 281–82, 505–7.

11. OC 139–40, 998; B 283, 507–9. See also the articles by Roger Little and Michael Spencer.

12. OC 141, 999–1000; B 285, 510–11.

13. OC 141–42, 1000–1001; B 286, 511–13.

14. OC 142, 1001; B 287, 513–14.

Chapter Nine

1. OC 143, 1002; B 289, 514–16.

2. OC 144–45, 1004–5; B 292, 518–20. See also the article by Margaret Davies.

3. OC 145–46, 1005–6; B 293, 520.

4. OC 146, 1006–7; B 294–95, 521–23.

5. See Fowlie, p. 237, and Peschel, p. 169.

6. OC 149–50, 1011–12; B 300, 527–28. See also the article by Nathaniel Wing.

7. OC 150, 1012–13; B 301, 528–30.

8. OC 1013.

9. OC 151, 1013–14; B 302, 530–31.

10. OC 151, 1014–15; B 303, 531–32. See also the article by Yves Denis.

11. Cohn, p. 381.

12. OC 152, 1015–16; B 304–5, 532–33.

13. OC 153, 1016–18; B 306, 533–35. See also the article by Margaret Davies.

14. Py, p. 221.

15. OC 154–55, 1019–20; B 308, 536–37.

Chapter Ten

1. Northrop Frye, *Anatomy of Criticism, Four Essays* (Princeton: Princeton University Press, 1957), p. 61.

2. R. C. Zaehner, *Mysticism sacred and profane, An Inquiry into some Varieties of Preternatural Experience* (New York: Oxford University Press, 1957 [1971]), p. 62.

3. William Barrett, *Irrational Man, A Study of Existential Philosophy* (New York: Doubleday, 1958 [1962]), p. 132.

4. Claude Lévi-Strauss, *Structural Anthropology*, trans. Claire Jacobson and Brooke Grundfest Schoepf, Harper Torchbooks TB 5017 (New York: Basic Books, 1958 [1963]), p. 202.

5. Edward Lucie-Smith, *Symbolist Art* (London: Thames and Hudson, 1972), pp. 54, 57.

6. Pierre Daix, *Nouvelle critique et art moderne, essai* (Paris: Seuil, 1968), p. 25.

7. M. H. Abrams, *Natural Supernaturalism, Tradition and Revolution in Romantic Literature* (New York: Norton, 1971), pp. 415–18.

8. Gabriel Josipovici, *The World and the Book, A Study of Modern Fiction* (London: Macmillan, 1971), p. 184.

9. Maurice-Jean Lefebve, *Structure du discours de la poésie et du récit,* Collection Languages (Neuchatel: La Baconnière, 1971), p. 59.

10. Rollo Myers, *Modern French Music, Its Evolution and Cultural Background from 1900 to the Present Day* (Oxford: Blackwell, 1971), pp. 61, 64, 65, 68.

11. Bernard Noël, *Le Château de Cène* (Paris: Pauvert, 1971), p. 84. The paraphrase reads: "Je cherche un long, immense et raisonné dérèglement de la réalité, car celle en qui l'on croit n'est que la part mesquine qu'il faut faire éclater. La surface."

12. Pierre Guyotat, *Littérature interdite* (Paris: Gallimard, 1972), p. 105.

13. James Ramsey Ullman, *The Day on Fire, A Novel Suggested by the Life of Arthur Rimbaud* (New York: World Publishing, 1958), 701 pp.

14. Yves Reboul, *"Une Saison en enfer,* film réalisé par Nelo Risi," *Arthur Rimbaud 1* (1972): *Images et Témoins, La Revue des Lettres Modernes,* nos. 323–26 (1972), pp. 144–46.

15. Christopher Hampton, *Total Eclipse* (London: Faber and Faber, 1969), 87 pp. First produced in 1968.

16. Clive Barnes, "Dance: 'Illuminations,' City Ballet Presents a Savory Portrait of Half of a Precious Pair of Poets," *The New York Times,* June 15, 1973, p. 25.

17. G. A. Bertozzi, "Arthur Rimbaud et Charles Cros," *La Revue des Lettres Modernes,* nos. 323–26 (1972), pp. 85–93.

18. Virginia A. La Charité, "The Role of Rimbaud in Char's Poetry," *Publications of the Modern Language Association,* no. 1 (January, 1974), pp. 57–63.

19. John MacCombie, *The Prince & the Genie, A Study of Rimbaud's Influence on Claudel* (Amherst: University of Massachusetts Press, 1972), xix&197 pp.

20. Paul-Louis Rossi, "Lautréamont et Rimbaud," *Action poétique,* no. 34 (1967), pp. 50–60.

21. Marcel A. Ruff, "Rimbaud's Relationship to Baudelaire," trans.

L. B. Hyslop and F. E. Hyslop, in *Baudelaire as a Love Poet, and Other Essays*, ed. Lois Boe Hyslop (University Park: Pennsylvania State University Press, 1969), pp. 65–86.

22. Brom Weber, "Arthur Rimbaud," in *Hart Crane, A Biographical Study* (New York: Bodley, 1948), pp. 144–50. James Robert Hewitt, "Rimbaud and Hart Crane: a comparative essay," *Ici*, no. 1 (1950), pp. 60–71.

23. Friedhelm Pamp, "Der Einfluss Rimbauds auf Georg Trakl," *Revue de littérature comparée*, 32 (July–Sept., 1958), 396–406. Herbert Lindenberger, "Georg Trakl and Rimbaud: A Study in Influence and Development," *Comparative Literature*, 10 (Winter 1958), 21–35.

24. Petre Ciureanu, "Rimbaud e Emanuele Sella," *Rivista di letterature moderne e comparate*, 13 (December, 1960), 296–98.

25. Enid Rhodes Peschel, "Themes of Rebellion in William Blake and Arthur Rimbaud," *The French Review*, no. 4 (March, 1973), pp. 750–61.

26. Julia Kristeva, *La révolution du langage poétique: L'Avant-garde à la fin du XIXe siècle: Lautréamont et Mallarmé*, Collection "Tel Quel" (Paris: Seuil, 1974), 646 pp.

27. Jean-Pierre Richard, *Poésie et profondeur*, p. 248.

28. Yves Bonnefoy, *Rimbaud par lui-même*, p. 178.

29. W. M. Frohock, *Rimbaud's Poetic Practice*, p. 6.

30. Jacques Plessen, *Promenade et poésie*, p. 19.

31. Jean-Louis Baudry, "Le texte de Rimbaud," *Tel Quel*, p. 46.

32. Marcel Lobet, *Classiques de l'an 2000* (Paris: La Francité, 1970), p. 88.

33. Pierre Gascar, "Rimbaud" in *Tableau de la littérature française III: De Madame de Staël à Rimbaud*, Preface by Dominique Aury (Paris: Gallimard, 1974), p. 450.

34. Octavio Paz, *Alternating Current*, trans. Helen R. Lane (New York: Viking, 1973), p. 4.

Selected Bibliography

Because the Rimbaud bibliography is so enormous, I have included only the essential and most recent works. The place of publication is Paris unless otherwise indicated.

PRIMARY SOURCES

Album zutique. Introduction, Notes and Commentaries by Pascal Pia. Le Cercle du livre précieux, 1961, vol. I: 30 pp.; vol. II: 255 pp.

Illuminations–Painted Plates. Critical Edition with Introduction and Notes by H. de Bouillane de Lacoste. Mercure de France, 1949, 203 pp.

Illuminations. Text edited, annotated, and commented on with an Introduction, A Summary of Themes and a Bibliography by Albert Py, Textes littéraires français. Geneva: Droz, 1967, xxxiv&244 pp.

Œuvres, Vers et proses. Checked against the original manuscripts and first editions, organized and annotated by Paterne Berrichon, rediscovered Poems, preface by Paul Claudel. Mercure de France, 1912, 401 pp.

Œuvres. Text edited by H. de Bouillane de Lacoste. Mrecure de France, 1950, 318 pp.

Œuvres. Text edited by Paul Hartmann. Strasbourg: Brocéliande, 1957, 311 pp.

Œuvres. Biographical summary, introduction, résumés, indication of variants and notes by Suzanne Bernard, Classiques Garnier. Garnier, 1960, lxx&569 pp.

Œuvres complètes. Text edited, introduced, and annotated by Antoine Adam, Bibliothèque de la Pléiade 68. Gallimard, 1972, liv&249 pp.

Poésies. Critical edition, introduction and notes by H. de Bouillane de Lacoste. Mercure de France, 1948, 261 pp.

Poésies. Edited by Elvire Choureau, preceded by "Views of Rimbaud" by Georges Duhamel, portrait of the author, gouache by Fantin-Latour. L'Artisan du Livre, 1952, 252 pp.

Poésies, Une saison en enfer, Illuminations. Preface by René Char,
text introduced, edited, and annotated by Louis Forestier, Collection Poésie 87. Gaillimard, 1973, 301 pp.

Translations

Illuminations and Other Prose Poems. Trans. Louise Varèse. Revised
edition. New York: New Directions, 1957, xxv&182 pp.
A Season in Hell & The Drunken Boat. Trans. Louise Varèse. New
York: New Directions, 1961, xx&108 pp.
Complete Works, Selected Letters. Translation, Introduction, and
Notes by Wallace Fowlie. Chicago: University of Chicago Press,
1966, xx&370 pp.
A Season in Hell, The Illuminations. Trans. Enid Rhodes Peschel.
New York: Oxford University Press, 1973, vii&181 pp.
Complete Works, Trans. Paul Schmidt. New York: Harper & Row,
1975, xx&309 pp.

SECONDARY SOURCES
1. Books

BONNEFOY, YVES. *Rimbaud par lui-même,* Ecrivains de toujours.
Seuil, 1961, 189 pp. Remarkably sound and sensitive appraisal.
————. *Rimbaud.* Trans. Paul Schmidt. Harper Colophon Books.
New York: Harper & Row, 1973, 145 pp.
BOUILLANE DE LACOSTE, HENRY DE. *Rimbaud et le problème des
"Illuminations."* Mercure de France, 1959, 268 pp. Important
landmark in Rimbaud criticism.
BRIET, SUZANNE. *Madame Rimbaud.* Biographical essay followed by
the Correspondence of Vitalie Rimbaud-Cuif including 13
unpublished letters, Avant-Siècle 5, Lettres modernes. Minard,
1968, 133 pp. Information about the mother revealing some-
thing about the son.
BRUNEL, PIERRE, *Rimbaud.* Collection Thema/anthologie. Hatier,
1973, 127 pp. Useful quick reference to Rimbaud's themes.
CARRÉ, JEAN-MARIE. *La Vie aventureuse de Jean-Arthur Rimbaud.*
New edition corrected and augmented with unpublished documents, with a map, notes, and 9 engravings. Plon, 1926 [1946],
ix&308 pp. Outdated biography but still interesting and useful.
————. *A Season in Hell: The Life of Rimbaud.* Trans. Hannah and
Matthew Josephson. New York: Macaulay, 1931, viii&312 pp.
CHADWICK, CHARLES. *Etudes sur Rimbaud.* Nizet, 1960, 154 pp.
Informative essays.

CHAUVEL, JEAN. *L'Aventure terrestre de Jean Arthur Rimbaud.* Seghers, 1971, 270 pp. Most recent biography, with only a few errors of fact.

CHISHOLM, A. R. *The Art of Arthur Rimbaud.* Melbourne: Melbourne University Press, 1930, ix&66 pp. Early but still illuminating essay.

COHN, ROBERT GREER. *The Poetry of Rimbaud.* Princeton: Princeton University Press, 1973, xii&447 pp. Many unusual insights into all of the poetry.

DELAHAYE, ERNEST. *Les "Illuminations" et une "Saison en enfer" de Rimbaud.* Messein, 1927, 201 pp. Sincere but frequently misleading information by a contemporary of Rimbaud.

————. *Rimbaud l'artiste et l'être moral.* Messein, 1947, 207 pp. Interesting but sometimes erroneous and often biased.

ETIEMBLE [RENÉ], et YASSU GAUCLÈRE. *Rimbaud.* New edition corrected and augmented, Les Essais XLIV. Gallimard, 1950, 260 pp. Extremely biased but frequently corrective interpretations.

ETIEMBLE [RENÉ]. *Le mythe de Rimbaud,* 4 volumes. *I Genèse du mythe, 1869–1949,* Analytical and critical bibliography followed by a supplement to the iconographies, second edition corrected and augmented, Bibliothèque des Idées. Gallimard, 1954, 536 pp. II *Structure du mythe,* new edition, reworked, corrected, and augmented with numerous passages censored in 1952 (1961), 453 pp. IV *L'Année du centenaire* (1961), 133 pp. The critical bibliography to end all critical bibliographies. Vol III in preparation.

FOWLIE, WALLACE. *Rimbaud.* Chicago: University of Chicago Press, 1966, viii&280 pp. A good general introduction.

FROHOCK, W. M. *Rimbaud's Poetic Practice: Image and Theme in the Major Poems.* Cambridge: Harvard University Press, 1963, 250 pp. Extremely useful introduction to the poetry.

GASCAR, PIERRE. *Rimbaud et la Commune,* Collection Idées. Gallimard, 1971, 184 pp. Settles nothing factually but draws some interesting conclusions.

GENGOUX, JACQUES. *La Pensée poétique de Rimbaud.* Nizet, 1950, 673 pp. Much that is enlightening and much that is mere speculation.

HACKETT, C. A. *Rimbaud,* Studies in Modern European Literature and Thought. New York: Hillary House, 1957, 109 pp. Brief useful introduction.

HOUSTON, JOHN PORTER. *The Design of Rimbaud's Poetry.* Yale Romanic Studies, Second Series 11. New Haven: Yale University

Press, 1963, 170 pp. Another very helpful introduction to the poetry.

IZAMBARD, GEORGES. *Rimbaud tel que je l'ai connu*. Preface and notes by H. de Bouillane de Lacoste and Pierre Izambard. Mercure de France, 1946, 227 pp. Again sincere but sometimes erroneous information by a contemporary of Rimbaud.

KLOEPFER, ROLF, and URSULA OOMER. *Sprachliche Konstituenten moderner Dichtung, Entwurf einer deskriptiven Poetic–Rimbaud.* Bad Hamburg: Athenäum Verlag, 1970, 231 pp. A structural approach that yields much.

MATARASSO, HENRI, and PIERRE PETITFILS. *Album Rimbaud.* Iconography collected and commented on by Henry Matarasso and Pierre Petitfils, Bibliothèque de La Pléiade. Gallimard, 1967, 321 pp. A gold mine of information and illustrations.

MILLER, HENRY. *The Time of the Assassins.* Norfolk: New Directions, 1956, xi&163 pp. Amusing, but reveals more about Miller than Rimbaud.

MONTAL, ROBERT. *Rimbaud.* Classiques du XXe siècle. Editions Universitaires, 1968, 124 pp. Brief sober introduction to Rimbaud.

MORRISSETTE, BRUCE. *The Great Rimbaud Forgery, The Affair of "La Chasse spirituelle"* with unpublished documents and an anthology of Rimbaldien Pastiches. St. Louis: Washington University Press, 1956, viii&333 pp. Scrupulous account of a scandalous affair.

NOULET, E. *Le Premier Visage de Rimbaud.* Eight poems of childhood, choice and commentary. Bruxelles: Palais des Académies, 1953, 326 pp. Still among the most sensitive appraisals.

PERRIER, MADELEINE. *Rimbaud, Chemin de la création,* Les Essais CLXXXVII. Gallimard, 1973, 166 pp. A promising beginning that does not lead to solid conclusions.

PLESSEN, JACQUES. *Promenade et poésie.* The experience of walking and of movement in the works of Rimbaud, Publications of the Institut d'Etudes Françaises et Occitanes of the University of Utrecht under the direction of H. E. Keller and B. A. Bary, I. La Haye-Paris: Mouton, 1967, 348 pp. Interesting and important existentialist interpretation.

RICHER, JEAN. *L'Alchimie du Verbe de Rimbaud ou les Jeux de Jean-Arthur.* Essay on the imagination of language, orientations. Didier, 1972, 251 pp. Interesting but not very convincing interpretations.

RIVIÈRE, JACQUES. *Rimbaud.* New Edition. Emile-Paul Frères, s.d. (1938), 234 pp. Early and still interesting but biased.

ROLLAND DE RENÉVILLE [ANDRÉ]. *Rimbaud le voyant.* Corrected and augmented edition. Vieux Colombier, 1947, 151 pp. Another early but informative introduction.

RUCHON, FRANÇOIS. *Jean-Arthur Rimbaud, sa vie, son oeuvre, son influence.* With a woodcut designed and printed by William Métein and two plates. Honoré Champion, 1929, 361 pp. An early biography now outdated but containing much useful information.

RUFF, M.-A. *Rimbaud,* Connaissance des Lettres. Hatier, 1968, 288 pp. Solid and sober introduction and interpretation.

STARKIE, ENID. *Arthur Rimbaud.* New York: New Directions, 1961, 491 pp. Still the most authoritative introduction in English.

WHITAKER, MARIE-JOSÉPHINE. *La Structure du monde imaginaire de Rimbaud.* Nizet, 1972, 192 pp. Promises more than it delivers but with some unusual insights.

WING, NATHANIEL. *Present Appearances: Aspects of Poetic Structure in Rimbaud's "Illuminations."* Romance Monographs No. 9. University [Mississippi]: Romance Monographs, 1974, 172 pp. A somewhat different approach that yields much that is soundly satisfying.

2. Articles

AHEARN, EDWARD J. "'Entends comme brame' and the Theme of Death in Nature in Rimbaud's Poetry." *The French Review,* no. 3 (February, 1970), pp. 407–17.

ASCIONE, MARC, and JEAN-PIERRE CHAMBON. "Les 'zolismes' de Rimbaud." *Europe,* no. 529–30 (May–June, 1973), pp. 114–32.

AUTRAND, CHARLES. "Approches de Rimbaud (1949–1959)." *Courrier du Centre International d'Etudes Poétiques,* no. 4 (s.d.), pp. 3–20.

AVICE, ROBERT. *"Les Illuminations de Rimbaud." L'Ecole des lettres,* no. 9 (Jan. 19, 1974), pp. 2, 49–51.

BACHELLIER, JEAN-LOUIS. "Rimbaldiane Miousic: Les maîtres-mots-chanteurs de Rimbaud.' *Sub-Stance,* no. 7 (Fall 1973), pp. 127–37.

BARTHES, ROLAND. "Nautilus et Bateau ivre." In *Mythologies,* Collection points. Seuil, 1957, pp. 80–82.

BAUDRY, JEAN-LOUIS. "Le texte de Rimbaud." *Tel Quel,* no. 35 (Autumn 1968), pp. 40–63. "Le texte de Rimbaud (fin)," *Tel Quel,* no. 36 (Winter 1969), pp. 33–53.

BLANCHOT, MAURICE. "Le Sommeil de Rimbaud." In *La Part du feu.* Gallimard, 1949, pp. 157–65.

BOULESTREAU, NICOLE. "Préliminaires à la biographie, Chronologie." *Europe*, no. 529–30 (May-June, 1973), pp. 151–70.

BRAUN, THEODORE E. D. "Phonetic and Visual Spires in 'Voyelles.'" *Publications of the Modern Language Association*, no 2 (March, 1974), pp. 353–54.

BREIT, SUZANNE. "La signification de 'Mémoire,' poème crucial de Rimbaud." *Etudes rimbaldiennes*, no. 3 (1972), pp. 35–41.

CHAMBERS, ROSS. "'Mémoire' de Rimbaud: essai de lecture." *Essays in French Literature*, no. 5 (November, 1968), pp. 22–35.

CHAROLLES, MICHEL. "Le texte poétique et sa signification, Une lecture du poème intitulé 'Mouvement' ('Illuminations') et de quelques commentaires qui en ont été donnés." *Europe*, no. 529–30 (May–June, 1973), pp. 97–114.

CHISHOLM, A. R. "Two Exegetical Studies (Mallarmé, Rimbaud)." *L'Esprit Créateur*, no. 1 (Spring 1969), pp. 28–36. ("Le Coeur volé")

COQUET, JEAN-CLAUDE. "Combinaison et transformation en poésie (Arthur Rimbaud: les *Illuminations*)." *L'Homme*, no. 1 (Jan.-Mar., 1969), pp. 23–41.

DAVIES, MARGARET. "Rimbaud's 'Bonne pensée du matin." *French Studies*, no. 3 (July, 1971), pp. 295–304.

————. "Le Thème de la voyance dans 'Après le déluge,' 'Métropolitain,' et 'Barbare.'" *Revue des Lettres Modernes*, nos. 323–26 (1972), pp. 19–39.

————. "'Dévotion' de Rimbaud." *The French Review*, no. 3 (February, 1973), pp. 493–505.

DENIS, YVES. "Glose d'un texte de Rimbaud: 'Après le déluge.'" *Les Temps Modernes*, no. 260 (January, 1968), pp. 1261–76.

————. "Glose d'un texte de Rimbaud: 'H.'" *Les Tempes Modernes*, no. 263 (April, 1968), pp. 1878–87.

————. "Le bain dans la mer à midi." *Les Tempes Modernes*, no. 275 (May, 1969), pp. 1067–74.

DUMONT, JEAN-PAUL. "'Littéralement et dans tous les sens,' essai d'analyse structurale d'un quatrain de Rimbaud." In A. J. Greimas, *Essais de sémiotique poétique*, Collection L. Larousse, 1972, pp. 126–39. ("L'Etoile a pleuré rose . . .")

ETIEMBLE [RENÉ]. "Les Sourciers ne sont pas sorciers: Les Sources littéraires du 'Bateau ivre.'" In *Hygiène des lettres*, IV: *Poètes ou faiseurs?* (*1936–1966*). Gallimard, 1966, pp. 23–55.

FAURISSON, ROBERT. "'Le Bateau ivre,' Essai d'explication." *La Bibliothèque Volante*, no. 4 (July, 1971), pp. 57–61. First published in *L'Information Littéraire*, no. 2 (Mar.–Apr., 1966), pp. 83–88.

————. "A-t-on LU Rimbaud?" *Bizarre*, no 21–22 (1961), pp. 1–48.

FREY, HANS-JOST. "Rimbaud's poem 'L'Eternité.'" *Modern Language Notes*, no. 6 (December, 1968), pp. 848–66.

GIUSTO, JEAN-PIERRE. "Explication de 'Mémoire.'" *Etudes rimbaldiennes*, no. 3 (1972), pp. 43–52.

HACKETT, C. A. "Rimbaud and the 'splendides villes.'" *L'Esprit Créateur*, no. 1 (Spring 1969), pp. 46–53.

HUBERT, RENÉE RIESE. "The Use of Reversals in Rimbaud's *Illuminations*." *L'Esprit Créateur*, no. 1 (Spring 1969), pp. 9–18.

HUNTING, CLAUDINE. "La Voix de Rimbaud: Nouveau point de vue sur les 'naissances latentes' des 'Voyelles.'" *Publications of the Modern Language Association*, no. 3 (May, 1973), pp. 472–83.

ISRAEL, ABIGAIL. "The aesthetic of violence: Rimbaud and Genet." *Yale French Studies*, no. 46 (1971), pp. 28–40.

LA CHARITÉ, VIRGINIA A. "The Role of Rimbaud in Char's Poetry." *Publications of the Modern Language Association*, no. 1 (January, 1974), pp. 57–63.

LAPP, JOHN C. "'Mémoire': Art et hallucination chez Rimbaud." *Cahiers de l'Association Internationale des Etudes Françaises*, no. 23 (May, 1971), pp. 163–75.

LITTLE, ROGER. "Rimbaud's 'Mystique': Some Observations." *French Studies*, no. 3 (July, 1962), pp. 285–88.

NIELSEN, LAUS S. "L'anti-conte chez Rimbaud à travers quelques-uns de ses *Illuminations*." *Revue Romane*, no. 4 (1969), pp. 61–82.

NOULET, E. "Rimbaud." In *Le Ton poétique*. Corti, 1971, pp. 81–165.

PESCHEL, ENID RHODES. "Ambiguities in Rimbaud's Search for 'Charity.'" *The French Review*, no. 6 (May, 1974), pp. 1085–93.

PETITFILS, PIERRE. "Les manuscrits de Rimbaud—leur découverte, leur publication." *Etudes rimbaldiennes*, no. 2 (1969), pp. 41–157.

PISCOPO, UGO. "Les Futuristes et Rimbaud." Trans. Bernadette Morand, *Europe*, no. 529–30 (May–June, 1973), pp. 133–46.

RICHARD, JEAN-PIERRE. "Rimbaud ou la poésie du devenir." In *Poésie et profondeur*. Seuil, 1955, pp. 189–250.

RICHER, JEAN. "Gautier en filigrane dans quelques 'Illuminations.'" *Europe*, no. 529–30 (May–June, 1973), pp. 69–76.

RUFF, MARCEL A. "Chronologie rimbaldienne." *Etudes rimbaldiennes*, no. 2 (1969), pp. 159–70.

SOMVILLE, LÉON. "'Fils du soleil,' un emprunt d'Arthur Rimbaud."

Courrier du Centre International d'Etudes Poétiques, no. 73 (s.d.), pp. 13–22.

SPENCER, MICHAEL. "A Fresh Look at Rimbaud's 'Métropolitain.'" *Modern Language Review,* no. 4 (October, 1968), pp. 849–53.

––––––. "Arthur Rimbaud ou le monde renversé." *Raison Présente,* no. 30 (1974), pp. 89–96. ("Mystique")

VLÉMINCQ, ALBERT. "Analyse de 'Bottom' de Rimbaud." *Courrier du Centre International d'Etudes Poétiques,* no. 48 (December, 1963), pp. 4–21.

WEINBERG, BERNARD. "Rimbaud, *Le Bateau ivre.*" In *The Limits of Symbolism, Studies in Five Modern French Poets.* Chicago: University of Chicago Press, 1966, pp. 89–126.

WING, NATHANIEL. "Metaphor and Ambiguity in Rimbaud's 'Mémoire.'" *Romanic Review,* no. 3 (October, 1972), pp. 190–210.

––––––. "Rimbaud's 'Les Ponts,' 'Parade,' 'Scènes': The Poem as Performance." *The French Review,* no. 3 (February, 1973), pp. 506–21.

ZILBERBERG, CLAUDE. "Un essai de lecture de Rimbaud: 'Bonne pensée du matin." In A. J. Greimas, *Essais de sémiotique poétique,* Collection L. Larousse, 1972, pp. 149–54.

Index

DATE DUE